Military Justice

Recent Titles in
Contemporary Military, Strategic, and Security Issues

Information Operations—Doctrine and Practice: A Reference Handbook
Christopher Paul

The National Guard and Reserve: A Reference Handbook
Michael D. Doubler

Returning Wars' Wounded, Injured, and Ill: A Reference Handbook
Nathan D. Ainspan and Walter E. Penk, editors

Manning the Future Legions of the United States: Finding and Developing Tomorrow's Centurions
Donald Vandergriff

The Process and Politics of Defense Acquisition: A Reference Handbook
David S. Sorenson

International Crime and Punishment: A Guide to the Issues
James Larry Taulbee

Serving America's Veterans: A Reference Handbook
Lawrence J. Korb, Sean E. Duggan, Peter M. Juul, and Max A. Bergmann

Military Doctrine: A Reference Handbook
Bert Chapman

Energy Security Challenges for the 21st Century: A Reference Handbook
Gal Luft and Anne Korin, editors

An Introduction to Military Ethics: A Reference Handbook
Bill Rhodes

War and Children: A Reference Handbook
Kendra E. Dupuy and Krijn Peters

Military Space Power: A Guide to the Issues
Wilson W. S. Wong and James Fergusson

Military Justice

A Guide to the Issues

Lawrence J. Morris
Foreword by Francis A. Gilligan

Contemporary Military, Strategic, and Security Issues

AN IMPRINT OF ABC-CLIO, LLC
Santa Barbara, California • Denver, Colorado • Oxford, England

Copyright 2010 by Lawrence J. Morris

All rights reserved. No part of this publication may be reproduced, stored in a retrieval system, or transmitted, in any form or by any means, electronic, mechanical, photocopying, recording, or otherwise, except for the inclusion of brief quotations in a review, without prior permission in writing from the publisher.

Library of Congress Cataloging-in-Publication Data
Morris, Lawrence J.
  Military justice : a guide to the issues / Lawrence J. Morris ;
foreword by Francis A. Gilligan.
        p. cm. — (Contemporary military, strategic, and security issues)
  Includes bibliographical references and index.
    ISBN 978-0-275-99366-5 (hard copy : alk. paper) — ISBN 978-1-57356-753-4
(ebook)   1. Courts-martial and courts of inquiry—United States.   I. Title.
    KF7620.M67   2010
    343.73'0143—dc22   2009043567

ISBN: 978-0-275-99366-5
EISBN: 978-1-57356-753-4

14 13 12 11 10   1 2 3 4 5

This book is also available on the World Wide Web as an eBook.
Visit www.abc-clio.com for details.

Praeger
An Imprint of ABC-CLIO, LLC

ABC-CLIO, LLC
130 Cremona Drive, P.O. Box 1911
Santa Barbara, California 93116-1911

This book is printed on acid-free paper ∞

Manufactured in the United States of America

For

judge advocates—

the guardians of the

military justice system.

Contents

Foreword by Colonel (Retired) Francis A. Gilligan		ix
Introduction		xi
Chapter 1	Why a Military Justice System: An Introduction to the Theory and History of American Military Justice	1
Chapter 2	Founding of the Republic to Modern Times: Military Justice Develops Alongside the Professional Military	14
Chapter 3	Basics of the Military Justice System: Structure and Levels of Military Courts	34
Chapter 4	Basics of the Military Justice System: The Investigative and Pretrial Processes	47
Chapter 5	Basics of the Military Justice System: Defining Criminal Conduct in a Unique Society	63
Chapter 6	Basics of the Military Justice System: The Trial and Appellate Processes	90
Chapter 7	Implementing the Uniform Code of Military Justice: A Generation of Change	122
Chapter 8	There's More to Military Justice than Courts-Martial: Nonjudicial Punishment and Administrative Separations	148
Chapter 9	Back to the Future: Military Commissions to Try War Criminals	174
Glossary		201
Bibliography		207
Index		209

Foreword

With the armed forces deployed throughout the world undertaking a wide range of critical missions from nation building to fighting terrorism, the military justice system is in the forefront. There have been significant trials of service members, unlawful enemy combatants, and civilians accompanying the armed forces.

These cases bring attention and scrutiny to the military justice system. In studying this system, all must know not only the text of the Constitution, the Uniform Code of Military Justice, and the Manual for Courts-Martial, but also develop an awareness of history, tradition, purpose, and precedent in analyzing, interpreting, and practicing in this system. This book sets forth the democratic pedigree of our form of government and how the three branches of government interrelate in the military justice system, making it easier to understand the rules and procedures that are unique to military justice. This treatise emphasizes constitutional rights but recognizes that greater rights are granted by the code and the manual.

Whether a novice or an experienced practitioner, it is important to examine the purpose of the military criminal system in light of history. The historical vignettes concerning jurisdiction, geographical reach of code, and purposes of sentencing put this treatise in perspective.

Practitioners have a great deal of discretion, whether it is the prosecutor deciding what to charge or the defense counsel shaping the theme and theory of a case. The material in this book will be helpful in exercising that discretion and prompt reflection and deeper understanding by those entrusted with administering military justice—not only the lawyers but also commanders and other leaders who are charged with bringing about good order and discipline, fairness, and justice.

For all, this book sets forth the basic underlying concepts on which the military justice system is built and addresses many fundamental topics in a refreshing manner that should be intelligible to experts, lay readers, and military justice practitioners. When you step back from the fray, you realize that the military justice system is about doing justice, and this book will be an excellent guide to how that happens—and keeping it on course.

Colonel (Retired) Francis A. Gilligan

Introduction

The goal of this book is to provide an overview of the theory and practice of military justice, so that the interested reader—especially the nonlawyer, but also the practitioner new to military justice—receives a thorough and balanced overview of the military justice system. The book provides a comprehensive treatment of the current military justice system, enriched by enough history to make current practices understandable and future changes foreseeable. It addresses the system from the standpoint of society, which invests in the military; the command, through which good order and discipline are administered; and those who participate in the trial process.

I believe it is a fundamentally just system—but, as with all honorable systems of justice, is only as good as its participants' practices and ethics, and can always be improved. This book is not an apologia, nor does it reflect every criticism I might lodge or every reform I might recommend based on a career's worth of trials, teaching, and thinking about military justice.

I am indebted to many colleagues, judges, and former supervisors for their guidance, critiques, and tutelage over the years. While any mistakes are solely mine, I am especially beholden to my mother and sister, who edited it without the burden of having law degrees, and most of all to my wife, who edited with the burden of a law degree, caring for our six children, my odd hours, and even more clutter than usual.

CHAPTER 1

Why a Military Justice System: An Introduction to the Theory and History of American Military Justice

The United States retains the most wide-ranging, complex, and vibrant military justice system in the Western world—both just and robust according to its proponents, intrusive and archaic according to its harshest critics. A fundamental tool of discipline and justice, the system governs all military personnel, thousands of whom receive some form of discipline every year—and, in theory, the system touches all military personnel by girding the foundation of discipline and justice for an effective fighting force. The current system is best understood by first examining how it came into being (why there should be a specialized military code at all) and then examining the changes that have been made over more than 200 years—especially since World War II—to strengthen, reform, and invigorate a military justice system that, while retaining features of the systems that shaped it, has taken on a distinctly American flavor.

Roots

A military justice system is not unique to and did not originate with the United States. As with so many aspects of the U.S. government and its legal system, the military justice system can be traced to Europe well before there was any thought of a United States, much less a New World or colonization. There has been a need for military discipline as long as there have been organized armies, and historians agree that many early versions of military discipline were summary, cruel, and unmonitored, with scant concern for anything other than retribution and deterrence. As the concepts of individual rights and due process slowly evolved in most societies, some rudimentary protections, if not rights, gradually developed for soldiers who faced military discipline.

Military judges were known as early as the days of the Roman Empire, though rights and protections for soldiers were negligible in a system in which command was supreme. Usually a military justice system—if system is not too generous a description for some early efforts—was specific to a particular leader or particular conflict. Richard the Lionheart issued an ordinance in 1190 that punished his offending crusaders with sanctions that included fines and ignominious expulsion as well as tarring and feathering and burial alive. Some credit Richard II with publishing the first comprehensive articles of war in 1385, as they contained features that could be expected in most any code—prohibitions against disobedience, pillage, and theft—and punishments more associated with the 14th than 21st centuries, including amputation of the left ear, drawing, and beheading.[1] Many historians trace the roots of modern military justice to Gustavus Adolphus, the 17th-century Swedish king, famous tactician, and military innovator. Although some argue that his codification was less than original, it had significant impact in the way that it formed a philosophical and structural basis for many of the military codes that followed. The first suggestion of legislative involvement arose in 1689, when William and Mary, near contemporaries of Gustavus Adolphus accepted the Bill of Rights,[2] which required Parliament's consent to raising and keeping armies.

As with so much of the U.S. legal system, the underpinnings of U.S. military justice derive mainly from British sources, particularly the British articles of war, which changed radically as they evolved from the 12th century to the version in place at the time of the American Revolution. The central reason for a modern military justice system—enforcing discipline among soldiers who are part of a separate society—remains a core concern today, especially in the United States, whose system of military justice has broadened and strengthened while other countries have constricted or eliminated their military justice systems. Contemporary U.S. military justice, which dates from the implementation of the Uniform Code of Military Justice (UCMJ) in 1951, is far more complicated, more rigorous—and, to most observers, more fair—than any of its predecessors. While the core concerns of discipline in a separate society remain the foundation of and justification for the military justice system, they are amplified and modified by the realities, demands, and limitations of operating a military justice system in a Constitution-based, sophisticated society that insists on both discipline and justice in its all-volunteer force.

Guiding Principles and Concepts

The contemporary military justice system is rooted in principles and traditions that predate the Republic but that have evolved with, and in some cases preceded, developments in U.S. criminal jurisprudence society. The U.S. system of military justice, originally a clone of its British ancestor, began to form its own path and traditions, based in part on the kind of wars it fought and, eventually, the oversight and involvement of civilian leadership, which reflected society's and soldiers' expectations.[3]

Separate Society

Soldiers traditionally form a separate society. While they are citizens of the greater society, the military makes unique demands of soldiers (especially immediate obedience), and society has unique expectations of them (willingness to risk life and well-being); these concerns merit a separate system of discipline and justice. Courts have made such findings throughout history and have reiterated the concept again since adoption of the Uniform Code of Military Justice. "Military law . . . is a jurisprudence which exists separate and apart from the law which governs in our federal judicial establishment," the Supreme Court held in 1953 and has repeated often since.[4] The concerns will be addressed in detail throughout this book, but, taken together, they provide the reason to have a military justice system at all and the reason that such a system endures, especially in the United States' all-volunteer military, into the 21st century. The Second Continental Congress acknowledged and foresaw this distinctive society, even at a time when a large standing army was antithetical to many of the founders, finding that all citizens would have the right to indictment by "Grand Jury, except in cases arising in the land or naval forces"[5]—explicit recognition in the Bill of Rights that not all civilian criminal protections are practicable in the military.

Discipline

If there is a single reason for a code of military justice, it is the enforcement of discipline to manage the peculiar demands of maintaining an effective fighting force. Most societies recognize the military as a separate society in many respects, with expectations of its members for which there is no civilian corollary, even in police departments. American tradition, the Constitution, and Supreme Court case law explicitly and repeatedly acknowledge this for the U.S. military. The core demand of a military organization is obedience to lawful orders, and in this regard military discipline is tied to military effectiveness. John Adams took special interest in military discipline, observing, "If I were an officer, I am convinced I should be the most decisive disciplinarian in the Army. . . . Discipline in an Army is like the law in a civil society. There can be no liberty in a commonwealth where the laws are not revered and most sacredly observed, nor can there be happiness or safety in an army for a single hour when discipline is not observed." Similar observations have been made by leaders ranging from Winfield Scott to Sherman to MacArthur. Military law, mainly embodied in the Uniform Code of Military Justice in the United States, provides a wide range of mechanisms through which to enforce military discipline, deter misconduct, and thereby enhance military effectiveness.

The paramount importance of discipline is reflected both in the substance of military law and in its procedures. Discipline means that offenses that might be inapplicable or trivial in civilian life become crimes when a civilian becomes a soldier or are treated much more seriously when soldiers are involved. Some military offenses such as absence from duty and disrespect have no civilian equivalents; the same with sleeping on guard duty, not to mention spying or treason.[6] Other offenses become more significant in a military setting when factors peculiar to military life—living in close proximity and an expectation of trust and honor—are breached by offenses such as larceny in the barracks or on a submarine. Some of the procedures in military law are designed to accommodate the strong emphasis on discipline coupled with efficiency in a manner that would not be considered lawful and perhaps not fair in the civilian world. Smaller juries with nonunanimous verdicts are one example, but the same interests in efficiency and discipline also provide unique flexibility to disapprove or radically reduce findings and sentences in a manner unavailable in the civilian world. The fact that discipline is the central organizing principal of the military justice system brings other related concepts to the fore.

Command-Run System

The most distinctive procedural feature of the military justice system is that decisions on what to charge, whether to prosecute, and at what level to prosecute are made exclusively by commanders. This reflects the concept that runs throughout the system—that commanders are in charge, not lawyers or other disciplinary officials. Judge advocates (the most accurate term for uniformed military lawyers regardless of their branch of service) advise commanders, and in some narrow circumstances commanders may not act without the advice of a lawyer,[7] but most decisions that are made by lawyers in the civilian world—such as the bringing of charges and determining their disposition—are made by military commanders. In practice, most commanders rely heavily on legal advice from their judge advocates, but in most instances that advice is nonbinding; commanders enjoy tremendous discretion and near plenary authority to bring charges, pick juries, approve (or disapprove) findings and sentences, and grant clemency. This concept might appear to run counter to the disinterest with which civilian prosecutors are expected to approach prosecutorial decisions and has been both the source of abuse and criticism and the cause of extensive protections, especially those instituted since World War II, meant to guard against and correct for unlawful command influence, addressed in more detail in chapter 7. Commanders are also expected to be disinterested, but their central role in the military justice system is based on their not being *un*interested—that is, they have a professional interest in the good order and discipline of their units but must not have a personal interest in the outcome of a particular case.

Justice

If the military justice system were only meant to enforce discipline, then it would be a much simpler system—more efficient, more summary, more draconian, and presumably much less trusted or effective. Providing discipline coupled with justice is the linchpin of the military justice system. A key factor that motivated the movement that resulted in passage of the UCMJ in 1950 was the perception by many in Congress that the UCMJ tilted too much toward discipline at the expense of justice. The reasons to reemphasize justice were both noble and practical.

Critics, reform advocates, and members of Congress repeatedly made the point that soldiers were citizens who must not lose the fundamental guarantees of citizenship when joining the military. While it was almost universally acknowledged that some Constitutional rights cannot be available to soldiers in the same way that they are to civilians—there are, for example, some restrictions on speech that would not apply in the civilian community—it was also emphasized that the only limitations that should be placed on soldiers' rights are those directly necessary for military effectiveness. The temptation for the military to overreach would create a class of citizen-soldiers unduly removed from the protections that their fellow citizens enjoyed.

There is a highly pragmatic component to the concern as well. A military justice system in a free society is only truly effective when it commands the broad respect of those whom it governs. The concern for justice, then, is grounded partly in the concern that good order and discipline are so important that they must be rooted in a system that soldiers essentially trust. If soldiers perceive that the system—popular or not—essentially produced just results, then it would be an effective tool for leaders to enforce discipline and produce a fighting force that is more cohesive and effective. Implicit in this concern is that the results of any criminal process are more likely to be reliable when they incorporate fundamental Constitutional protections, especially the fundamental guarantees of due process, such as the right against self-incrimination and the right to call and confront witnesses.

Inherent Authority

Military commanders have wide-ranging authority to take actions to accomplish their missions. At its most elemental level, this means to make decisions to fight and win a nation's wars. To accomplish that mission, and always to be prepared to accomplish that mission, a commander must be able to rely on a trained and ready force. Inherent authority, then, derives directly from concern for mission accomplishment, of which readiness and its major component, unit discipline, is an indispensable part.[8] Every commander has this authority, informed by his mission and limited and clarified by the leaders above him, irrespective of any formal grant or further authorization. This authority is as plenary as it is because it serves a military and societal purpose: inherent authority corresponds to and is meant to reinforce the tremendous responsibility that society in general and the military in particular places on a leader. If we expect her to do anything—anything lawful—to accomplish her mission, then we must entrust her with the authority, broad but not unchecked, to execute that mission.

Individualized Treatment

This corollary of command authority is one of the most controversial—most praised *and* most criticized—aspects of the military justice system. There are very few instances in the Uniform Code of Military Justice or the Manual for Courts-Martial where a particular disposition of a case is mandated. A few of the most serious offenses carry mandatory punishment at general courts-martial (e.g., premeditated murder and treason), but the great majority of offenses carry no required level of disposition, and commanders have all but unlimited authority to dispose of them in the manner they see fit. As discussed in chapter 4, commanders are encouraged to consider a wide range of factors when making recommendations and decisions regarding disposition of misconduct—but the decision ultimately is theirs and is intended to be unique for each case. Unlike most civilian jurisdictions, there are no sentencing guidelines (again, but for the rare case of mandatory punishments), and courts have struck down commanders' efforts to issue templatelike punishment guidelines, even when those efforts have been motivated by commanders' desire to ensure consistency in treatment.[9]

Lowest Level of Disposition

One principal that further amplifies, and in many instances moderates, the bedrock principals of command control and individualized treatment is the expectation that offenses will be disposed of at the lowest level consistent with good order and discipline. Although this is not an unfamiliar concept in the civilian world, there are distinctly military factors that make it more important—and perhaps easier to execute—than in the civilian world. The military justice system features a wider range of disposition options than are available in the civilian world. Because there are numerous nonpunitive, administrative, and corrective measures available to address conduct that also could be characterized as criminal, and there are also three levels of criminal disposition, commanders can more carefully calibrate the disciplinary option to the needs of the military and of the soldier.

At its root, this reflects other factors for which there are no civilian parallels. The military—and, by extension, U.S. society—already has invested resources (and hopes) in any soldier who gets in trouble, starting with the sunk cost of recruiting the all-volunteer force, through the educational and training costs that are considerable at the outset of a military career and that continue throughout every soldier's career. As discussed earlier, the system always seeks to balance mission and discipline with justice and due process. The preference for the lowest level of disposition is meant to ensure that good order and discipline are served by meting out punishment no harsher than necessary and by imposing corrective measures whenever possible to try to retain most who commit misconduct, ideally setting an ethic of accountability moderated by common sense. When commanders are seen to have carefully and appropriately selected a disposition option, then those who observe their conduct are more likely to believe the system is just—and to conform their conduct accordingly.

Reliability

A justice system that does not produce reliable results has no credibility. Reliability is a shared concern of all participants in the system, starting with commanders, who seek good order and discipline but who base discipline-related decisions on finding and knowing accurate information. Judges and juries insist on accurate information in making their judgments. Besides the accused's obvious interest in accuracy, however, observers and the rank and file base much of their perception of the system's justice on its ability to produce reliable results and on their sense that the justice they observe being carried out is fundamentally fair. Because the Military Rules of Evidence are so similar to the Federal Rules of Evidence, and because the Rules for Courts-Martial have similar sophistication (and many similar provisions) to the Federal Rules of Criminal Procedure, it is only where there are specific military needs (such as the readiness concerns that drive the policies that permit inspections of military units, discussed in chapter 8) that the military justice system significantly deviates from the civilian world. As in the civilian world where there are fewer procedural protections in contesting a parking ticket compared to a felony, there are gradations of due process that accompany the various levels of discipline in the military.

Worldwide Applicability

Soldiers deploy, face danger, and represent the United States wherever they serve.[10] Consequently, there is a need for discipline everywhere. Most U.S. laws do not have extraterritorial jurisdiction, but the UCMJ specifically applies to all soldiers anywhere in the world.[11] In some narrow circumstances, it can apply to U.S. civilians, civilians in occupied territories, and enemy belligerents.

The main reason the UCMJ applies everywhere is obvious—we tend to fight wars on foreign soil, and if discipline is at the center of military justice, the military needs to have jurisdiction wherever soldiers are deployed. Such jurisdiction is also a function of the United States' sovereignty. A nation's ability to prosecute its own citizens for their violations of domestic law is tied directly to its independence and character. Because the projection of U.S. fighting power is a distinctively American function, then the ability to hold soldiers accountable for their conduct in such settings is fundamental to the effectiveness of the fighting force as well as American accountability. The fact of worldwide applicability is essential to reducing the risk that U.S. service members undertake when they serve outside the United States and a recognition that they should not ordinarily be subject to the jurisdiction of a foreign nation that might be adversarial, if not hostile. Although the military justice system might ultimately be used to prosecute a U.S. soldier who engages in misconduct overseas, reserving and asserting jurisdiction of the military justice system is based on the belief that such a prosecution would be more just and would be consistent with U.S. notions of due process than a trial by a foreign government that might be politically motivated or brought under a system that provides lesser due process protections than the UCMJ.

As discussed several places in this book, there are circumstances in which the United States cedes some of that sovereignty for soldiers stationed overseas, but usually in peacetime locations and always as a function of negotiated agreements, usually Status of Forces Agreements (SOFAs) with established host nations with whom the United States enjoys friendly relations. For example, after our troops in Western Europe, Japan, and Korea became invited forces[12] after World War II and the Korean War, the United States and those nations negotiated—and periodically revised—agreements under which U.S. personnel became subject to host nation laws under certain circumstances. The SOFAs set out a process for determining under what circumstances the host nation might be able to assert jurisdiction over U.S. military personnel.

The balance between U.S. sovereignty and accountability for soldier misconduct also arose in recent times, when the International Criminal Court (ICC) was implemented as a result of the Rome Treaty of 2002. The treaty set up an international court with the power to try citizens of all signatory nations for various crimes when their host nations had shown a refusal or inability to try them. Although the United States signed that treaty, it also took advantage of a provision that permitted bilateral agreements between signatories to opt out of the ICC for conduct by U.S. soldiers on that nation's soil. The United States signed at least 95 such Article 98 agreements, based on Article 98 of the Rome Treaty, encountering considerable criticism from some quarters, although it was seen by U.S. military and diplomatic leaders as a predicate to being able to station military personnel in those countries.

An offshoot of worldwide applicability is the inherent difficulties of managing a justice system in far-flung places. While this is less true in the age of instant communications and easier transportation, it remains true that the stresses of the battlefield alone make it more difficult to manage a fully functioning system of military justice away from U.S. soil. In addition, there are purely practical factors, such as making lawyers and supporting resources available, which are made more difficult by distance and are subject to variables such as host-nation comity and laws.

Judicial Deference

The military has its own appellate courts (addressed in detail in chapter 6) that are concerned with reviewing courts-martial convictions and do not have jurisdiction to hear disputes regarding other forms of discipline, including nonjudicial punishment or administrative sanctions or separations. Disputes involving military discipline in areas other than courts-martial occasionally find their way to civilian courts, most often when a soldier claims that his administrative separation was unlawful and, at times, to assert that he should not have to serve in the military based on conscientious objection, unlawful enlistment, or inability to perform duties. When the issues before civilian courts involve the exercise of discipline or commander discretion tied to the good order and discipline of the unit or of the military as a whole, courts are most likely to defer to the judgment of the commander in question. This concept of judicial deference has been reinforced in decisions that have found that commanders have the right to regulate the distribution of petitions on a military installation,[13] that soldiers cannot sue commanders based on decisions with which they disagree, and that the military's rulings forbidding the wearing of distinctive religious garb are permissible, based on the military assertion of the need for uniformity, tied to good order and discipline.[14] Civilian federal courts also will not permit soldiers facing courts-martial to jump the court-martial process and seek relief in ordinary federal courts.[15] Not all of these cases relate directly to the criminal aspects of military justice, but they reflect the strong inclination of civilian courts, including the Supreme Court, to defer to the military as a separate society and to set a lenient standard of review for decisions that are within the judgment of commanders, leaders, and policymakers.

Balancing Military Needs, Soldier Rights, Society's Expectations

This concern is treated elsewhere in greater detail, and it is the central concern of courts and policymakers as they carefully strike the balance between a system that is grounded in the unique demands of the military and that is grounded in the Constitution and must be consistent with the fundamental principles of U.S. law and procedure. In many respects, soldiers yield some of the protections and liberties of their civilian contemporaries. Some Constitutional rights clearly do not apply in the same manner to soldiers—for example, the rights of free speech and association are circumscribed in the military. Soldiers do not, however, stand outside the Constitution, and they gain, under the UCMJ, some procedural protections that their civilian counterparts lack. For example, Article 31 of the UCMJ gives soldiers greater protection than the *Miranda* ruling; the Article 32 pretrial investigation gives soldiers greater protections than a civilian grand jury; and, after trial, the commander may disapprove or reduce the findings and sentence in almost all cases. On the other hand, the system features numerous compromises or efficiencies that are tied to military demands—such as the rule declaring witnesses farther than 100 miles away to be unavailable for Article 32 investigations.

Because U.S. military commanders swear an oath to uphold and defend the Constitution[16]—they do not swear allegiance to the president or to commanders above them—their authority is circumscribed by the Constitution and the U.S. system of laws. While inherent and broad, then, military authority is not unlimited, and many of the details of the military justice system concern balancing inherent authority and the principles underlying inherent authority (discipline, effectiveness, society's high expectations and confidence in national defense) with concepts that are fundamental to the U.S. system of law (due process in all its variations). That combination yields the complexity and, it is hoped, the credibility and effectiveness of the military justice system.

Sources of Military Law

Military law is sometimes misunderstood by both its critics and its proponents as a legal discipline that is so distinctive that its sources and contours are hard to discern. This is not the case. Although military law, like much of U.S. law, has its roots in principles and practices that predate the formation of the republic, the starting point for military law is the Constitution, and the process of finding and analyzing military law follows a firm and predictable rubric.

Constitution

Notwithstanding the common supposition in the barracks or on the streets that the Constitution does not apply to the military, it does, though differently at times because of the factors that are a common theme in military justice—essentially the unique demands of military readiness and good order and discipline. The Constitution is the primary source of military law, as with all domestic law, in that it expressly empowers Congress to "make Rules for the Government of the land and naval Forces."[17] The Constitution also makes the president the commander-in-chief, and, because of this, the president has a unique role to play in the promulgation of military law, and the executive branch has greater authority and responsibility in military law than it does in other areas of federal criminal law. The ways in which the Constitution applies differently to the military will be addressed throughout the book; the differences only arise in areas in which military necessity collides with the freedoms, expectations, and procedural guarantees of the Constitution. For example, military members enjoy fewer First Amendment protections (they can read and write what they want but cannot, for example, march in a partisan parade while in uniform), narrower Fourth Amendment protections (their military barracks and gear—and bodies—can be inspected without probable cause), and some aspects of the Sixth Amendment are made expressly inapplicable to them (no right to indictment by grand jury).

Statute (Uniform Code of Military Justice)

Congress has exercised its Constitutional authority to make rules governing the military since its first passage of the British-influenced Articles of War and most recently by enacting the UCMJ in 1950, in its amendments to the UCMJ in the Military Justice Act of 1968, and with periodic changes in the UCMJ in subsequent years.

Regulation

Most statutory schemes require detailed implementation by regulation. The same is true for the UCMJ. In addition, because of his unique status as commander-in-chief, the president plays a greater role in promulgating the military justice system than, for example, a governor might play in enacting a state criminal code. The president publishes the Manual for Courts-Martial, which contains the Rules for Courts-Martial (essentially the rules of criminal procedure for the military), the maximum punishments for military offenses, and the Military Rules of Evidence; both of these are treated in detail in chapter 6.

Military Regulations

The Department of Defense and each of the military services have authority to publish regulations that govern all aspects of military operations. Each service has many dozens of regulations, a few of which are especially relevant to military justice, because they either criminalize certain conduct (such as sexual harassment or improper use of computers) or set standards of performance, which set duties that can be breached, holding soldiers liable for derelictions of duty. Only regulations that are made expressly punitive may be used as the basis for charging someone with violating a lawful general regulation (again, treated in detail in chapter 5), but any regulation that sets military standards can be the basis for a charge of dereliction of duty. In addition, certain ethics and procurement regulations have punitive elements, the violation of which could subject a service member to military disciplinary sanctions.

Local Regulations and Orders

Almost every military organization has its own sets of orders, regulations, and procedures. Those published by a general officer and made expressly punitive (usually by plain language that says that those who violate it are subject to the UCMJ) can also form the basis for criminal liability under the UCMJ. Local regulations can address a wide range of conduct, from carrying knives longer than three inches to wearing headphones while jogging on a military installation. Commanders receive great deference in publishing such orders, and courts test them by evaluating the extent to which they foster good order and discipline. In recent years, commanders have issued orders in areas such as requiring off-post wear of motorcycle helmets or limiting the amount of alcohol drunk while on liberty, raising questions, occasionally litigated, on whether they exceed the scope of a commander's responsibility for and authority over his troops. Some of these questions can be traced to a balancing act that started the first time a military leader began to codify military law.

Notes

1. See Nicole E. Jaeger, "Maybe Soldiers Have Rights After All," *Journal of Criminal Law and Criminology* 87 (1997).

2. Gustavus Adolphus's vigorous reign concluded with his death in battle, at age 41, in 1632. William and Mary jointly took the throne in 1689.

3. The best contemporary treatise on military justice, the modern rival and supplement to William Winthrop's seminal *Military Law and Precedents*, is the two-volume Francis A. Gilligan and Frederic I. Lederer, *Court-Martial Procedure* (3d ed., 2007), on which I drew in several instances in thinking about military justice and writing portions of this book.

4. *Burns v. Wilson*, 346 U.S. 137, 140 (1954).

5. United States Constitution, Amendment V.

6. As will be discussed later, it is not that such conduct is necessarily overlooked in the civilian world—it can get a person fired and harm his reputation—but that the conduct cannot generally form the basis of a criminal prosecution.

7. A commander may not refer a case to a general court-martial, the highest level of military court, without receiving the advice of a judge advocate (military lawyer) and without that judge advocate's certifying that there is jurisdiction over the offense, that the charge properly states an offense, and that evidence is available to prove the offense. See Rule for Courts-Martial 406, discussed in detail in chapter 4.

8. This is not to say that good order and discipline is paramount over all other factors, including technical competence and morale; most leaders would agree that overemphasis on discipline and commander inflexibility can be just as corrosive as laxness or inconsistency.

9. In *United States v. Martinez*, 42 M.J. 327, 334 (C.A.A.F. 1995), the Court of Appeals for the Armed Forces expressed its disapproval of a policy letter, published by an Air Force base commander, that set specific punishment guidelines, tied to the offender's rank, for those who committed drinking-related offenses.

10. Military law applies to members of all of the military services. I use the term *soldiers* throughout the text generically to apply to soldiers, sailors, airmen, and members of the Coast Guard.

11. "This chapter [of Title 10, United States Code] applies in all places." 10 USC sec. 805 (Art. 5, UCMJ).

12. Such invited forces are not considered to be invaders but to be allied with the host nation, serving at the host nation's pleasure on their soil. U.S. forces in Iraq transitioned to such status in several stages starting in 2008 and concluding in 2009.

13. *Brown v. Glines*, 444 U.S. 348 (1980) (Air Force personnel protesting Air Force grooming standards could be required to have their petition approved before distributing it and seeking signatures on a military installation).

14. In *Goldman v. Weinberger*, 475 U.S. 503 (1986), the Supreme Court deferred to the military's judgment that regulating the wear of such distinctive apparel (a yarmulke was at issue in this case) was worthy of deference, because the military was best equipped to

evaluate the impact on good order and discipline, and to consider the difficulty in implementing an accommodationist policy (though they eventually did).

15. *Schlesinger v. Councilman*, 420 U.S. 738 (1975).

16. The commissioning oath for military officers, last modified in 1959, is the following:

"I, _____, having been appointed an officer in the Army of the United States, as indicated above in the grade of _____ do solemnly swear (or affirm) that I will support and defend the Constitution of the United States against all enemies, foreign or domestic, that I will bear true faith and allegiance to the same; that I take this obligation freely, without any mental reservations or purpose of evasion; and that I will well and faithfully discharge the duties of the office upon which I am about to enter; So help me God." (DA Form 71, August 1, 1959.) The terms of the oath are set by federal law. See 10 U.S. Code 502 (which does not include the phrase, "So help me God").

17. U.S. Constitution, art. I, sec. 14.

CHAPTER 2

Founding of the Republic to Modern Times: Military Justice Develops Alongside the Professional Military

The United States has had some form of a code of military conduct about as long as it has had an army—and longer than it has been a country. The Army was created on June 14, 1775. A couple of weeks later, on June 30, the Second Continental Congress approved the Articles of War to govern the conduct of the Continental Army (the Judge Advocate General's Corps was established on July 29). Reflecting the aspiring nation's continued close cultural association with the country against whom it was rebelling, the 69 Articles of War that Congress approved were virtually identical to the 74 contained in the British Code at that time. These were not, however, the first military codes in the Colonies, as several of them had passed military codes earlier that year, starting with Massachusetts Bay's act of April 5, 1775 (two weeks before the battles of Lexington and Concord) and followed shortly by similar enactments in Connecticut, Rhode Island, and New Hampshire.

The initial Articles of War were reenacted in 1776, slightly altering and enlarging the 1775 version. Meanwhile, commanders already were employing the system and seeking changes to it. In 1776, Thomas Hickey, one of George Washington's trusted aides, was arrested for attempting to poison Washington's peas. In a court-martial that began 11 days after Hickey's arrest, he was found guilty and ordered to be hanged. Washington approved the sentence the day after it was handed down, and Hickey was hanged the next day in front of 20,000 onlookers, mostly soldiers—an obvious exercise of the commander's desire to deter future such misconduct by others. The framers, though rebels, seem to have placed great stock in military discipline. The same year of the Hickey court-martial, Washington's request to increase the maximum number of lashes from 39 to 100 was approved (though still short of the British maximum of 1,000), and there were minor changes in 1778 and 1786. The 1786 Code, of which John Adams was a primary drafter, reduced the size of a court-martial from 13 to 5 members, in recognition of the difficulty of finding sufficient numbers in an army that had begun to establish remote outposts. This statute also provided that no sentence of life or dismissal of an officer could be approved unless reviewed by the secretary of war and approved by Congress—the first introduction, however slight, of post-trial due process.

> ### *Swift Justice: Public Execution for Anti-Washington Plotter*
>
> In 1776, George Washington brought court-martial charges against Thomas Hickey, one of his guards, for a conspiracy to assassinate him as well as for other misconduct. It was thought that one of Hickey's co-conspirators was Washington's female cook, who apprised Washington of the plot. He was tried by a court of 13 officers and sentenced to death, which was carried out in front of perhaps 20,000 other soldiers brought together for the occasion, because General Washington thought the public execution would serve as a deterrent to future such misconduct. Washington, who approved the sentence the day after the court issued it (it was executed the following day), also issued this statement along with the execution:
>
>> The unhappy fate of Thomas Hickey, executed this day for mutiny, sedition and treachery, the GENERAL hopes will be a warning to every soldier in the army to avoid these crimes, and all others, so disgraceful to the character of a soldier and pernicious to his country, whose pay he receives and whose bread he eats. And to avoid those crimes the most certain method is to keep out of the temptation of them, and particularly to avoid lewd women, who, by the dying confession of this poor criminal, first led him into practices which ended in an untimely and ignominious death.[1]

The Code of 1806, still known as the Articles of War, was Congress's most comprehensive treatment of military justice to this point in the history of the young nation. It expanded to 101 articles and included spying as an offense for the first time but left unchanged the bulk of the 1775 act and its procedures. It still featured punishments that reflect the tenor of the day (ear cropping, head shaving, dunking, ball and chain, marking with indelible ink), and for the first time it prohibited "contemptuous words" against the president, vice president, Congress, and the leaders of the state in which the soldier was located. This code remained intact, with occasional very minor changes (and a technical reenactment in 1878), until the 20th century. It spanned a period of tremendous change in the United States' identity as a nation, its willingness and ability to be engaged militarily beyond its borders, and its concept and operation of a standing army—all of which had some impact on the need for and nature of a military criminal code. The Articles were in effect during the War of 1812 and during the first two significant engagements outside U.S. soil, the Mexican-American War (1846–48) and the Spanish-American War (1898); the Articles also, obviously, were in effect during the protracted and bloody Civil War.

Two midcentury incidents contrasted the traditions and legitimacy of U.S. military justice. In 1842, Philip Spencer, rebellious son of Secretary of War John C. Spencer, had entered the Navy after dropping out of college. After brawls and an assault on an officer, it took his father's extraordinary intercession to keep his nascent career alive. He was reassigned to the *USS Somers,* and, on a voyage home from Liberia, he was suspected of mutiny. He was shackled at the orders of the ship's leadership, and names were found in his razor case written in Greek (he had founded the Chi Psi fraternity at Union College) that appeared to implicate him in planning for a mutiny. Two other men were arrested, and the ship's officers met, deciding to hang Spencer by the yardarm of the ship—which they did five days after he was apprehended. This incident highlighted the summary nature of discipline on a ship at sea, not grounded in any meaningful sense in procedure, much less a sense of justice.

In 1857, the Supreme Court for the first time had the opportunity to address whether courts-martial had a valid constitutional basis, ruling in *Dynes v. Hoover*[2] that the court-martial of a sailor for desertion and other crimes was proper, because the Articles of War were rooted in Congress's authority to "provide and maintain a navy" as well as the authority, also in Article I, to make rules for governing the land and naval forces. It further supported the constitutionality of the court-martial by pointing to the Constitution's intentional excepting of the military from the requirement that a grand jury indictment precede a felony trial. "These provisions show that Congress has the power to provide for the trial and punishment of military and naval offenses in the manner then and now practiced by civilized nations," the majority held, adding that the judicial power found in Article III and the legislative power located in Article I "are entirely independent of each other."

Over time, it became clear to most practitioners that the Articles fulfilled their main purpose, enforcing good order and discipline, but that they were too inflexible and too formal to swiftly address soldier misconduct, especially minor misconduct. There were two main disciplinary options: the general court-martial, with its fairly strict procedures and due process, and the summary court-martial, with its minimal due process and correspondingly minimal punishment. Sentiment built for change that would provide a range of disciplinary choices that would enable commanders to adjudge discipline in a more precise manner, leading to better justice as well as procedural efficiency. As always for the first hundred years of U.S. military history, the nation looked to the British.

Navy Sails Alone

The singular military justice-related development of the mid-20th century was the enactment of a military criminal code that embraced all services. From the beginning of the U.S. military, the Navy had sailed alone, with a distinct disciplinary culture that was generally harsher and more summary in nature than the Articles of War—heavy on the corporal discipline and especially heavy on the commander's prerogatives. The nature of naval recruitment often meant that naval officers had the challenge of commanding a ship mainly populated by "townies" who felt little affinity or loyalty to the imposed leader. There was no U.S. Navy from 1783 to 1797, so, when President John Adams reinstated the Navy, he looked to the Royal Navy for guidance in establishing a disciplinary system. The British, in turn, had borrowed from the Romans, meaning that, on the cusp of the 19th century, the navy of the world's newest nation, framed by idealism and moored to a Constitution, featured flogging, keel hauling, the liberal use of irons, and the threat and occasional employment of capital punishment. Congress passed the Act for Government of the Navy in 1799, and in 1800 it enacted the Articles for the Government of the Navy, which established crimes, rules, and procedures for the Navy that were different from the Articles of War. Although many provisions were similar or identical, there were significant differences, the most notable being the authorized punishments. Nearly daily floggings during the five-month-long voyage of the *Congress* in 1845–46 bothered crew member and future Senator Robert F. Stockton so much that he successfully introduced legislation four years later to abolish flogging. The abolition of flogging, which Congress approved in 1850, had less to do with concern about sailors' welfare than it did with slavery: Northern legislators wanted to abolish flogging as a way of emphasizing a practice frequently used against slaves, while Southern congressmen wanted to legitimize such corporal punishment on slaves by pointing to its use in the military. Southern withdrawal from Congress in 1861 provided an opening for reform that was quickly exploited. Gideon Welles, Lincoln's secretary of the Navy, had little tolerance of what he considered to be archaic provisions, such as the rules that permitted courts-martial to settle disputes between officers. Although he had served for three years as chief of the Bureau of Provisions and Clothing for the Navy from 1846 to 1849, he was a lawyer, journalist, and politician, not a career Navy man, and was willing to make other changes, including a drastic reduction in the types of offenses that warranted courts-martial, because serving on courts-martial was consuming enormous amounts of officers' time, made even more draining by the fact that only career officers (about 20% of the force) had been permitted to serve on courts-martial. The 1860s were the period of greatest change in the Articles for Government of the Navy until the mid-20th century, when initial attempts to reform them ultimately resulted in their abolition.[3]

Introducing Military Corrections

While very little changed in the laws and procedures governing military justice during most of the 19th century, there was a major change in the rules, process, and philosophy governing what came to be known as military corrections. In the early days of the standing Army, military prisoners were held at Governor's Island, New York, or in state penitentiaries. In 1871, Secretary of War William W. Belknap, prompted by Thomas Barr, an Army major who later became judge advocate general, became concerned about the quality and effectiveness of military confinement. As with the Articles of War, the United States looked to the British for guidance, and Belknap sent a study committee to examine military confinement in Canada, the result of which was a plea for a system "more in consonance with humanity and the enlightened views of the present day." The report urged adopting the British primary goals for its confinement facilities—"to maintain discipline in the army, to reform offenders, and to repress repetition of military offenses"—as well as its main features, including rules and physical layout, which emphasized what was considered to be the optimal combination of work and rehabilitation. By 1874, when Congress passed a final bill establishing the United States Disciplinary Barracks at Fort Leavenworth, Kansas, it had codified very similar goals for the institution, which remain virtually unchanged today: essentially, to return soldiers to productive civilian life. Policy leaders had four major goals and motivations: to (1) standardize the treatment of military prisoners, (2) deter desertion (and implicitly military crimes in general, though desertion was a particular scourge at that time), (3) minimize the mixing of "good" and hardened prisoners, and (4) restore soldiers to duty or prepare for return to civilian society those who could not or should not be restored to duty. The rules for governing military confinement facilities are addressed in chapter 6.

Early 20th Century

The concerns of leaders and practitioners are well documented in a set of documents, extraordinary for the quality of analysis, detail, and plain English, generated by the secretary of war and judge advocate general in 1912. As with later changes to the military justice system (see chapter 7 for the timing of military justice reforms in relation to the Korean and Vietnam Wars), a major proposal for systemic change in the early 20th century came on the (of course unforeseen) cusp of major conflict, as World War I started two years later. In a letter of transmittal dated April 19, 1912, Secretary of War Henry L. Stimson wrote to Congressman James Hay, Chairman of the House of Representatives Committee on Military Affairs.[4] In his letter, Secretary Stimson explained what he characterized as the urgent need for change in the Articles of War and advocated that Congress promptly enact the first significant changes in a century. This letter was accompanied by a letter from Major General Enoch H. Crowder, the judge advocate general, to Secretary Stimson, in which General Crowder made a detailed and articulate case for the substantial revisions by citing fluently and persuasively to the history of the Articles of War and the theories on which they were based.

Secretary Stimson's brief letter highlights concepts that General Crowder then develops in more detail. The secretary writes that the disciplinary structure under which the military then operated—general courts-martial or summary courts-martial, with nothing in between—"impair[s] the efficiency and discipline of the Army." He cites the requirement for 13 panel members (jurors) for the felony-level general court-martial, made even more complicated by the prohibition against regular army officers serving on courts-martial for other forces, such as regulars, volunteers, and militia—a procedural rigidity made even more unworkable by the fact that military members from all such forces were typically brigaded together and fought together. (Such distinctions among the forces have evaporated over time, especially in the latter 20th century, but they were matters of cultural and operational significance at the time, and the law reflected that.) The general court-martial was the felony-level court that could adjudge any punishment up to death and dishonorable discharge. The summary court-martial could adjudge only one month's confinement and forfeitures and could not be employed against officers. Regimental or garrison courts had been introduced, but they had essentially the same attributes as summary courts-martial, and consequently they were rarely used—they did not provide the flexible, efficient intermediate disciplinary vehicle that commanders sought, because they only had marginally greater authority (maximum three months confinement as opposed to maximum one month at a summary court-martial and similar authority on forfeitures), insufficient in the eyes of most commanders to be worth the investment in a court proceeding with multiple court members, compared to the one-officer summary court-martial. Secretary Stimson characterized the general court-summary court dichotomy as "unsystematic and unscientific" and told Congress, "there is need of an intermediate disciplinary court to deal with that large proportion of cases midway between the grave offenses calling for dismissal, dishonorable discharge, or detention, to be disposed of by general court-martial, and the minor offenses calling for very light punishment."

General Crowder developed the secretary's main points, providing detail and analysis in support of his perspective. The ratio of general courts-martial to summary courts-martial was, to his and most leaders' perspectives, greatly unbalanced in that there were too many summary courts-martial compared to general courts-martial. Their point was not that any of the summary courts-martial necessarily should have been a general court-martial, but that not all summary courts-martial necessarily merited such comparatively modest disposition; it was not a desire for greater discipline but a desire for more disciplinary choices, especially an intermediate option between summary and general courts-martial. In 1910, there were 5,206 general courts-martial and 42,275 summary courts-martial, a less than one-to-eight ratio; in 1911, the only other year for which he provided data, there was a similar imbalance: 3,851 general courts-martial and 33,082 summary courts-martial, a nearly one-to-nine ratio. The numbers themselves, of course, are not necessarily illustrative of a problem—if, in fact, 10 percent to 15 percent of the cases merited general court-martial and 85 percent to 90 percent merited the lighter punishment options of a summary court-martial. The problem, however, was in the rigid choice—a general court-martial that had felony-level powers including death (when authorized) and dishonorable discharge or the summary court-martial whose maximum was a month's confinement and a month's forfeiture of pay. As General Crowder wrote, general courts-martial were plagued by an "unwieldiness" that stemmed from their having to address all "charges [that were] too serious for summary court-martial." He illustrated the problem further by drawing a contrast with the British experience at a time when British military justice practices still were considered to be the most illustrative and relevant in analyzing U.S. military justice. This comparison, Crowder believed, reflected the differences in their approaches to discipline.

The British had five levels of courts-martial, with clearly different jurisdictional levels and corresponding levels of evidentiary and procedural complexity. Some only applied during war time and during expeditions in which the increasingly adventurous British found themselves deployed. The courts were general court-martial, field general court-martial, disciplinary court-martial, regulatory court-martial, and summary court-martial. General Crowder cited statistics showing that, during an eight-year period from 1905 to 1913, Great Britain, with an army of about 250,000 personnel, half of them stationed abroad, held a total of 180 general courts-martial, 168 of them abroad. During the same period, the U.S. military was about half the size of Great Britain, and it held 41,726 courts-martial, a rate of 4,636.2 per year compared to 20 per year in Great Britain. Crowder concluded that the general court-martial in the United States was being used to address offenses that belonged somewhere between the summary court-martial and the felony-level general court-martial. He observed that, "because of the difficulties of bringing them to trial," cases were "delayed until the cases are nearly or quite forgotten by those cognizant of the facts, and all that salutary disciplinary influence resulting from prompt trial is lost." Because of the "unwieldiness" of the general court-martial and the fact that many less serious offenses cluttered its docket, Crowder believed that the "practical result is that . . . the grave offenses have, in many instances, immunity from prompt and adequate punishment." He believed that an intermediate court should try about 40 percent of all cases and proposed three tiers of courts: general courts-martial for grave offenses that would require significant confinement and dishonorable discharge; special courts-martial, where the accused should likely be retained but whose offense merits significant discipline; and the summary court-martial for minor offenses with limited punishments.

The marked contrast between the poles of the U.S. military justice system (full-level felony court or low-level summary court) and the carefully stratified British system was all the more notable because the U.S. military justice system had such deep British roots. It would have immediate consequence because of the proposal by some congressional reformers to assign judge advocates to each trial, which Crowder thought was unworkable in light of the relatively small legal corps then in existence. It also sparked discussion about whether that judge advocate's rulings on evidentiary matters should have the sort of binding finality we have come—generations later—to associate with trial judges both inside and outside of the military. While Crowder agreed with extending authority to the judge advocate, he noted that the British practice bound the court-martial to the "decision of the judge advocate except for very weighty reasons," a policy that "practically exonerates the members of the court-martial from liability" for legal decisions. He believed that the proposed language that the judge advocate "shall

Founding of the Republic to Modern Times

govern the court-martial" was a radical step, as, "[t]he judge advocate of the British court has not that authority." He did not offer a strong recommendation on this issue, because he seemed mainly interested in bringing it to the committee's attention, saying it was "rather a weighty matter to consider whether you want to do it or not." He did, however, balk at a provision that would permit the judge advocate to overrule the directions of the convening authority. "I assume that is error in drawing the bill," he testified to Congress in 1919, adding, "I believe in maintaining the responsibility of the court for a decision of the legal questions."[5] The debate concerning the extent to which courts-martial verdicts could be reviewed or revised captivated the government as Congress worked after World War I to make the first substantial revisions to the Articles of War.

The Ansell-Crowder Dispute

Major General Crowder had been the judge advocate general before being detailed as provost marshall general, at which time General Samuel T. Ansell became, effectively, the acting judge advocate general. It developed that both men, close professional associates in the elite of military lawyers, had distinctly different perspectives on the authority of senior officers and their military advisors in reviewing and revising the results of courts-martial, a dispute that led to press and public attention and congressional scrutiny, ultimately yielding significant reforms in the military justice system and providing the spark for reforms that continued, piecemeal, throughout the 20th century. One of the most frequently cited examples of imperfections in the court-martial process occurred on U.S. soil in 1917.

In September 1917, a group of enlisted soldiers at Fort Bliss, adjacent to El Paso, Texas, was under arrest for minor disciplinary infractions. Army regulations at the time prohibited those under arrest from attending drill, but these individuals were ordered to attend drill, which they refused to do, resulting in their being charged with mutiny at general courts-martial. They were found guilty and received dishonorable discharges and sentences of substantial confinement, ranging from 10 to 25 years. In accordance with the procedures at the time, the cases were approved by the commander who convened the court, and the record of trial was sent to the judge advocate general for review. Section 1199 of the Revised Statutes of 1877 provided that the judge advocate general "shall receive, revise and have recorded the proceedings of all courts-martial." The extent of that authority became a matter of tremendous contention.

General Ansell, acting as the judge advocate general because of General Crowder's detail to serve as the provost marshall general, believed the courts-martial were obviously unjust, because of the catch-22 of the soldiers being unable to perform drill in light of the regulation that forbade their attending drill while under arrest. He wrote an opinion directing that the result of the trial be set aside. General Crowder believed that the judge advocate general did not have authority to make such a revision after the officer who convened the court had made his decision. The dispute was considered especially critical because of the lack of confidence in many quarters in the results of courts-martial.

The result proved unsatisfactory for nearly all serious observers, prompted an outcry from many politicians and newspapers, and resulted in congressional hearings more than a year later. Both Generals Ansell and Crowder gave extensive written and oral testimony before Congress. The positions of both men have been characterized by their extremes in the ensuing years; Ansell is often portrayed as the progressive voice of reason and ally of the soldier and Crowder as the fusty pillar of the establishment and status quo. Crowder did support several reforms to the UCMJ but also looked to the British experience not only for guidance but also for distinctions in the sources of authority. The essence of the dispute was whether and under what circumstances the judge advocate general could revise sentences and findings. Ansell believed the authority was plenary, under what he took to be a plain reading of the language of section 1199, which empowered the judge advocate general to "revise and review" courts-martial records. He believed that "'revise,' whether used in its legal or ordinary sense . . . can have but one meaning. It signifies an examination of the record for errors of law upon the face of the record and the correction of such errors as may be found." Without such an interpretation, Ansell testified, the system could not make "amends to the injured man," could not "restore him to his honorable position," and could only "grant pardon for any portion of the sentence not yet executed." Ansell could not definitively state, and was careful in his testimony not to overstate, whether prior judge advocates general interpreted the provision as broadly and acted on that interpretation. He did quote General Lieber, when serving as secretary of war late in the Civil War as suggesting that the judge advocate general's authority to revise and review was "an exercise of a judicial function," with independence equivalent to the courts.

Ansell was bitterly critical of the current system, arguing that a soldier could go all the way through the military justice system, even to a death sentence, "without requiring or contemplating the participation of a single man of legal qualifications at any phase." While recognizing that a recent general order had inserted a review process for courts-martial, he said it was only "done now administratively to modify [courts-martial's] asperities and correct their blunders." A process that he argued was "done extralegally, is insufficient, and is subject to change at the mere whim of military power." He called for "revisory power at the top of the system," characterizing the absence of such authority as "the worst possible deficiency in the existing code." His ardor for enhanced revisory power was hinged in no small part to his belief that the Articles of War, as administered, featured such opportunities for unfairness and capriciousness that swift and comprehensive correction had to be made available—but he also believed that the underlying system clearly needed reform. He cited instances of grossly disproportionate sentences, inadequate sentences, and poor judge advocate review. He called for eliminating junior officers from courts-martial, suggesting a scenario in which a second lieutenant on a court-martial panel with senior members simply would not speak his mind. "I do not think we need mince matters. A second lieutenant does not take a very aggressive stand or attitude in behalf of the law if a colonel is opposing him." He claimed that "legal deficiencies" in courts-martial had "become the custom," producing a "lax system" lacking rigor and respect.

While Crowder joined in the concerns for improving an appellate process that corrected errors and rectified injustices, he did not believe that the law as then operating permitted such a broad and unreviewable exercise by the Judge Advocate General. He distinguished the U.S. system from British authorities in this area, arguing that the equivalent official to the judge advocate general in the British system arose "out of an executive power of the sovereign himself," as opposed to the legislative source of authority in the U.S. system. In other words, the fact that the senior legal official in the British system enjoyed the authority that Ansell advocated was irrelevant to Crowder, because he believed the authority of that British officer derived from the crown, whereas the judge advocate general's authority in the U.S. military justice system was limited by legislative enactments.

While the debate was intensive and closely followed by the press and public and resulted in strengthened authority in the 1920 act, it concluded one debate and presaged and framed another that would continue for several generations. Eliminated was the long-standing practice by which commanders could send cases back to courts for revisions—including reconsideration of acquittals. The newer and more intensified debate concerned the extent to which noncommanders (lawyers, albeit military lawyers who served the command) could exercise independent authority to review the processes and results of a military justice system whose core justification was that it was a function of command's interest in good order and discipline.

The Houston Riots

Of course the services were strictly segregated at the time, which gave rise to another opportunity to highlight structural inequities in the military justice system in the World War I era. An all-black unit, the third battalion of the 24th U.S. Infantry, had been guarding a construction site at the Houston Ship Channel in the months after the United States entered World War I in spring 1917. Members of the unit faced routine harassment when they went into Houston while off duty, prompting some Army leaders to restrict the liberty of the black soldiers, seldom permitting them to leave their camp.

On August 23, 1917, Houston police detained a black soldier for a minor incident, prompting Corporal Charles Baltimore of his unit to go to the police station and check on the soldier. By most accounts, police hit Baltimore over the head, and he ultimately was apprehended after fleeing and being shot at by Houston police. Rumors spread quickly, one of them reporting inaccurately that Corporal Baltimore had been shot dead (no shots had hit him) and that a white mob was marching toward the black battalion's camp (also apparently groundless). Spurred by the rumors, more than 100 of the black soldiers grabbed rifles and marched into Houston. Details of the riot that followed come from police reports, court-martial testimony, and sources that are affected by limited opportunities to observe, as well as the soldiers' own perspectives. There is a consensus that the black soldiers killed 15 whites, four of them policeman, and that 12 other white citizens of Houston were injured, including another police officer who died of his wounds. Four of the black soldiers were killed, two of them apparently having been accidentally shot by their own men. Among the tragedies of the event was the accidental shooting by the black soldiers of an officer of the Illinois National Guard, as they believed he was a police officer. This led to internal quarreling among the soldiers and, ultimately, to their return to camp—it also troubled Sergeant Vida Henry, who led the march to Houston and who shot himself in the head a few hours later.

Martial law quickly was declared, and the 24th Infantry was removed from Houston. Three courts-martial were held between fall 1917 and March 1918. In the first trial, which convened in November 1917, more than 200 witnesses, including members of the unit who testified under the promise of clemency, testified over more than three weeks before a panel of 13 officers that included three generals and eight West Point graduates. Thirteen soldiers were sentenced to hang, 41 received life sentences, and 4 received relatively minor sentences. The case was reviewed by the judge advocate for the command in early December and was approved by General John Wilson Ruckman, who convened the court, on December 9, 1917. The 13 were hanged before sunrise on December 11. Less than a week later, 15 soldiers were tried in the second court-martial stemming from the riots. Ten of them were sentenced to hang, and General Ruckman approved their sentences on January 2, 1918. Many believe that it is inconceivable that General Ruckman was not aware, when he acted on January 2, that the Army had issued an order on December 29, 1917, that prohibited carrying out court-martial death sentences until they were reviewed by the judge advocate general's office. Regardless, the War Department issued another order in January 1918 that suspended all death sentences until the president could review them.

Meanwhile, the third and final court-martial on the Houston riots tried 40 more soldiers and on March 26 issued its verdict, finding 23 guilty, sentencing 11 to hang and the remaining 12 to life in prison. While General Ruckman approved those sentences as well, all death sentences awaited President Wilson's action. On August 31, President Wilson commuted 10 of the death sentences. He issued a statement, an uncommon practice for him, in which he expressed satisfaction with all three of the courts-martial, finding them to be fair and the members to be "officers of experience and sobriety of judgment." President Wilson praised the black units' "splendid loyalty," while deploring the death of "peaceable disposed civilians of the City of Houston." Notwithstanding President Wilson's endorsement and putting aside the probable guilt of many who were tried, the Houston Riots became emblematic of many of the shortcomings of the military justice system (which reflected deeply rooted inequities in society a half century after the Civil War), including its swiftness, the lack of meaningful access to competent and independent defense counsel, and the cursory, inconsistent nature of post-trial review, especially in capital cases.

Postwar Analysis and the Military Justice Act of 1920

The war ended in November 1918, and Congress launched into analysis of the military justice system shortly thereafter, holding hearings in February and March 1919, which featured the most comprehensive analysis and testimony about the military justice system to that point in history. Congress was concerned with all aspects of the system—broadly, its justice and its efficiency—and wrestled with the procedures, rights, and protections that aimed to strike the proper balance between those considerations. Generals Ansell and Crowder ultimately presented their views on a wide range of issues, including the pivotal and controversial question of the role of the judge advocate in reviewing and revising the results of courts-martial. While this seems an arcane dispute, it was critical at the time and crucial to the development of military justice, because analysis of this question touched issues and procedures, including the authority of lawyers compared to commanders, the need for and extent of post-trial and appellate review, and the influence and role of commanders in military justice. Both public opinion and the final legislative product leaned toward General Ansell's view that favored greater latitude in reviewing court-martial results. The broader concern, however, recurred throughout the periodic reforms of the 20th century and remains a matter of debate—the extent to which a commander and his lawyer own the military justice process and the extent to which justice, fairness, and the credibility of the system require and justify levels of independent review.

Members of Congress, then, were well aware of the Houston riots when both Generals Ansell and Crowder testified in February 1919 before the Senate Committee on Military Affairs. The testimony included questions of technical precision, but the broader concerns went to service members' and society's confidence in the justice and fairness of such a system. Much of the testimony before the committee concerned section 1199, but the background included other ignominious episodes of military justice, including the Houston Riots and a detailed report on several courts-martial, including capital sentences handed down overseas.

The hearings and debates on the military justice system received considerable attention, landing Crowder and others on the front page of the *New York Times*. In March, Secretary of War Newton D. Baker wrote to Crowder, who had resumed his position as judge advocate general earlier that year, outlining his concerns about military justice while expressing confidence in the system. He said the "recent outburst of criticism and complaint . . . has been to me a matter of surprise and sorrow" and that, while he did not believe "that justice is not done to-day (sic) under military law . . . [i]t is highly important that the public mind should receive ample reassurance on the subject." Crowder responded with some asperity ("It is my belief that the intelligent public . . . would welcome such an exposition of the facts"), a defense of his own reformist bona fides (he noted that he had advocated specific reforms in 1888, 1896, 1903, and 1911), and then a detailed, nearly 100-page analysis of what he considered to be the 14 main critiques of the military justice system (it is not known whether the superficial similarity to Wilson's Fourteen Points of 1918 was intended). While some of Crowder's points were straw men (number two was "That the military Criminal Code itself is not modern and enlightened, but is an archaic code which systematically belongs to medieval times"), several others accurately captured the most prominent critiques of military justice, to which he offered his replies. Some of Crowder's characterizations of the critiques and his analysis provide insight into matters of debate that continued even after Congress settled on its legislation:

- *"That the general treatment of accused soldiers is not according to the rigid limitations of law as embodied in the Criminal Code, but is according to the arbitrary discretion of the commanding officer in each case."* Crowder quoted a congressman's statement that the system effects "the more or less arbitrary discretion of the commanding officer," arguing there was "only [a] kernel of correctness . . . [in] that the *theory* of military justice is in its general purpose somewhat different from the theory of civilian criminal justice." He quoted General Sherman as having observed that, "The object of military law is to govern armies composed of strong men." Crowder emphasized that the military justice system is "one of law and order and not one of arbitrary discretion," then asserted that it "follow[s] the fundamental of our criminal common law," including the right to counsel, protections against self-incrimination, and a record of proceedings and was therefore fundamentally just, because it tracked the civilian system in its most important attributes.
- *"That a soldier may be put on trial by a commanding officer's arbitrary discretion, without any preliminary inquiry into the probability of the charge."* He responded by noting the trend away from grand juries in the civilian system and toward presentation of "an information . . . which France and other continental nations arrived [at] some centuries ago," arguing that it is most important to apprise an accused of the charges against him. Nevertheless, his argument here was less passionate, and, as discussed below, he recommended strengthening the pretrial investigative process, the absence of which was a major vulnerability of the system, providing the opportunity for commanders to force charges through the system with no check on them before they reached a panel in court.
- *"That Commanding Officers do thus put on trial a needlessly large number of trivial charges."* The number and type of courts-martial, a matter of considerable concern in 1910, remained a matter of detailed analysis and concern after the war. Though Crowder had been—and remained a proponent of intermediate levels of court and, in general, greater flexibility in the system, he cited statistics that he believed reflected sociological reasons for the use of particular levels of courts during the Great War. In responding to congressional criticism suggesting harsh treatment, he pointed to a decline in courts-martial of all types by the second year of the war. This decline stemmed, in his view, from the fact that more than 90 percent of the suddenly conscripted forces were "new men, . . . unfamiliar with military discipline," which produced "an unusual proportion of minor breaches of discipline." In 1917, the first year of the mobilization, the rate for general courts-martial was 1 per 20 servicemen, for special courts-martial 1 per 42, and for summary courts-martial, "representing extremely petty disciplinary penalties," 1 per 2.7 men. The following year showed stark declines in the rates in each category: 1 general court-martial per 200 men (1 per 275 in the second half of that year), 1 special

court-martial per 165, and 1 per 11.4 summary courts-martial. He drew a final contrast that he believed showed "conclusively that commanding officers were more lenient and liberal with the men fresh from civilian life": in 1918, when the overall rate for general courts-martial was 1 per 200, the rate for regulars (veteran troops, essentially the standing army) was 1 per 107, while the rate for new soldiers was 1 per 785. These statistics seem to justify Crowder's inference that discipline earlier in the war (the United States did not enter the war until April 1917) produced a higher rate of courts-martial that quickly subsided as green recruits became seasoned and well-disciplined troops.

- "*That the court-martial is composed of and the defense is conducted by men not acquainted with military law.*" Crowder argued that military justice was different from the civilian system in which ignorance of the law by jurors was expected. Because of the absence of a trial judge, it was appropriate, Crowder argued, to have legally trained personnel on the panel. He expressed confidence that West Point graduates and mobilized reservists, who were required to pass examinations on military law and who regularly served not just as commanders but also as prosecutors and defense counsel, produced a just system. While many of the postwar discussions anticipated later changes in the system, there was very little discussion of lawyers as prosecutors and independent defense counsel practicing before independent judges with authority to issue binding rulings.
- "*That second lieutenants 'knowing nothing of law and less than nothing of court-martial procedure' are assigned to the defense of 'enlisted men charged with capital or other most serious offenses.'*" Crowder conceded this was sometimes the case[6] but argued that it was "impracticable," especially under wartime conditions (in which most capital cases were generated at the time) to assign defense counsel "already qualified as a civilian lawyer." He argued that convening authorities were scrupulous in finding the most experienced possible defense counsel but that there were "almost insuperable obstacles to any other practice." He conceded that it was ideal—but again, unrealistic—to make defense counsel equivalent in rank to the senior member of the panel. The best check against ineffective defense counsel, according to Crowder, was the automatic appeals guaranteed in the military system, a process that included the review of all possible legal errors—in sharp contrast, Crowder argued, to the civilian system that only considered on appeal the objections raised at trial.
- "*That the Judge Advocate combines incongruously the functions of prosecutor, judicial advisor of the court, and defender of the accused.*" Crowder believed this confusion resulted from not realizing that the trial judge advocate, who typically was not a lawyer, fulfilled the roles commonly associated with an ordinary prosecutor. Crowder emphasized that the trial judge advocate not be the same person and did not fall under the supervision of the staff judge advocate, whose role was "to supply the professional and technical legal knowledge" needed "in all stages of the trial." He characterized the staff judge advocate as a neutral party, "a kind of superintendent of justice" who "aids the accused quite as much as he aids the prosecution . . . as impartial as the Comptroller of the Treasury" who dispassionately pays the government's bills. He said that after trial the staff judge advocate was "essentially an appellate judge." Obviously the roles of both individuals developed significantly in the generations following Crowder's observations, as legally trained prosecutors (and, for many years, defense counsel) came to work directly for the staff judge advocate, though the system continued to entrust that official with the ability to both supervise the prosecution and advise the convening authority, a practice that remains in effect today. The staff judge advocate remains the key legal figure in the military's legal architecture, especially in the military justice system, and is the official

(see chapter 4) who must advise the convening authority regarding the legal sufficiency of a case and its disposition.
- *"That commanding generals, as reviewing authorities, send back for reconsideration judgments of acquittal."* Crowder conceded this was the case, and, although he made a spirited defense of the practice—arguing that it was both rare and just—he acknowledged that it was time to change. While calling the commanding general's review "essentially a first appellate stage," he asserted that returning an acquittal to a panel to rethink its verdict implied nothing other than that the panel had the opportunity "to reconvene and reconsider its judgment freely and independently." Crowder examined 1,000 cases, 95 of which were acquittals. Of the acquittals, 39 were returned "only for formal corrections"; of the 56 others, 38 were unchanged but 18 resulted in conviction of some offense. Crowder concluded that "[i]t seems plain, therefore, that in no appreciable number of cases has the exercise of this power resulted in a change of verdict," though another interpretation would be that changing 18 of 56 cases represented nearly a third of all cases returned to juries in his sample. He conceded, however, that "it can not be denied that the [military] practice differs radically from the traditions of civil justice . . . which on first impression is repugnant." Known for his adherence to the British system, Crowder noted that the British had removed the authority to reconsider acquittals two years earlier, and, because "it does not appear that it is a necessary or fundamental one to the maintenance of military discipline," he recommended removal of the authority of a commander to return an acquittal to a panel, recommending in addition that the commander "should not have the power to revise a sentence upward."
- *"That the sentences imposed by courts-martial are as a rule excessively severe."* A related point was that "sentences imposed by courts-martial are variable for the same offense." Crowder clarified the differences and then applauded and endorsed the unpredictability of courts-martial sentences. He noted the prevailing view that desertion should be treated harshly, arguing that it was tempered by policy that did not seek to make arbitrary examples of the first offenders in the war. He said "death was imposed in only 24 cases," of the approximately 3,000 desertion convictions during the war and that all were commuted or remitted. He noted that the average desertion sentence was 7.58 years and that nearly 24 percent were for less than two years. In examining more than 3,000 convictions for the related offense of absence without leave (it does not contain the element of intent to remain away permanently), Crowder noted that 11 percent of them received no punishment at all, the average sentence was 1.59 years, and that 67 percent received a sentence of less than two years. He also defended the aggressive prosecution of disobedience of an officer, deflecting public citations "of one or two instances . . . of trivial consequence,"[7] and emphasizing that "it is not the thing commanded that is material; it is the act of deliberate disobedience." Crowder dismissed "a sentimentality toward offenders of every sort," returning to his frequently cited theme of the unique needs of military good order and discipline. On the issue of sentences that varied for the same offense, Crowder emphasized that it was a strength of the system, not a reflection of justice of "the most erratic and whimsical variety." He said that the military system enabled panels to take into account the many variables afoot in any circumstance. "This very matter of variation in sentences is one of the triumphs of modern criminal law." To this day, as seen in chapter 6, the military has continued to resist determinate sentences, and, except for a few mandatory sentences of death or life in prison, a sentencing authority is free to issue a sentence ranging from no punishment at all to the maximum authorized by law.

- "That the Judge Advocate General's office either partakes in the attitude of severity or makes no attempt to check it by revisory action." Another of Crowder's 14 points also addressed the fact that decisions of the judge advocate general's office were comparatively ineffectual, because, lacking the authority of the Supreme Court, they could be disregarded by commanders. Crowder again recurred to statistics, in part to support his position that the judge advocate review was meaningful. He examined a 12-month period from 1917 to 1918 in which 7,624 sentences were imposed for the nine most common major military offenses, of which the judge advocate general's office furnished relief in 947 cases, about 12.5 percent of the total. Assessing the extent of the relief, he characterized "the action of this office [as] radical," in that the sentences of the 947 were reduced by 89.5 percent. He then addressed, with passion and at considerable length, the issue of the judge advocate general's authority to revise sentences, a presentation made more ardent by his belief that he had been misportrayed by General Ansell and misunderstood by many on this issue. Crowder insisted that not even the president had clear authority, except in the instances in which he was the senior convening authority, to modify the findings or sentence of courts-martial. He addressed anew the notorious Fort Bliss mutiny cases, stating that the episode "was a genuine case of injustice" and that the "impropriety and illegality of the sentence in this case was immediately recognized" and placed quickly on the path to correction. Crowder bristled at the "groundless charge that I have opposed the reforming efforts" of Ansell and others, saying his "chief concern . . . has been to remove the slurs" cast on the system and "that admirable band of conscientious and able officers" who administered it. Then he concluded with his own recommendations.

Crowder's Recommendations

Crowder acknowledged that he could seem defensive in his effort "to remove the slurs" on the military justice system and "to redeem . . . the honor of that admirable band of conscientious and able officers who managed the system," but he returned to his theme that the system could be improved and offered several recommendations for reform:

- Require the summary court-martial authority to conduct an investigation of an accused or "to depute it to an officer of experience" before the case is submitted to the general court-martial convening authority. The process should confront the accused with witnesses and summarize the evidence, "substantially as in the British practice." This represented a tremendous change and was the precursor to the Article 32 investigation.
- Require that a case may not be sent to general court-martial without the written advice of the staff judge advocate, a stipulation that he believed would "guard against any possibility of (a) hasty, ill-considered, or arbitrary action by any commanding officer, (b) ordering any person to trial without full and careful, as well as impartial, investigation. . . , or (c) trivial cases going before general courts." This remains an essential feature of the military justice system and the place where the legal influence of the staff judge advocate is strongest.
- Increase the jurisdiction of special courts-martial to adjudge two years confinement and grant the authority to suspend sentences. This reflected a debate that continued until the increase of the maximum punishment of special courts-martial from six months' to one year's confinement in 2002—how to calibrate the jurisdiction, punishment authority, and attendant due process for the intermediate-level court-martial.

- Create a preference for using lower-level courts by requiring that trial by general courts-martial may be ordered "only where the punishment that might be imposed by a special or summary court . . . would be under all the circumstances of the case clearly inadequate." The Manual for Courts-Martial has since structured the referral process to implement the preference that all known charges be tried together[8] and that all known charges and the lowest level of disposition appropriate.[9]
- Publish a general order "appointing an especially qualified member on the court, who is required to be present at the trial of all serious, difficult and complicated cases." The person should be a judge advocate when "reasonably available." This reflected concerns that a court-martial was insufficiently trial-like in one fundamental way: the absence of an official with the authority traditionally associated with a trial judge, especially power to rule conclusively on legal issues and manage the courtroom. While the military judge was not instituted until 1968, Crowder presaged increasing discomfort with a "law member" who sat with the panel but did not have the binding authority of a judge; rather, his rulings could be countermanded by the vote of fellow (lay) panel members.
- Clarify the controversial section 1199 to provide more flexibility during the postconviction review process that "leaves the final power of ultimate decision in the President" or "allows the President to correct, change, reverse, or set aside any sentence of a court-martial found by him to have been erroneously adjudged," a change that Crowder believed "would supply the needed appellate jurisdiction over court-martial sentences," locating authority in the president, who, he believed, "would normally act [favorably] on the recommendation of . . . the Judge Advocate General." The essence of the "Ansell-Crowder debate," this represented a clear grant of review authority, clarifying any ambiguity surrounding terms such as *revise*. It also constituted implicit recognition that justice, especially as reflected in confidence in the results of courts-martial, demanded an independent and binding post-trial process by which to evaluate and, if necessary, correct significant errors at the trial level.

Path to Enactment

While Congress debated the product that yielded the 1920 Articles of War, Senator George Chamberlain, the Oregon Republican who chaired the Senate Military Affairs Committee, introduced a bill that became known as the Ansell-Chamberlain Bill (Ansell left the military in 1919), which proposed these changes:

- Permitting a sufficient number of enlisted members to sit on courts-martial involving enlisted accused that the enlisted bloc could affect the actions of a court-martial (for example, more than one-third enlisted members on the ordinary court-martial, which required two-thirds to convict).
- Establishing an independent military appeals court of three life-tenured judges to review all cases of a certain minimum level of sentencing severity.
- Requiring that charges be sworn and investigated before trial.
- Establishing a court judge advocate who would perform judgelike functions at trial.
- Abolishing the reviewing power of the officer who convened the court—but retaining his power to grant clemency after trial.

Although that bill did not pass, it ensured the ferment and continued analysis that resulted in future changes to the military justice system. The 1920 Articles, as finally approved by Congress, reflected most of the recommendations of the Stimson Report and the central focus of the 1919 hearings. The major changes:

- Simplification of Special Courts-Martial so that they could be convened more readily, in accord with the recommendations of the military and the drafters' intent of increasing the proportion of special courts-martial and reducing the proportion of general courts-martial.
- Created the authority for "company punishment," by which commanders could give minor punishment (small forfeitures, extra duty, and confinement for short periods of time) to soldiers for minor offenses, thereby avoiding the court-martial process. This provision, a precursor to the modern Article 15, is treated in greater depth in chapter 8. It also contributed to the broadly shared goal of reducing the total number of courts-martial out of a desire not to consume personnel and other resources for courts-martial unless the severity of the conduct warranted them.
- Broadened the definition of soldier, in establishing jurisdiction, to include "a noncommissioned officer, a private, or any other enlisted man."
- Anyone "subject to the code" could now prefer (swear) charges, meaning it was no longer the exclusive function of officers. An affidavit of support was required.
- Strengthened the requirement for a pretrial investigation before sending charges to a general court-martial, adding an accused's right to cross-examine any witnesses whom the government presented. This was an improvement on the prior law that provided, among other things, that no one may be held in arrest more than 8 days without charges and that trial normally should be held within 10 days.
- Barred using proceedings in revision to increase sentences or to reconsider acquittals (codifying a General Order issued in July 1919).
- Created boards of review, composed of military officers who would review records of trial in cases in which punitive discharges or confinement were adjudged before submitting them to the judge advocate general for review. This was the first step toward a formal appellate process, which was expanded in each major change in the military justice system during the 20th century.
- Omitted the preference for 13 members of a general court-martial, retaining the minimum of 5.
- Set the minimum number of members of a special court-martial at three, omitting the "three to five" wording of the prior act.
- Strengthened the role of the law member, requiring that he be a judge advocate unless not available, in which case the appointing authority would be required to select an officer "specially qualified to perform the duties."
- Designated for the first time the prosecutor as the "trial judge advocate" to ensure no confusion with the role and title of the staff judge advocate.
- Increased the commitment to defense support of accused soldiers by providing that those accused could choose their own counsel, including civilians and that military counsel may be appointed for them (note that military counsel did not necessarily mean members of the bar). This improved the prior practice in Article 17, which blurred the functions of advocates in providing that, when there was no defense counsel, the

prosecutor "will from time to time throughout the proceedings advise the accused of his legal rights."
- Expanded the definition of desertion to include those who quit their "organization or place of duty with the intent to avoid hazardous duty or to shirk important service." Concerns about the gravity of desertion and the belief that it was tacitly approved in some quarters were major points of discussion and resulted in Congress's defining an additional offense, "entertaining a deserter."
- Codified other crimes that reflect concerns of the time:
  - False muster of a man or animal.
  - Dealing in captured or abandoned property. Prohibited buying, selling, "or in any way deal[ing] in or dispos[ing] of captured or abandoned property, whereby he shall receive or expect any profit, benefit, or advantage to himself, or to any other person . . . connected with himself."
- Required a unanimous vote for the death penalty both on findings and sentence (two-thirds were required to convict in ordinary cases, and a three-fourths majority was required to impose sentences of 10 years or more).
- Granted the president the authority "in time of war as well as peace" to set the punishments for offenses. Previously, the president only had the authority during peacetime, and this represented an expansion of presidential authority to the part in the court-martial process when flexibility might be most valuable. It also reinforced the concept that Congress defined offenses and that the president set punishments and procedural rules, a relationship to be contested all the way to the Supreme Court (and affirmed) generations later.
- Some provisions were rescinded, perhaps reflecting a belief that the provisions were archaic or desuetudenal:
  - Rescinded Article of War 53, which penalized "anyone who uses any profane oath or execration shall . . . forfeit and pay $1," which went to a fund for sick soldiers.
  - Rescinded Article 52, which provided that "anyone who behaves indecently or irreverently at any place of divine worship shall be . . . publicly and severely reprimanded" and pay a fine that also went to a fund for sick soldiers.
  - Rescinded the requirement that "all members of a court-martial shall behave with decency and calmness," presumably in recognition of its purely hortatory nature.

Implementation of the postwar changes in the UCMJ occurred at the same time as a swift and dramatic decline in the strength of the Army. The most intensive mobilization in U.S. history was followed by a reduction of nearly equal speed and scope. The military peaked at about 4.3 million service members in 1918, and, by 1920, the United States, which clung to a tradition of a minimal peacetime standing military, had about 150,000 soldiers and sailors on active duty, a number that stayed at about that level until Congress gradually began to increase the size of the military in 1935. Consequently, the revised military justice system had about 20 years to operate before the next major crisis and mobilization put it to a stringent test, an opportunity to adapt military culture to significant changes in its disciplinary environment and to test General Ansell's axiom that "prevention of injustice is better than any attempted cure."

Notes

1. James C. Neagles, *Summer Soldiers: A Survey and Index of Revolutionary War Courts-Martial* (Salt Lake City, UT: Ancestry, 1986).

2. 61 U.S. 65 (1857).

3. Some of the information in this section derives from "Rocks and Shoals," by James E. Valle (1996), and *Naval Discipline Prior to the Civil War,* U.S. Naval Landing Party, at <http://74.125.95.132/search?q=cache:ONrw6k8nZmkJ:www.navyandmarine.org/handouts/USNLP_NavalDisciplinePriorToCivil%2520War.doc+naval+discipline+prior+to+the+civil+war&cd=1&hl=en&ct=clnk&gl=us>,

4. Hay was not related to John Hay, the statesman and Lincoln intimate who died in 1905.

5. This goes to the broader, frequently debated question of whether the military justice system is fundamentally commander run, as remains the case with U.S. military justice, or lawyer run, as has become a trend in other Western nations.

6. Crowder referred to 21 capital sentences on review. The ranks of the defense counsel were: four second lieutenants, nine first lieutenants, six captains, one major, and one chaplain.

7. One involved the command to turn over tobacco unlawfully in his possession, and another was a command to clean a gun.

8. "Ordinarily all known charges should be referred to a single court-martial." Rule for Courts-Martial 601(e)(2) Discussion.

9. "Allegations of offenses should be disposed of . . . at the lowest appropriate level of disposition." Rule for Courts-Martial 306(b).

CHAPTER 3

Basics of the Military Justice System: Structure and Levels of Military Courts

As chapter 1 makes clear, the notion of military law predates the United States; it has existed as long as there have been armies. As the military became a more integral part of American life, military law gradually emerged as a distinct, complex, and sophisticated legal discipline. This chapter provides an overview of military justice today—who is subject to the law, the key components of military criminal law, and the unique procedures and protections that the system provides to soldiers.

Military Jurisdiction

The jurisdiction of a court or legal system derives from authority granted to it by a Constitution and codified by a legislature. In the case of the military, it comes from the Congress, which received authority under the Constitution to "make Rules for the Government of the land and naval Forces." The class of persons subject to military law and the offenses that it encompasses, then, are set primarily by the Congress but have been the subject of considerable litigation and modification over the years.

Who Is Subject to the UCMJ: Jurisdiction over the Person

With few exceptions, someone must be a member of the military to be subject to military justice. Any soldier serving on active duty is subject to the Uniform Code of Military Justice (UCMJ). Theoretically, civilians can be subject to the UCMJ under certain circumstances. In practice, it is rare and intentionally difficult to try a civilian under the UCMJ, a practice made considerably more unlikely by a 1957 Supreme Court decision, *Reid v. Covert*,[1] in which the Court ruled that the conviction of an airman's wife for murdering her husband overseas violated her Constitutional right to a trial by jury. Military trials are not jury trials—that provision of the Fifth Amendment is expressly inapplicable to the military (discussed in chapters 1 and 4)—and the Court found that Mrs. Reid's status as a military dependent living overseas was not enough to confer jurisdiction on the military. The UCMJ, in a provision unchanged since the murder of Air Force Sergeant Covert, provided that it applied to individuals "accompanying the force." The Court interpreted that provision narrowly and found that the mere fact that Mrs. Covert lived with her husband, an Air Force sergeant stationed in Great Britain, was an insufficient basis to give authority to the military to try her for murder—even for murdering her husband, an American service member living overseas. It also did not matter that Great Britain was willing to let the U.S. military exercise jurisdiction in the case. The main point was that there was nothing other than the accident of her being married to a service member stationed overseas that would take her out of the ordinary U.S. criminal justice system and apply the peculiarities and limitations of military justice to a civilian spouse. Implicit in this analysis, of course, is that there are such differences and limitations—and that while they are intended and defensible when applied to soldiers, they do not have the same justification when applied to civilians, especially civilian family members.

Reid was a precursor, however, to a gap in jurisdiction, and therefore in accountability, that emerged in a more dramatic fashion over the following years. If a civilian overseas were not accountable under the UCMJ, and if most U.S. laws—and certainly most federal criminal laws—did not apply overseas, how could the United States hold civilians accountable for criminal conduct overseas that had an impact on U.S. persons or missions? This was less a problem for military family members, because most of them remained subject to host nation laws, as affected by provisions in Status of Forces Agreements (SOFAs) with most countries that spell out the fine details of such relationships. The greater concern was civilians who worked for the military but were not military members. It was a common problem—made more common and often more acute during wars and deployments—that Department of Defense civilians and contractors would commit misconduct overseas and, largely because of *Reid*, not be accountable to the U.S. government. This was made more glaring in places where there was no SOFA or where it was so weak that the host nation was unable—or, for reasons of U.S. relations or political weakness, disinclined—to assert jurisdiction against the civilian. Whereas family members had the plausible argument, endorsed by the Supreme Court, that the "accident" of their location overseas should not deprive them of Constitutional protections, the concern with civilians and contractors was that their misconduct was beyond the reach of U.S. law and that this was unjust because it harmed U.S. effectiveness, credibility, and prestige and highlighted an inequity in accountability, because soldiers overseas remained subject to the UCMJ.

In response and after years of intermittent debate and failed proposal, Congress passed in 2000 the Military Extraterritorial Jurisdiction Act, which, under certain circumstances, makes civilians overseas subject to U.S. law—not the

UCMJ. In addition, in 2006, Congress passed changes to the UCMJ under which Department of Defense civilians and contractors working overseas would be subject to the UCMJ under certain circumstances. This was in response to concerns that U.S. personnel who were not military members, though working in support of the military, received undue protection and near–immunity for non–duty-related misconduct (often sexual misconduct, but this has not been the exclusive concern), emboldening them to disobey the law and harming the United States' strategic posture in those places. The contrary concern has been that defining duty-related misconduct can be vague, and that U.S. personnel, military or not, could face exploitation and manipulation by local authorities when it was known that they no longer had immunity from indigenous law enforcement and courts. No doubt these new laws will be appealed in federal court once they are asserted, giving the courts, and perhaps the Supreme Court, the opportunity to interpret it in light of the 50-year-old *Reid* opinion.

Mainly, of course, the UCMJ defines the crimes with which the military can charge members of the military and enforces discipline through the nonjudicial means that the UCMJ also provides. The UCMJ is only a criminal or disciplinary tool, and, in this sense, it is no different from the criminal code of any state, so it cannot be used for private actions or enforcement of individual disputes such as debts.

Members of the Reserve also are subject to the UCMJ when they are performing military duties. Because reservists are civilians except when performing military duties, they are not subject to the UCMJ for the ordinary offenses they commit during civilian life. When they are performing Reserve functions, when activated or mobilized, but also on Reserve drill periods, reservists are subject to the UCMJ for any offenses they might commit.[2] It is a slightly different matter for members of the National Guard. In most ordinary circumstances, members of the National Guard are under the control of their state governors, so not in federal status. Members of the Guard are subject to the UCMJ only when in federal status. Commonly, they are referred to as being in Title 37 status and not subject to the UCMJ when under ordinary state control, a reference to Title 37 of the United States Code that broadly governs the National Guard. They are referred to as being in Title 10 status when federalized—and thereby subject to the UCMJ.

What Can Be Charged: Jurisdiction over the Offense

Individuals subject to the UCMJ can be charged under the UCMJ for almost any conduct committed anywhere in the world. Once it is clear that a soldier's status makes her subject to the UCMJ, the next question is whether the offense is one that the UCMJ can address. This question, which became highly complicated for almost 20 years due to a series of confusing Supreme Court opinions, is now quite clear: Soldiers can be tried for any offense committed anywhere, regardless of whether the offense might also be a crime under some other laws in the jurisdiction where the offense occurred.

The Tangled Path of Service Connection

The path to *Solorio* tracks several other judicial and political trends that also developed between the 1969 *O'Callahan*[3] decision and the 1987 *Solorio* decision. The Warren Court heard the arguments in *O'Callahan* three days after the inauguration of President Nixon, when the Vietnam War was highly unpopular, issuing its ruling near the end of its term that June. Writing for a five-to-three majority (one seat was vacant), Justice Douglas, a Roosevelt appointee in his 31st year on the Court, used it as an opportunity to lambaste the "so-called military justice" system. He wrote that a "court-martial is not yet an independent instrument of justice but remains to a significant degree a specialized part of the overall mechanism by which military discipline is preserved." In light of this and other criticisms, Justice Douglas's majority held that off-duty, off-post offenses committed by soldiers out of uniform generally did not have a "service connection" and therefore could not be tried by the military justice system.

The case involved a 1956 incident (note how long it took the case to reach the Supreme Court) in which a soldier in Hawaii was court-martialed for rape and other offenses stemming from an incident with a Hawaiian woman. He was convicted of all charges and sentenced to 10 years' confinement and a dishonorable discharge. (The case is also discussed in chapter 7.) The case featured extensive and withering criticisms of the military justice system, and its impact was tremendous confusion in the military—raising the question of whether the ruling was as simple and clear as barring courts-martial for all offenses that occurred off post, off duty, committed by soldiers out of uniform. What was the relevance of other possible factors, including the military status of the victim, the civilians' willingness to prosecute, and commanders' concerns about impact on good order and discipline?

The concept of "service connection" turned out to be so unclear to practitioners that the Court sought and found the opportunity to clarify—or attempt to clarify—the concept just a couple of years later. In *Relford v. Commandant*,[4] issued in 1971, the Court listed 12 factors that prosecutors and trial courts could use to evaluate whether the offense in question was "service connected." While most of the factors were instructive, if not logical or intuitive, the Court emphasized that they were nonbinding, not exclusive, and not a checklist—leading only to further contention and litigation about which factors or combinations of factors carried more weight, as well as claims of inequitable treatment by similarly situated accused service members. The *Relford* Court said these factors should be considered in deciding whether court-martial was appropriate:

1. The serviceman's proper absence from the base.
2. The crime's commission away from the base.
3. Its commission at a place not under military control.
4. Its commission within U.S. territorial limits and not in an occupied zone of a foreign country.
5. Its commission in peacetime and its being unrelated to authority stemming from the war power.

6. The absence of any connection between the defendant's military duties and the crime.
7. The victim's not being engaged in the performance of any duty relating to the military.
8. The presence and availability of a civilian court in which the case can be prosecuted.
9. The absence of any flouting of military authority.
10. The absence of any threat to a military post.
11. The absence of any violation of military property.
    One might add still another factor implicit in the others:
12. The offense's being among those traditionally prosecuted in civilian courts."

While *O'Callahan* was decided by a sharply divided court—the slender five-to-three margin that featured considerable rhetorical clash—*Relford* was a unanimous opinion written by Justice Blackmun, one of the *O'Callahan* dissenters. The unanimity likely derived from the strong sense that the Court needed to clarify *O'Callahan* so that it gave greater certainty to military and civilian criminal law practitioners as they tried to determine whether or where their criminal jurisdiction overlapped. It also commanded a majority because it was couched as a clarification of *O'Callahan* that only sought to explain *O'Callahan*'s intent. Justice Blackmun's *Relford* opinion said that the 12 factors it outlined came directly from the facts of *O'Callahan* and that the Court's explication of them would make it easier to guide practitioners in an analysis of whether a service connection is present. Notwithstanding the Court's best efforts, *Relford* represented a gallant but ultimately futile attempt to bring clarity and certainty to the service-connection analysis. The Court seemed to anticipate as much in acknowledging that *Relford* probably did not represent the final word on the topic:

> We recognize that any ad hoc approach leaves outer boundaries undetermined. *O'Callahan* marks an area, perhaps not the limit, for the concern of the civil courts and where the military may not enter. The case today marks an area, perhaps not the limit, where the court-martial is appropriate and permissible. What lies between is for decision at another time.[5]

The concept of service connection—and ultimately the requirement by the military's highest court that it be affirmatively pled in every court-martial charge[6]—was litigated ceaselessly from the time of *O'Callahan* forward. Notwithstanding extensive parsing of the concept of service connection by the military courts, there was little clarity and a strong argument by the military services that *O'Callahan* and *Relford* left the law an inconsistent jumble that deprived commanders and military communities of predictability and certainty and left open the possibility and perception that military justice was inconsistently if not capriciously administered, owing in part to the vagaries of service connection.

Structure and Levels of Military Courts

The concept changed completely in 1987, when the Supreme Court abandoned the concept of service connection in *Solorio v. United States*.[7] This case involved a Coast Guardsman who was court-martialed in New York for the off-post sexual abuse of two minor daughters of a fellow Guardsman while they were stationed in Alaska. The Court majority, in an opinion by new Chief Justice Rehnquist, held that the Constitution, which gives Congress the power to govern the land and naval forces,[8] and the UCMJ, which Congress expressly made applicable to all soldiers everywhere in the world, meant that there was no need for additional tests to determine whether military members could be subject to military courts for their misconduct. The Court said that no further analysis was required, and it expressly overturned *O'Callahan*. The Chief Justice wrote of *O'Callahan*, "we have decided that the service connection test announced in that decision should be abandoned." In contrast to the highly charged language of *O'Callahan*, *Solorio* was a short and comparatively straightforward opinion, but it was also unequivocal, not only in its abandonment of *O'Callahan*—the Court is rarely so explicit when overturning precedent—but also in its reiteration of several fundamental principles regarding military jurisdiction, including maximum deference to Congress on managing military affairs (there is no requirement that there be a UCMJ at all, but the *Solorio* Court's point was that, if there is to be one, the judiciary is loathe to referee the points of overlap in the civilian and military justice systems).

Only three members of the *O'Callahan* Court took part in the *Solorio* decision. Two of the three, Justices Marshall and Brennan, were in the *O'Callahan* majority, as were two of the three *Solorio* dissenters (the third dissenter, Justice Blackmun, was a Nixon appointee). The other justice who was on the Court for *O'Callahan*, Justice White, who had been appointed by President John F. Kennedy, was part of the *Solorio* majority—also consistent with his *O'Callahan* dissent. It is important to remember what also had occurred between the time of *O'Callahan* and the time of *Solorio*. President Nixon had been elected and re-elected, and President Reagan followed the four-year term of Jimmy Carter with consecutive terms. (Carter was the first president since Andrew Johnson to serve a full term and not nominate a justice for the Supreme Court.) The public had also come to terms with Vietnam and entered a period not only of prosperity but of Cold War stability. The military gained steadily in prestige—and, not incidentally, the military justice system had been substantially changed.

The Military Justice Act of 1968 made the greatest changes to the military justice system since passage of the UCMJ in 1950. Its most striking innovation was the introduction of the military judge (treated in detail in chapter 7), which was the most significant step toward making a court-martial similar to a civilian trial. Before these amendments, the judge was known as the "law member," literally a member of the court-martial, albeit a nonvoting member. He sat with the panel that he advised throughout the trial and deliberations, though he did not vote on findings and sentence. In addition, though he ruled on evidentiary motions and objections in a way similar to a traditional trial judge, the panel had the ability to overturn his rulings upon appeal by either the prosecutor or defense counsel. President Johnson signed the 1968 Act in fall 1968, so it preceded the June 1969 ruling in *O'Callahan*, but the changes had not yet been implemented and clearly had not entered the consciousness of the Supreme Court majority, whose sting applied to the pre-1968 UCMJ, as well as to provisions of the UCMJ that remained unchanged by the tremendous changes in the 1968 legislation (obviously, the Court had to analyze the military justice system in effect at the time of O'Callahan's trial, but the majority opinion makes no reference to the 1968 changes).

Overlapping Jurisdiction

Although there is no longer any question that soldiers anywhere and in proper status are always subject to the UCMJ, individuals can be subject to the laws of more than one sovereign at the same time, a conflict of laws for which there is no necessary solution. For example, a soldier who commits an offense off the installation still can be charged by that civilian community for an offense over which the military can also claim jurisdiction. In practice, these are normally worked out as matters of comity, products of consultation between senior legal officials from the military and civilian communities. In the case of conflicts, however, it can be something of a race to the courthouse, in which first-charged ultimately prevails, though other factors such as ownership of evidence—and in some cases, control of the accused's body—can effectively determine the outcome.

As is discussed in the double jeopardy section, it is possible but rare for someone to be tried consecutively in military and civilian jurisdictions based on the fact that each is a separate sovereign. There are similar issues overseas, as military members in most countries in which U.S. troops routinely are garrisoned (for example, Germany, Japan, and Korea) are subject to local laws under the terms of detailed Status of Forces Agreements. These SOFAs spell out under which circumstances the host nation or the United States has primary jurisdiction and the many ramifications and procedural steps involved in making such determinations. In countries in which the United States is at war or conducting short-fuse military operations, the United States claims, or receives as a condition of its invited entry, immunity for its personnel. A contemporary illustration of how immunity can evolve into a SOFA is the U.S. presence in Iraq, which began with the March 2003 military invasion, during and after which the United States claimed and then received immunity for military personnel. As the intensity of the war abated and the Iraqi civilian government broadened its control, the Iraqis were motivated by multiple concerns—sovereignty, public affairs, and international relations—to temper the immunity of U.S. soldiers. A long negotiation process culminated in a SOFA implemented in December 2008 that retained significant protections for U.S. personnel but softened the prior near-absolute immunity, bringing the arrangement in that country more in line with those governing U.S. forces in largely garrison settings elsewhere overseas.

Levels of Courts-Martial—and Deciding Which Level Is Appropriate

There are three types of court-martial: summary court-martial, special court-martial, and general court-martial. They are distinguished by their maximum punishments, the level of command that has the authority to convene the court or order it into being, and the extent of the appellate process available.

The special court-martial and the general court-martial are easiest to comprehend—the special court is akin to a misdemeanor court, and the general court is akin to a felony court. The summary court-martial is a unique mechanism that, because of features such as the absence of a defense attorney and jury, is not considered a federal conviction because such a court is not a criminal prosecution under the Sixth Amendment.[9] Because the stakes increase with each level of court-martial—the levels of potential sanctions differ at each level—the amount of due process and procedural protections accorded to an accused increase at each level; all are factors that commanders consider when deciding what level of court-martial to convene. Courts-martial are best understood by reference to the maximum punishment they can adjudge, or their jurisdictional limit.

Convening Authority

A court-martial can be ordered into existence only by a commander with the authority to do so. There are no exceptions to this rule. The authority to convene a court-martial is tied to the level of command. Although the individual military services can alter this authority by regulation, certain thresholds of command correspond to the levels of courts-martial:

- Summary court-martial can be convened by battalion or equivalent-level commanders (commonly Army or Air Force lieutenant colonels or Navy commanders).
- Special courts-martial can be convened by brigade or equivalent-level commanders (commonly Army or Air Force colonels or Navy captains).
- General courts-martial can be convened by division or wing or equivalent commanders (commonly two-star generals or admirals, though they can be full colonels and Navy captains).

Not every commander in such a position has the corresponding level of courts-martial authority. The military services commonly alter and define court-martial convening authority by regulation. By such measures, they can expand the authority for some commanders beyond their formal command and limit others, usually in the interests of geography and efficiency. The services can impose such limitations by regulation, but they can never grant a level of court-martial jurisdiction to an individual unless the command position held meets the minimum requirements of the UCMJ. It has been common in overseas environments to implement some version of what is commonly referred to as area jurisdiction, by which a commander, otherwise qualified under the UCMJ, exercises court-martial authority over individuals within her geographic footprint even though she has no command authority over them. Similarly, on some military installations, there are several commanders who qualify as general courts-martial convening authorities. It is common for a superior authority, perhaps a service secretary, to designate one general court authority for such an installation or cluster of military organizations or to limit or redraw the authority of commanders that might not reflect command lines.

This system has the advantages of efficiency and consistency, because it means that fewer individuals have the ability to set the tenor of the command and make justice decisions regarding good order and discipline. On the other hand, such a structure or adaptation means that a senior leader in charge of an organization yields disciplinary control over those whom he commands and for whose good order, discipline, and readiness he remains responsible. Many observers, critics, and participants in the military justice system believe that the advantages of efficiency and consistency outweigh the interests of discrete commanders in personally managing good order and discipline. Still, some commanders and observers believe that such efficiencies undermine commanders' ability to place their imprints on their organizations. They believe that good order and discipline is tied so intimately to a unit's effectiveness that removing their court-martial jurisdiction deprives them of an essential element of command, distracting and diluting their troops' sense of accountability, authority, and loyalty.

Summary Court-Martial

A conviction at a summary court-martial generally is not considered to be a federal conviction, because these proceedings do not have a judge or jury in any traditional sense, defense counsel are not present at the proceeding, and appellate review of the conviction is internal to the military and does not reach any judicial authorities. A soldier may be charged at a summary court-martial for any offense under the UCMJ—and only offenses under the UCMJ. A summary court-martial may not discharge anyone, and the maximum forfeiture is two-thirds pay for one month. Only enlisted soldiers in the pay grade of E-4 and below may be reduced to the lowest enlisted grade at a summary court-martial; soldiers in the pay grade E-5 and above may be reduced only by one enlisted grade ("lose a stripe"). The maximum confinement that can be adjudged is 30 days, but only enlisted soldiers in the pay grade E-4 and below may be sentenced to confinement.

These limitations reflect the tradition that soldiers serving in the pay grades E-5 and above generally are considered to be noncommissioned officers (NCOs), and the consequence of losing NCO status is considered to be worthy of increased protection. Officers may not be reduced in rank by any court-martial. The summary court-martial consists of a single officer (called the summary court-martial when handling these duties), who hears all of the evidence, examines all the evidence, conducts witness examinations if any, and determines guilt and the sentence. She need not be—and in practice rarely is—a legally trained officer but should at least be pay grade O-3 (captain in the Army, Air Force, and Marines; lieutenant in the Navy). The summary court-martial has access to legal advice, but the legal advisor is not a judge (typically it is an officer who works for the staff judge advocate, the chief lawyer for the command), need not have judicial training, and need not have court-martial experience. In practice, the legal advisor most often is an officer or civilian attorney who works in the command or installation legal office but not in the prosecution section—though the advisor often has the same senior supervisor as the prosecutors. Normally the summary court-martial will receive a legal and procedural briefing before conducting the court-martial, though that is not required, and normally the legal advisor is available, in person or by telephone, for consultation during the summary court-martial, but again such consultation is not required.[10]

The main function of the summary court-martial is to punish and correct soldiers who have committed minor offenses for which nonjudicial punishment (addressed in chapter 9) is not considered sufficient, but for whom a higher level court-martial is considered inappropriate, based on factors that include the nature of the offense, background of the individual, and perhaps operational requirements. Because of the diminished procedural rights that account for its summary nature—the summary court is intentionally tilted more toward internal military discipline than to due process—a guilty verdict from a summary court-martial not only does not qualify as a federal conviction, but no soldier is obliged to accept trial by summary court-martial. Soldiers have an absolute right to object to trial by summary court, which then gives the command the option of sending the case to a special court-martial or higher. (The soldier has the right to object to trial by summary court-martial even if he already has exercised the right to object to a case being disposed of through nonjudicial punishment.) Obviously, the potential impact of a higher-level court-martial is greater—longer periods of confinement, greater forfeitures, loss of rank as well as punitive discharge—but the right to turn down a summary court is intended to protect soldiers against possible capriciousness or manipulation by the command. Because summary courts-martial are convened at a relatively low level—battalion command or its equivalent—there is a greater chance of command influence and hasty, incomplete, or amateurish investigations. The investigation is not always as professional as it is for other levels of court (it may have been in-house, depending on the offense), and there is less direct judicial involvement in the process of referring a case to a summary court, as well as in trying and reviewing the case. Consequently, an accused soldier has the right to bear the risks of greater punishment at a higher level in exchange for the greater due process, such as a legally trained and tenured trial judge, the option of a jury (panel) trial, and the right to independent defense counsel to represent her in court.

Though there is clearly less formality and less rigor to a summary court-martial when compared to other levels of courts-martial, it is not a mere administrative proceeding, and the summary court-martial is expected to follow the elements of proof, provided in the UCMJ and the Manual for Courts-Martial, in determining guilt or innocence and to follow the same rules of evidence and the same sentencing strictures that the Manual for Courts-Martial dictates for all courts.

The post-trial process for special and general courts-martial is treated in detail in chapter 6. The post-trial process for summary courts is necessarily truncated (lesser consequence and stigma generally equates to less elaborate procedures), so the process outlined in chapter 6 does not apply to those courts. Recalling that a central purpose of the summary court-martial is speedy disposition of minor offenses, but also recalling the military justice system's commitment to due process at every stage of the proceeding—due process that, just as in the civilian world, is more robust as the stakes of the proceeding are greater—there is a procedure for a relatively swift review of summary courts-martial that ultimately can lead to independent review outside the chain of command that convened the summary court. After the summary court-martial is concluded, the government is required to review the jurisdiction, findings, and sentence. The review must be conducted by someone who was uninvolved in the process.

- *Personnel.* A summary court-martial consists of one officer appointed by the battalion-level commander or higher. He hears all of the evidence, rules on objections, and determines the findings and sentence. The accused soldier has no right to enlisted composition on the summary court-martial and no right to object to the summary court-martial officer; if she objects, she has a right to demand trial by a higher level of court-martial altogether.
- *Voting.* All decisions at the summary court-martial are the exclusive decision of the summary court-martial.

Special Court-Martial

This is the military's misdemeanor-level court. Special courts-martial can adjudge confinement up to one year, can reduce enlisted soldiers to the lowest enlisted grade (or any intermediate grade), can require forfeiture of up to two-thirds pay per month for up to 12 months, and can adjudge up to 12 months' confinement. Officers may not be reduced in grade and may not be discharged by a special court-martial, but all other punishments apply to them. Until 2003, there were two types of special courts-martial: the "straight special," which could adjudge forfeitures of two-thirds pay per month for six months, confinement for up to six months, and reduction of enlisted soldiers to the lowest pay grade; and "BCD special courts-martial," which could adjudge all of those punishments as well as a bad-conduct discharge (BCD) for enlisted personnel. A convening authority may still convene a "straight special" by intentionally withholding the authority to adjudge a BCD. Officers cannot receive BCDs.

- *Personnel.* A special court-martial is composed of at least three members (jurors). Accused soldiers may choose to be tried by judge alone. Enlisted soldiers may insist that at least one-third of the members be enlisted personnel.
- *Voting.* Two-thirds of the members must vote to convict, and two-thirds must agree on a sentence.

General Court-Martial

This is the military's felony-level court. All accused soldiers can receive the maximum punishment as provided in the Manual for Courts-Martial. Most maximum punishments include total forfeiture of pay and allowances and reduction to the lowest enlisted grade. The Manual for Courts-Martial sets the maximum confinement for each offense. Enlisted soldiers can receive either of two punitive discharges: the bad-conduct discharge or the dishonorable discharge, the more severe of the two, though a court is not necessarily required to adjudge a discharge at all regardless of what other components of the sentence (forfeitures, confinement) it imposes.[11] The only punitive discharge that can be adjudged against an officer is a dismissal. Any offense that provides for the possibility of a bad-conduct discharge or a dishonorable discharge will also provide for a dismissal for an officer. Soldiers can receive a maximum of total forfeiture of pay and allowances or any lesser level of forfeiture of pay, including no forfeitures at all. Allowances are only forfeited in the event of total forfeitures (allowances are payment for housing and subsistence, as well as pay such as special-duty pay for those filling airborne or other hazardous slots and special pay for those in unusual specialties, which can range from medicine to obscure musical instruments). Enlisted soldiers can be reduced to the lowest enlisted grade, but officers are not reduced in rank, even when dismissed. All services currently provide for interim reductions in rank—for example, a soldier in the pay grade of E-7 can be reduced to anywhere from E-1 to E-6 (or not at all), but these are service-specific decisions determined by regulations published by each service. In the absence of such a regulation, any enlisted soldier who receives any confinement, even if suspended, must be reduced to the lowest enlisted grade by operation of law.

- *Personnel.* A general court-martial is composed of at least five members (jurors). Accused soldiers may choose to be tried by judge alone. Enlisted soldiers may insist that at least one-third of the members be enlisted personnel.
- *Voting.* Two-thirds of the members must vote to convict, and two-thirds must agree on the sentence, except for sentences of 10 years or more, which require agreement by at least three-quarters. (There are additional rules for capital cases, including a minimum 12-member panel, pleading and finding of aggravating factors, and several unanimous votes, all of which are addressed in greater detail in chapter 6.)

The decision of what level of trial to convene, then, has an impact on procedures available to the accused.

Notes

1. 354 U.S. 1 (1957).
2. In *United States v. Chodara,* 29 M.J. 943 (A.C.M.R. 1990), the Army Court of Military Review (now the Army Court of Criminal Appeals) ruled that a court-martial's having personal jurisdiction did not always mean it had subject matter jurisdiction. In the case

of a reservist given a urinalysis test on the second day of his mobilization, the prosecution was unable to establish conclusively (limited by the science of urinalysis testing) whether the soldier had used an illegal drug before he came on active duty—and therefore was precluded from obtaining a conviction.

3. *O'Callahan v. Parker,* 395 U.S. 258 (1969).
4. 401 U.S. 355 (1971).
5. Relford, 401 U.S. at 369.
6. In *United States v. Alef,* 3 M.J. 414 (C.M.A. 1977), the Court of Military Appeals (now the Court of Appeals for the Armed Forces), ruled that the government must affirmatively assert and establish, "through sworn charges/indictment the jurisdictional basis for the trial of the accused and his offenses." So-called Alef pleadings continued until after the *Solorio* decision.
7. 483 U.S. 435 (1987).
8. U.S. Constitution, art. 1, cl. 14.
9. *Middendorf v. Henry,* 424 U.S. 25 (1976).
10. The Guide for Summary Court-Martial Trial Procedure, DA Pam 27-7 (June 15, 1985) provides general guidance to summary court-martial officers in the Army, consistent with the idea that the procedures should be easily understood and managed by a layperson but administered with the sense of justice, fairness, and consistency that is expected of any system of justice. Such a guide is not meant to substitute for a summary court-martial officer's ability to consult with a legal advisor.
11. In reality, it would be extraordinarily anomalous, and suggestive of an extraordinary jury dynamic or misunderstanding, for an accused to receive a significant sentence of confinement such as 10 years and not receive a punitive discharge.

CHAPTER 4

Basics of the Military Justice System: The Investigative and Pretrial Processes

Military law has several features and protections that are unique to the military or that developed in the military independently of the civilian criminal justice system. Among the many examples is that Article 31 of the Uniform Code of Military Justice (UCMJ) provides far greater protections against self-incrimination than the *Miranda* rule that it well predates. All of the unique rules stem from the concerns of balancing good order and discipline rooted in the military mission with essential justice for suspects and accused soldiers operating in a system that is subject to the inherent pressures of command control.

Investigation

Almost anyone in the military can investigate an offense, though it is not wise or common for investigations to be conducted by other than commanders or law enforcement organizations. It is most common for the military law enforcement organs of each of the services to lead most investigations, but that is not required, and many investigations are a collaborative process between law enforcement and the command. Military commanders have an affirmative obligation to "make or cause to be made a preliminary inquiry into the charges or suspected offenses" under the UCMJ. In that sense, military law enforcement works for the command—a reflection at the outset of the process that the system is command-run, even though there are numerous participants in it. Military law enforcement may also collaborate with civilian law enforcement, including host nation law enforcement when investigations occur overseas.

Most military investigative organizations do not strictly work for the commanders who administer discipline. Each service has its own criminal investigative organization: Criminal Investigative Command (CID)[1] in the Army; Naval Criminal Investigative Service in the Navy and Marines, and Air Force Office of Special Investigations for the Air Force. Because of occasional scandals as well as a desire to reinforce investigators' institutional independence and professionalism, the regulations and directives that govern the military law enforcement organizations have been altered in recent times to reinforce that independence. All are what the military calls stovepiped organizations, meaning that they are tenants on military installations, because their higher headquarters is at another location. Military criminal investigators serve the local commander, but they do not report to that commander, who has limited ability to direct their operations and no authority over budgets, efficiency reports, personnel assignments and evaluations, and other factors that could inhibit their independence. Although CID and the other organizations are the detectives of the military, the services also have ordinary street police, military police in the Army, and equivalents in other services; these individuals often report directly to the installation commander, especially when not working in an investigative capacity. The Army also has military police investigators who are a sort of junior detective body entrusted to investigate minor offenses, sometimes under the general supervision of CID. The Navy also has a unique profession, masters at arms, a law-enforcement related field with competence to investigate crimes and handle prisoners.

It has become more common in recent times, as military jurisdiction applies on and off post and on and off duty, for military law enforcement organizations to collaborate with civilian organizations in investigations of crimes that are not purely military in nature. While various memoranda of agreement—or Status of Forces Agreements overseas—govern such relationships, the fruits of such investigations are as admissible at courts-martial as they would be if they were conducted by military law enforcement. In some circumstances, overseas offenses, especially those that occur off U.S. military installations, are investigated exclusively or primarily by host nation law enforcement entities. The criminal rules and procedures of many of these nations are less strict than those of the United States, especially with regard to searches and seizure and questioning of suspects. The results of such investigations still can be used to prosecute soldiers in military courts as long as the process does not "shock the conscience." Typically, for example, a soldier might not be read his rights in the Article 31 or *Miranda* sense before being questioned by a German or Japanese police officer. The product of such an interrogation would be admissible as long as, under the totality of the circumstances, the result of the interrogation would be considered to be reliable, and the fact that such procedures might make the statement inadmissible in a court-martial would not be determinative.

Preference for Continued Liberty

Most soldiers facing serious charges are still expected to go to work. Pretrial confinement generally is permitted only when a soldier is charged with a serious offense and there is a showing that she is not likely to be present for trial (soldiers may not be placed in pretrial confinement for summary courts-martial, the lowest level of court-martial) or is so severely disruptive as to seriously affect the functioning of her military unit. In general, the system expects soldiers to continue to perform military duties while pending charges. If a soldier is placed in pretrial confinement, the military must follow Constitutional requirements for review of confinement, along with military rules that regulate the process and terms of such confinement. Commanders may place other reasonable conditions on the liberty of the accused soldier, but those restraints must be tied to a combination of the seriousness of the offense and the need to ensure the accused's presence for trial. Soldiers placed in pretrial confinement receive day-for-day credit against any confinement that a court-martial adjudges. In addition, soldiers who are not literally confined but are found to have been in the functional equivalent of pretrial confinement (e.g., they are escorted everywhere, have to forfeit their civilian clothes, etc.) will receive credit against their sentence as though they have been in pretrial confinement.

A soldier placed in pretrial confinement must have his case reviewed by a military magistrate within 48 hours of being placed in confinement, and again by an impartial judicial official within seven days. After 72 hours, the commander of the confined soldier must prepare a memorandum stating her reasons for placing the soldier into pretrial confinement. Failure to comply with these requirements can result in releasing the soldier or his receiving multiple days' credit for every day spent in illegal pretrial confinement. This is an area in which the military has adapted its procedures to the clear mandates of the Supreme Court.[2] The factors that a commander considers in deciding whether to impose pretrial confinement are similar in many respects to factors that civilian authorities use in making bail determinations—the nature of the offense; ties to the community; and the accused's record, including any history of failing to appear at or fleeing from prior proceedings.

Pretrial Punishment

Consistent with concerns about undue command control and authority (see chapter 7), and commanders' ability to affect justice in ways that might not be obvious or easily discovered, two provisions of the UCMJ are designed to protect against illegal pretrial punishment. Article 10, UCMJ, requires commanders to inform a soldier of the charges against him as soon as he is placed in pretrial confinement. Article 13, UCMJ, prohibits pretrial punishment. Obviously, this is meant to reinforce the concept that accused soldiers are innocent until proven guilty—military jury pools come from relatively small communities—but it also is meant to reinforce justice and not to let informal corrections displace or undercut the formal system of justice. Examples of pretrial punishment include singling out soldiers before trial—mentioning their cases publicly, having accused soldiers fall out of a formation, referring to them disparagingly—or imposing corrective training that does not relate to an offense (such as fatiguing physical training) or precautionary measures such as chaining soldiers to a radiator.

Military judges who find illegal pretrial confinement can give multiple days' credit for every day of illegal confinement. In addition, if pretrial confinement facilities are found not to meet military standards, then soldiers may also receive multiple days' credit for having been subject to such conditions. This has been a greater problem in recent years as many military confinement facilities have closed, and many units and military installations have contracted with local civilian facilities for pretrial confinement.

Privilege against Self-Incrimination

Because the pressure of command is always considered to be present in any interaction between a soldier and a superior, the soldier enjoys additional protections against self-incrimination that are not available to U.S. civilians.

The right not to be forced to be a witness against oneself is one of the fundamental guarantees of any legal system that claims to be based on justice and of course is explicit in the Fifth Amendment.[3] Still, the outlines of this right vary greatly even among Western nations. Among such nations, practices vary on factors such as when or whether the right applies in the investigative process, whether individuals should be informed of this right, whether it applies at trial, and whether the government may comment on the exercise of this right. The Fifth Amendment guarantees that citizens have the right not to be witnesses against themselves. For this right to be effective at trial, it has been found to extend to custodial questioning by police that could produce incriminating information—and it famously was extended, through the 1966 *Miranda* decision, to require police to inform suspects of their right against self-incrimination whenever they are subject to custodial questioning.

Because they are citizens, soldiers enjoy the full protections of the *Miranda* decision and the many Supreme Court cases that have interpreted it. Soldiers, however, have additional rights against self-incrimination that predate *Miranda* and have a different rationale. Article 31 of the UCMJ provides that any soldier subject to official questioning has the right not to answer the question and the right to know the offenses about which she is being questioned. Both of these rights are broader than *Miranda* in these respects:

- *Miranda* only applies to custodial questioning by law enforcement officials, while Article 31 applies to all official questioning of a military suspect or accused by military officials or superiors. Article 31 obviously applies to police-soldier exchanges in the military, but it also is designed to neutralize the pressure that is inherent in any superior-subordinate relationship in the military. Because of the assumption that soldiers will feel compelled to talk when questioned by a superior, even when they know the answer could hurt them, Article 31 was created to give soldiers the freedom not to cooperate in official questioning directed at them. As with *Miranda*, the terms of Article 31 have been the subject of contention and litigation. Military appellate courts have wrestled with when Article 31 applies—what constitutes official questioning, how comprehensive the warning/rights advisement must be, and how this limitation squares with commanders' operational needs for information. Courts generally have erred on the side of the soldier, but in circumstances in which there is a clear operational need for information—life

or death or catastrophic mission failure (e.g., asking a disruptive soldier in charge of an aircraft whether he was on drugs) courts have permitted the use of the admissions, despite the failure to give the normally required warnings.
- *Miranda* only applies to questioning when the suspect is in custody. Article 31 applies to all official questioning, regardless of whether the soldier is in custody. There has been a fair amount of appellate litigation over what constitutes official questioning, and while in some narrow circumstances impromptu questioning has been found to fall outside the ambit of Article 31, courts generally have interpreted it expansively, applying it to almost any exchange between an official or superior and a soldier that might reasonably be said to call for an incriminating response.
- Article 31 requires that the soldier be advised of the offense of which she is suspected. *Miranda* has no such requirement, and most civilian courts repeatedly have rebuffed any efforts to broaden it in this regard. This has not been a major area of contention in the military—precision is not required in advising a soldier about the topic of questioning, but a fair sense of the topic and likely potential offenses is expected—but it removes from military investigators and commanders one aspect of the tool of lawful deception or uncertainty that is available to civilian police.
- The *Miranda* decision imposed an exclusionary rule that keeps prosecutors from using statements taken in violation of *Miranda*. This rule is judge-made and subject to considerable interpretation—for example, on whether statements made as a result of a *Miranda* violation are also barred or whether the statement is admissible for impeachment if the soldier testifies in contradiction of the statement. Article 31 specifically provides that statements taken in violation of it or through the use of coercion, unlawful influence, or unlawful inducement may not be used at trial. This exclusion is far broader than *Miranda* and, because it is based in statute, rests on more solid legal footing. The exclusionary rule also has been the subject of considerable litigation and interpretation, compounded by issues such as what constitutes coercion, but, taken together with the other provisions of Article 31, it forms an intended, powerful bulwark against the explicit and implicit authority and potential for coercion that naturally inheres in the unique, hierarchical society of the military.
- *Miranda* provides for the right to counsel but only provides free counsel to the indigent. Article 31 guarantees the right to counsel for all soldiers, regardless of ability to pay.

Bringing Charges—The Preferral Process

A soldier is charged—in the parlance of the UCMJ, a charge is "preferred"—when anyone in the military swears to a set of charges and certifies that the charges are true or that he has reason to believe that they are true. Anyone subject to the UCMJ may prefer charges, but it takes command action to get a charge to trial. Preferral alone, however, is only the start of the process and has relatively little formal impact until a commander takes action.

- Typically, a commander at the level closest to the accused—company command in the Army and the Air Force—swears out charges, or the charges are preferred by someone in that unit (no one may be pressured to bring charges).
- A charge is a violation of the UCMJ. For example, a violation of Article 86, absent without leave (AWOL), constitutes a charge. A specification is a detailed assertion of

the infraction of the charge. There must be at least one specification for each charge, and there may be as many as needed to capture and characterize the misconduct. If, for example, a soldier is AWOL on three different occasions, then there could be one charge of violating Article 86 and three different specifications, each of which would carry the maximum punishment for that offense. The Manual for Courts-Martial provides sample specifications to assist in the drafting of charges.

- A preferred charge, standing alone, has no further impact unless commanders take action on it. Therefore, although anyone may prefer a charge, the charge is inchoate—ineffective—until a commander begins to move it through the recommendation and action process.

Disposing of Charges—The Command Starts to Make Decisions

Once a commander concludes, normally after consulting his judge advocate, that an offense has been committed, commanders are told to consider the offense in light of a unique combination of factors that include many that are common to civilian authorities (seriousness of the offense, availability of evidence, cooperation of the accused, victim impact) and some that are distinctly military in nature (for example, character and military service of the accused, impact on morale, health, safety, welfare, and discipline). This is not a formal, binding, or exhaustive checklist, but its placement in the Manual for Courts-Martial reinforces several fundamental principles of the military justice system, introduced in chapter 1:

- *Command control.* Anyone in the military may prefer charges, but the charge can go no farther without command action, because the purpose of the military justice system is to reinforce, define, and limit command authority and responsibility for the readiness of troops. For this reason, a charge cannot advance beyond preferral without a decision or recommendation by the first level of command.
- *Individualized disposition.* There is no requirement to dispose of any type of case at a certain level.[4] The factors from the manual, cited above, guide a commander through a set of criteria that prompt an evaluation of the facts of a particular case and the specific record and reputation of the accused soldier. There are no templates.
- *Good order and discipline/military as unique society.* A commander may dispose of a case in a manner that might seem relatively harsh or relatively lenient because of her judgment about the impact on good order and discipline. If a commander perceives that an infraction goes to a core concern that affects readiness or morale (thefts in the barracks, for example), she might recommend disposition or convene a court at a relatively high level; conversely, she might dispose of an offense with seeming lenience when she sees relatively little impact on the unit.
- *Lowest level of disposition.* Commanders are expected to dispose of offenses at the lowest level consistent with good order and discipline. Because of this, there is no rule that sets a particular level of disposition for a particular offense, and the decisions vary according to the host of factors that commanders are expected to—trusted to—evaluate. It is unusual for felony-type offenses to be disposed of at other than the general court-martial level, but many offenses, especially military offenses, often are addressed at levels ranging from reprimand to court-martial, ideally because of a commitment to unique treat-

The Investigative and Pretrial Processes

ment and disposition at the lowest level and the fact that the context of the offense often determines its seriousness.

- *Other measures.* The great majority of disciplinary actions are handled via mechanisms other than court-martial. There are hundreds of incidents of nonjudicial punishment and other lesser measures for every court-martial that is convened.[5] Other dispositions are covered elsewhere in this book; the rest of this chapter will address considerations and requirements governing the court-martial process.

Processing Charges through Levels of Command

As mentioned earlier, a fundamental principle about the military justice system is that charges should be disposed of at the lowest level consistent with good order and discipline. Two related principles are that commanders have inherent authority to discipline their troops and that commanders must make independent decisions and recommendations regarding the disposition of charges (for a broader treatment of command influence, see chapter 7). Consequently, after a soldier is charged with an offense, the charge works its way through each level of command, where each commander may exercise any of several options: dismiss the charges, forward them with a recommendation as to disposition, or act on them by imposing nonjudicial punishment or convening a court. Commanders are expected to make these disposition decisions and recommendations independently, and they are barred from consulting superior commanders about the particulars because of the belief that such consultation invites unlawful command influence and undermines the system's expectation that commanders are entrusted with the authority and independence commensurate with their level of command.

Ordinarily this is accomplished by subordinate commanders providing written recommendations to the next higher authority in the UCMJ chain that has authority to dispose of charges. In practice, the level of disposition for many offenses is relatively obvious—traditional felonies generally land at general courts-martial—but many offenses, especially military offenses, are harder to categorize and are highly dependent on the circumstances, including experience and reputation of the soldier and the impact on the unit. Defense lawyers likely will scrutinize commanders' decisions and recommendations as they try to ensure that their clients' rights are protected by such mechanisms, instead of their becoming so routine that commanders do not exercise independent discretion or that informal communication between levels of command subverts the intent of the independent recommendation process.

A concern of the system and of senior commanders is that junior commanders might take action that they consider precipitous or unwise. If a junior commander takes action on a case, it generally precludes—or at least complicates—the senior officer's ability to dispose of a case. There are procedures, however, that mitigate these possibilities while also seeking to protect the right of accused soldiers.

While any commander who receives charges for disposition has authority to dispose of them (including to dismiss them), such dismissal does not occur with prejudice. Therefore, charges can be reinstated and again passed through the chain of command.

Consistency and independence, however, would suggest that the junior commander would again take the same action. If a junior commander were to take different action, especially action that recommends or executes more severe disposition, it would raise the question of unlawful command influence—that is, whether the junior commander had been improperly influenced by a senior officer. To guard against that possibility, the Manual for Courts-Martial provides that a senior officer may always withhold a case—or type of cases or series of cases—from junior officers. This removes the specter of unlawful command influence, because when a senior officer feels strongly enough about a case, he should remove it from the lower levels of command rather than pressure the junior officer, indirectly or otherwise, to dispose of a case in a certain manner.

If, however, the junior officer disposed of a case in a manner that a senior officer believed was too lenient (for example, by imposing nonjudicial punishment when the senior thought that court-martial was appropriate), the senior commander could still cause charges to be preferred against the soldier and then act on the case and move it toward court-martial (nonjudicial punishment, because it is not a judicial proceeding, does not raise the issue of double jeopardy). Ultimately, if the soldier is convicted, the sentence would have to be offset by the terms of the nonjudicial punishment already served (for example, the punished soldier would be credited for prior forfeitures adjudged at nonjudicial punishment for the same offense).

The Requirement to Investigate

Commanders are obligated to investigate when they have reason to believe that a crime may have been committed. In practice and for most serious offenses, commanders refer information to military law enforcement and consult their judge advocates during the investigative process. They do, however, have independent authority to conduct investigations on their own—and it is not uncommon for them to do so, especially for minor offenses for which they contemplate minor disciplinary action or corrective actions. The services have their own traditions and preferred structures for investigating offenses, and there are also administrative processes (JAGMAN investigations in the Navy and AR 15–6 investigations in the Army) that can discover evidence that results in criminal charges. It is only when a general court-martial is contemplated that there is a statutory requirement.

The Article 32 Investigation

Commanders who are considering the possibility of a general court-martial must send the case to an investigation under Article 32, UCMJ, which requires a thorough and impartial investigation of all charges. Ordinarily this means that an officer considers all the evidence that has been developed against an individual and holds a hearing at which she considers testimony from any witnesses she considers relevant, as well as any witnesses suggested by the prosecution or requested by the defense who are found to be reasonably available.

This procedure has been analogized—frequently and inaccurately—in the press and elsewhere to a grand jury procedure. It is analogous only in the sense that it precedes a decision to send a case to a felony-level court. In fact, its purpose, and therefore its procedures, differs from a grand jury's. The essential purpose of an Article 32 investigation is to protect the accused and ensure against commander error—reducing the chance of a railroad. Interposing an officer who is not in the accused's chain of command (though a member of the command) before a case can be referred to a felony-level court is considered to be additional insulation against command influence and a greater guarantor of thorough examination of the case against an accused. Not only is it a statutory right of the accused, but it also is a command tool meant to reduce the chance that a senior commander (the only kind who can convene a general court-martial) does not commit resources to a case that is not as serious as it might sound, sorting for bias, weak evidence, and other factors that might militate against convening a general court-martial. The Article 32 investigation differs from a grand jury in several important respects:

- Unlike a grand jury, the Article 32 investigation is generally open to the public, meaning that other soldiers may attend, as well as members of the press and the public. There are rare exceptions that permit closure for sensitive or classified material, but the UCMJ and recent case law establish a strong preference for openness. The preference for openness became a matter of contention in 1997, when an Article 32 investigation involving the sergeant major of the Army, the highest-ranking enlisted soldier in the Army, was closed, a decision contested by ABC News and ultimately overturned by the Court of Appeals for the Armed Forces.[6] While most Article 32 investigations are open to the press and public, there is no requirement that the convening of an Article 32 hearing be announced to the public; consequently, most occur with no one present but the parties, witnesses, and support personnel.
- The accused has a right to be present at the Article 32 hearing, whereas he has no authority to be present at a grand jury for other than his own testimony.
- Unlike a grand jury, the accused has a right to have her defense counsel present at the Article 32 hearing.
- Unlike a grand jury, the accused and his counsel may cross-examine government witnesses.
- Unlike a grand jury, the accused and counsel have a right to a transcript of the Article 32 investigation testimony, which can be used at trial to cross-examine, impeach, or rehabilitate witnesses.
- Unlike a grand jury, the accused has a right to know the subject matter of the investigation. She must be charged before the Article 32 is convened; obviously this is not the case with a grand jury, when, at best, a suspect might receive a target letter informing her of the likelihood of future charges.
- Unlike a grand jury, the accused and counsel have the right to request that the investigating officer call witnesses and produce or consider evidence that they suggest.

Operational requirements may limit the availability of witnesses, but every effort should be made to obtain in-person testimony while recognizing that substitutes such as depositions, video teleconferences, and telephonic testimony sometimes are required. The use of such witness substitutes can limit the ability of either party to seek to admit such evidence at trial if the witness is found to be unavailable. The defense's ability to compel the attendance of witnesses also is limited by the rule that defines a witness as reasonably available if the witness is "located within 100 miles of the situs of the investigation and the significance of the testimony and personal appearance of the witness outweighs the difficulty, expense, delay, and effect on military operations of obtaining the witness' appearance."[7]

While many of the features of the Article 32 investigation requirements work to the benefit of an accused and are more extensive than grand juries, there are limitations as well, most significantly the fact that the Article 32 investigating officer's recommendation is not binding on the convening authority—that is, the investigating officer can recommend no charges, altered charges, or a lower level of disposition, and the convening authority may disregard those recommendations and refer the case to general court-martial. The convening authority also may disregard the recommendation in the other direction and dispose of a case at a lower level of disposition (or dismiss charges), notwithstanding the investigating officer's recommendation. The investigation is most often ordered by the commander who serves as the "special court-martial convening authority," ordinarily the commander just below the general court-martial convening authority. This means that the special court-martial convening authority still has jurisdiction over the case and has the freedom to act on the results of the investigation at his level—as well as the option to send the charges and the investigation to the general court-martial convening authority (the most common path) or return to lower level for disposition. He also may dispose of it himself, as every commander may do when the charges are before him.

The Article 32 investigating officer is not obliged to find any new evidence in the case. She may rely, if she chooses and neither party insists to the contrary, on the evidence developed by others, including law enforcement and the chain of command. Typically the investigating officer assembles all of the documentary evidence regarding the case and then finds out from both parties what evidence they would like to be produced and what witnesses they would like to call. It is not common, and generally not recommended, that the investigating officer actually investigate in the sense of going to a crime scene or conducting fresh or even initial interviews of witnesses. Law and regulation do not bar an investigating officer from doing so, but such conduct would reduce the role of investigative professionals, consume time, and increase the chance of investigative or legal error, as well as potentially call into question the impartiality of the officer. Such impartiality often is at issue, as the Article 32 investigating officer is a member of the command—the commander has no authority to task anyone who is not a member of his organization—and the best defense to such charges or skepticism is the manner in which the investigation is conducted. While the investigating officer is discouraged from conducting his own investigation, it is appropriate for him to ask law enforcement organizations for additional information or documents.

Witnesses must testify under oath and in the presence of the accused and her counsel, subject to their cross-examination. While privileges (such as the physician-patient privilege) apply at Article 32 investigations, the Military Rules of Evidence do not otherwise apply at this stage. This sometimes complicates the investigating officer's analysis, because evidence he hears at the investigation—especially hearsay—may properly be considered at this stage and in his report to the convening authority, even though it might not be admissible at trial. Ordinarily the prosecutors and staff judge advocate include such factors in their pretrial analyses so that the convening authority has proper perspective when considering the investigating officer's report and the potential issues at trial.

The Article 32 investigating officer must be a commissioned officer, and there is a general preference but not a requirement that the person be a field grade officer (major or lieutenant commander, pay grade O-4). In some places, it is common, or at least not unusual, for a judge advocate to serve as the Article 32 investigating officer, especially in legally complex cases. Some favor this practice based on the belief that a legally trained individual is best equipped to ferret out complicated material and provide careful, sophisticated, and independent advice to a convening authority. The contrary school of thought argues that the drafters of the UCMJ intentionally and advisedly chose not to require that the investigating officer be a lawyer and that, while unobjectionable, the practice of assigning a judge advocate as Article 32 investigating officer means the command forfeits the opportunity to receive a lay perspective that might be useful in deciding whether or how many resources to commit to a general court-martial.

In practice, a typical Article 32 investigation can last a few hours to a day or two. Usually they are conducted in a conference room on a military installation in duty uniform (dress uniforms normally are worn for courts-martial), and, while testimony is sworn, it is taken with less formality (examining counsel remain seated). There is no requirement that testimony be taken verbatim, though that is sometimes accomplished when requested by defense counsel or in cases of greater gravity.

A case may not be referred to general court-martial unless an Article 32 investigation has been completed or the defense waives the investigation—a frequent component of pretrial agreements (see chapter 4). A defense offer to waive an Article 32 investigation need not be accepted by the government, however, as the prosecution has its own and the system's interest to evaluate in deciding whether to go forward with the investigation.

Seeking and Receiving Legal Advice

Commanders are expected to seek the advice of military attorneys when evaluating evidence and disciplinary options. They are not required formally to receive legal advice, except before referring a case to general court-martial, but it has become an established practice for them to do so at all decision points in the disciplinary process. The advice usually comes from the military prosecutor who handles cases from her jurisdiction, but the services have some differences in this practice, because the legal staff on a ship tends to have clearly defined functions, and the Army assigns specific prosecutors to specific jurisdictions, while the Air Force has local prosecutors who advise the command but it generally deploys courtroom prosecutors on a regional basis. Regardless of these variations, it bears emphasis that the UCMJ is a command-driven system that it is fundamentally a tool of good order and discipline. While commanders are expected to seek and rely on the advice of military lawyers, the system depends on the independent judgment and recommendations of commanders. This principle is tied not only to good order and discipline, but also to the system's expectation that cases be disposed of at the lowest possible level and the related expectation that this will enhance good order and discipline, because it will reinforce the rank and file's trust in the system. Therefore, notwithstanding the availability of legal advice and the expectation that commanders rely on it (though they are not bound by it), the decisions and recommendations must be theirs alone. Legal advisors have to be careful that they are not conduits for unlawful influence by transmitting, intentionally or unwittingly, a senior leader's expectations or preferences to the junior commander. If the junior leader becomes aware that the senior leader wants, for example, a special court-martial when the junior commander prefers nonjudicial punishment, the legal advisor, though without official authority to dispose of offenses, can be an agent of command influence by making the junior commander aware of the senior's preferences—and if the junior adjusts his recommendation accordingly, then his recommendation no longer would be independent.

The Referral Process—A Commander's Decision to Send Charges to Trial

After all investigations are complete, a case ultimately is presented to the convening authority who has the power to determine whether to send it to court-martial and, if so, the level of court to convene. The level of court is limited only by the authority that accompanies the convening authority's level of command. As discussed earlier, a summary court-martial convening authority is typically at the battalion or equivalent level, whereas a general court-martial convening authority is commonly a division commander or equivalent. The charges must be accompanied by recommendations from all levels of command, even if they are preferred above the lowest level of command.[8] The recommendations are not binding, but charges may not be referred unless all levels "chop" on the charges or the higher level commander has withheld authority from lower levels of command, as discussed earlier in this chapter. In addition, the statute of limitations is "tolled" when charges are received by the summary court-martial convening authority; this means that the time elapsed for calculating possible violations of the statute of limitations stops when the summary court-martial records the hour and date of receipt of charges.[9] The convening authority must receive the advice

The Investigative and Pretrial Processes

of the staff judge advocate before making a decision to refer a case to a general court-martial, but there is no formal requirement to receive advice, written or otherwise, before convening a special court-martial or below. The pretrial advice for a general court-martial, required by Article 34, UCMJ and R.C.M. 406, must address these factors in writing:

- A conclusion about whether the specifications and charges actually state an offense under the UCMJ.
- A conclusion about whether each charge is supported by the evidence available.
- A conclusion about whether there is jurisdiction over the accused under the UCMJ.
- A recommendation about what action the convening authority should take, which could include the full range of options from dismissal of the charges to convening a general court-martial.

This is a very significant document, the only place in which a military lawyer has a statutory role in the process. The requirement to personally sign the pretrial advice sometimes yields questions of who prepares it, because there is a technical requirement that prosecutors not prepare this advice. While the purpose of that requirement is to ensure that the staff judge advocate exercise independent judgment, in practice, prosecutors provide much of the information for the pretrial advice, while the staff judge advocate nevertheless is obliged personally to consider and evaluate the evidence and adopt the document as her own. Infrequently an issue arises regarding whether the staff judge advocate exercised independent judgment in the preparation of the advice, but in circumstances in which that might be called into question—for example, someone close to her was a victim of an offense or the staff judge advocate was a witness—then it should be transferred to a staff judge advocate from another jurisdiction to generate the advice, while the case remains with the same command. Most importantly, this is an area in which the balance in the military justice system that generally gives most disposition authority to a layperson, the convening authority, is balanced back toward a noncommander. If the staff judge advocate does not certify, in writing, any of the four factors above, including whether there is jurisdiction and whether the charge is supported by the evidence, a referral decision by the convening authority would be void. The recommendation as to disposition of the case itself, however, is not binding.

Selecting Court Members

When a convening authority makes a decision to refer a case to trial, he also selects court members, sometimes for the particular case and sometimes referring a case to a standing panel. The services vary in the practice of using standing panels. It is common in the Army to convene courts that hear all cases for a period of time, often six months to a year. It is also common at large installations to have more than one court-martial panel sit during the same period and to alternate the assignment of cases to multiple panels. It is common in the Marine Corps, however, to convene a new court—that is, to select new jurors (court members) for each trial. All of these practices are lawful as long as commanders comply with the requirements of Article 27, UCMJ, to choose members best qualified by virtue of these six factors: age, education, training, experience, length of service, and judicial temperament. Rank is conspicuously missing from these factors but is effectively implied by the heavy weighting of the first four factors toward seniority, and most panels of most courts-martial skew toward greater representation of higher-ranking individuals. It is also common, however, to include some members of lower ranks and more common to have junior officers than to have enlisted members who are not at least noncommissioned officers. Courts occasionally have had to rule on a convening authority's decisions in this area (see chapter 7 on unlawful command influence), but there is no expectation that there be a proportionate array of ranks and no requirement for certain representation of other demographic categories such as race or sex (though some case law supports inclusion of racial minorities and women as an affirmative factor in the convening authority's judgment in selecting panel members). The key is for the convening authority to be able to certify that she followed the Article 27 criteria and did not have an inflexible attitude in excluding categories or ranks from consideration.

Pretrial Agreements

Pretrial agreements or plea bargains are available at all levels of courts-martial, including summary courts-martial. The accused may bargain for any terms, but most commonly they involve limitations on the most significant portions of the sentence—length of sentence to confinement, and sometimes forfeitures or characterization of discharge—in exchange for pleas of guilty as well as waiver of procedural rights or options, such as Article 32 investigations, and production of in-person witnesses.

Another unusual protection for military accused is that they receive the best of both worlds with regard to pretrial agreements. In most civilian jurisdictions, a defendant receives the sentence for which he bargains, and it is not uncommon for the final sentence to depend on postconviction cooperation. In the military, the accused soldier enjoys the protections of a pretrial agreement *and* the opportunity to beat the deal, because the sentencing authority is not informed of the terms of the pretrial agreement before adjudging a sentence and consequently issues a sentence uninfluenced by the bargain struck between the accused and the convening authority. Therefore, for example, an accused can have an approved agreement that limits her confinement to 36 months, but if the panel or judge—which always will remain ignorant of the terms of the deal while deliberating about an appropriate sentence—sentences the accused to 12 months confinement, then the convening authority will be foreclosed from approving confinement in excess of 12 months. This is an extraordinary protection for an accused, unknown in most civilian jurisdictions.

- *Initiating discussions and the negotiation process.* Several years ago, the military eliminated the archaic and unworkable requirement that all discussions of pretrial agreements had to be initiated by the defense—an awkward Kabuki more honored in the breach. Its intent, as with so many unique provisions of military criminal law, was to protect an accused from the potentially overbearing authority of the government—charging a case and suggesting terms of a deal. Now that either party may suggest terms of a pretrial agreement, the most common process is that prosecutors and defense counsel discuss the case between themselves and gain some sense of the offenses to which the defense would be inclined to plead guilty and some possible terms. Because the counsel do not ordinarily have authority to bind the government, they suggest terms to their superiors, and ultimately the staff judge advocate (senior lawyer in the office) advises the convening authority whether to accept the proposal.
- *Terms of pretrial agreements.* There are multiple potential areas of negotiation in pretrial agreements, but these are the most common areas of bargaining:
  - *Offenses.* The accused may plead guilty to all or any combination of the charged offenses or lesser included offenses. For example, someone charged with aggravated assault might offer to plead guilty to simple assault, someone charged with murder might offer to plead guilty to manslaughter. There are as many possibilities as there are charged offenses, and the local practices vary widely, with some adhering to a "plead to the sheet" philosophy (i.e., plead guilty to all charges) and others bargaining robustly. It is not uncommon, of course, for the government to be more willing to accept a plea, including a plea to a lesser included offense, when it feels evidence might be weak or there are concerns about witnesses or other proof-related factors.
  - *Waivers.* The accused who pleads guilty may waive most procedural rights and protections—and must waive some. He must, obviously, waive his right to plead not guilty and have a trial on the merits and must waive his right against self-incrimination, because he will be required to assure the military judge, under oath in open court, that he is truly guilty. He may, and often does, waive procedural rights or options, including the right (at a general court-martial) to an Article 32 investigation and the right to seek to call certain witnesses during the sentencing phase of trial. Courts generally have found that he may not waive his right to appeal, though he may and commonly will waive certain procedural motions, such as a claim of an illegal search or violation of his right to speedy trial.
  - *Convening authority action.* Once the accused and her counsel sign the pretrial agreement, the government, usually the staff judge advocate, will present it to the convening authority for a decision. The convening authority may reject the agreement, approve the agreement, or counter-offer by lining through a provision and returning it to the defense or sending an alternative agreement back to the defense. Counter-offers, available only since 1984, are still relatively rare. The most common practice is for a subordinate of the convening authority, most often the staff judge advocate or prosecutor, to communicate to the defense alternative terms that the convening authority is likely to support.
- *Binding the government.* The convening authority is the only person with formal power to bind the government to the terms of a pretrial agreement. There are rare circumstances, however, in which there is a question of whether someone who is subordinate to the convening authority, such as the staff judge advocate or prosecutor or a subordinate commander, can be seen to have bound the government in such a sense that due process and fundamental fairness counsel that the agreement should be enforced. The most famous case for this proposition is *Cooke v. Orser*,[10] a 1982 case in which a commander ap-

peared to have promised an Air Force lieutenant suspected of spying that he would not be prosecuted if the information he provided were verified by polygraph tests. Although the convening authority was ignorant of and did not approve such a representation, the military appellate courts chose to enforce this promise in the interests of justice. Because of such sensitivity, prosecutors typically will tell defense counsel while negotiating pretrial agreements that they will support a certain sentence limitation but make clear to the defense counsel that they do not formally represent or bind the government—and then send their recommendations through the legal office, who may or may not choose to present them to the convening authority.

- *Presenting the agreement in court.* Unlike most civilian courts, the process for ensuring that an accused person is freely pleading guilty is extensive in military court. (See chapter 6 for details of this part of the process.) Because the statement made during the providence inquiry is made under oath, case law has developed by which the prosecution may introduce some of those statements during the sentencing phase of trial. Courts are cautious about permitting the use of such statements, because, although they are made under oath in the presence of a defense counsel and after an advisement by the judge, they are still made under circumstances that, though not coercive, have their primary purpose of further developing, amplifying, and sometimes certifying the guilt of the accused. Courts are not at all reluctant to permit introduction of such information if the accused takes the stand during the sentencing phase of trial and testifies—or exercises her right to an unsworn statement and presents information—inconsistent with statements made during the providence inquiry.

Notes

1. Strictly, there is no D in CID; the anachronistic terminology survives from the time that it was known as the Criminal Investigation Division. The abbreviation has survived the name change to Criminal Investigation Command.

2. The services revised their procedures for review of pretrial confinement to comply with *County of Riverside v. McLaughlin,* 500 U.S. 44 (1991), in which the Supreme Court set strict timetables for judicial review of municipalities' decisions to place charged individuals into confinement pending trial.

3. The relevant part of the Fifth Amendment reads: "No person . . . shall be compelled in any criminal case to be a witness against himself."

4. As is discussed in chapter 5, a small number of serious offenses have mandatory minimum punishments, but they are the exception in a system that generally sets maximum punishments and requires no minimums.

5. For example, in fiscal year 2009, the Army tried about 1,500 courts-martial] but adjudicated about 38,293 incidents of nonjudicial punishment, a ratio of about 25 instances of nonjudicial punishment for every court-martial.

6. In *ABC Inc. v. Powell,* 47 M.J. 363 (1997), the Court of Appeals for the Armed Forces ruled that Article 32 hearings must be open to the public (and therefore to the press) unless the government made a specific and substantial showing of the need for secrecy.

7. Rule for Courts-Martial 405(g)(1)(A).

8. See Rule for Court-Martial 401.

9. See Rule for Court-Martial 403(a), and Article 43, UCMJ. The statute of limitations for most offenses under the UCMJ is five years, though several, such as murder, have no statute of limitations.

10. 12 M.J. 335 (A.C.M.R. 1982).

CHAPTER 5

Basics of the Military Justice System: Defining Criminal Conduct in a Unique Society

Defining and codifying criminal conduct is one of the elemental functions of a civil society. The sovereign, through legislatures that make laws, decides what conduct is so contrary to an ordered society that it will be prohibited and that criminal sanctions will attach. This is true for the military as well. Most conduct that is criminal in U.S. society is also made criminal in the military (rape, murder, larceny, most common law crimes). Additionally, however, a substantial portion of the Uniform Code of Military Justice (UCMJ) is devoted to defining offenses that are unique to the military, whether disrespect and disobedience or potentially grave crimes of disloyalty to the nation.

Making Military Law: Defining Crime

Just as state legislators define crimes for their states, the Congress defines federal crimes. Most federal crimes appear in Title 18 of the United States Code. The UCMJ, however, appears in Title 10, the part of the U.S. Code that governs the military. The first few punitive articles of the UCMJ, which begin at Article 77, do not define discrete crimes, but they do provide explicit legal support for ways in which to hold someone criminally responsible for conduct.

For example, Article 77 provides that someone subject to the UCMJ may be tried as a "principal," meaning that he can be criminally responsible for any offense when he is not actually a perpetrator but takes substantial, intentional steps toward enabling others to accomplish the offense. This is a long-established concept, sometimes short-handed as "aiding and abetting," that ensures that someone who shares criminal intent and helps a crime happen can be tried as though she actually committed the offense. This recognizes that criminal conduct can have its source and owe its success to those who do not actually pull the trigger or steal the item, and Article 77 is the foundation for punishing any soldier who "aids, abets, counsels, commands, or procures" the commission of an offense. When a soldier is charged with an offense as a principal, he would not be charged with a violation of Article 77, but would be charged with a violation of the substantive offense as though he had committed it. Charging in this manner relies on Article 77 as the legal theory that makes the person subject to prosecution for that crime, but she is charged with a violation of the actual crime; therefore, someone charged as a principal for larceny has a charge sheet that shows Article 121, and it is then up to the prosecution to make clear that the theory of legal guilt is built on the person's acts as a principal as made criminal by Article 77. A person convicted as a principal faces the same potential maximum punishment as someone convicted as a perpetrator.

Just as Article 77 recognizes that those not on the scene can be just as responsible for a crime as those who complete the crime, the crime of conspiracy, codified in Article 81, recognizes that a crime is more likely to occur when more than one person is involved in its planning—and it makes punishable the fact of coming to an agreement to commit a crime and taking any act, even an act that is itself innocent, toward completion of the crime. Conspiracy is one of the more heavily litigated concepts in the law, centering on issues such as what actually constitutes an agreement, but prosecutors embrace it as a way to hold responsible those who might not actually accomplish the completion of the crime but whose collaboration and planning made the crime more likely to happen. It naturally is meant to deter crime by subjecting such individuals to prosecution. Again, this concept is long established in common law, and the military's implementation is consistent with that body of law: The government must show that there was an agreement to commit a crime, and the person charged must have taken some step—an overt act—toward that crime. The overt act need not be and often is not in itself criminal; it can be conduct such as purchasing a plane ticket. Someone convicted as a conspirator faces the same maximum punishment as someone convicted of the offense that he conspired to commit. Unlike Article 77, which is a theory of criminality but not actually an offense, someone can be charged under Article 81 for the crime of conspiracy, because the crime about which the accused conspired need not have been brought to conclusion. In addition, the conspiracy also can be charged under Article 81, and the service member can be separately charged, convicted, and punished for the completed crime itself—because this is consistent with the main reason for prosecuting conspiracy, that an agreement to commit a crime makes it more likely to happen. Finally, a soldier may be convicted of conspiracy under the UCMJ even if the co-conspirator is a civilian and beyond the reach of the UCMJ.

Skip Work, Talk Back to the Boss—and Go to Jail? A Survey of Unique Military Offenses

Many military offenses qualify as crimes only because the person is in the military. Of the punitive articles of the UCMJ, 34 (articles 83–115, 133, and 134) are military-specific, and 17 (articles 116–132) are common law crimes that would also be offenses in civil society. Most of the common law offenses are structured in

Defining Criminal Conduct in a Unique Society 65

a manner similar to those in the civilian world and consequently are not treated in detail in this book. The most notable of recent changes was the military's restructuring of Article 120, the major offense regarding rape and sexual misconduct, early this century. Among other changes it removed the requirement for force in charging sexual assaults, and created gradations of sexual assault more in line with many civilian jurisdictions. The following examination of some of the military offenses best illustrates the sweep of the UCMJ and the variety of conduct that it reaches.

Sneaking in: Fraudulent Enlistment; Sneaking out: Fraudulent Separation

Even in an all-volunteer military, a person does not get to serve unless the military chooses to enlist or commission him. Because of this principle, the military must be able to discharge those who enlist fraudulently. Although the military does have administrative authority to discharge those who do this—and, in fact, the administrative option is the one most commonly employed—it is also a crime to enlist fraudulently, meaning that someone who sneaks into the military may be prosecuted by the military and then punitively discharged, even though the military did not accept that person in the first place. Under Article 83, a person can be found guilty of fraudulent enlistment (or appointment) if she is accepted into the military based on a knowing misrepresentation or concealment of a material fact—typically misrepresenting age or concealing important medical information—and then receives pay or allowances. Fraudulent separation, also prosecuted under Article 83, punishes someone who is separated from the military based on a similar misrepresentation or concealment of information. Among the possibilities here are exaggerating or misrepresenting medical data, information from family that could trigger a hardship discharge, or like information that misleads the military into permitting a soldier to separate who otherwise would be obligated to continue to serve. In a similar vein, it is a crime under Article 84 to bring about the unlawful enlistment or separation of another. Recruiters are most commonly liable for the offense of effecting unlawful enlistment, a crime that naturally is much more prevalent in the era of the all-volunteer military—a military that also places significant pressure on recruiters, and often rewards them with bonuses, praise, and high performance ratings based on the number of individuals recruited. Almost anyone in a position of authority could be liable for the crime of effecting unlawful separation—medical personnel, leaders, and personnel officers whose representations are relied on in making decisions about whether to separate soldiers for a variety of administrative reasons, including unfitness, physical and mental shortcomings, and extraordinary family hardships.

Walking Out: Unauthorized Absences

In the civilian world, a person who fails to show up for work can be fired. In the military, he can go to jail. Obviously, fundamental to good order and discipline is the requirement that soldiers serve where they are told when they are told. Being late for duty (failure to repair) is a crime, as is absence without leave (AWOL), failing to show up for a deployment (missing movement), and leaving a duty station with the intent to remain away permanently (desertion). The offense of missing movement applies when a soldier, "through neglect or design," misses the movement of a ship, aircraft, or unit. It is not necessarily a wartime offense, because it can apply to failure to show up for any operation in which a group of soldiers are to move to another location—including on foot. When AWOL or desertion is committed in time of war, or when it is terminated by apprehension, or when it is committed with the intent to avoid hazardous duty or "shirk important service," the potential punishment is increased. Obviously, these offenses are central to good order and discipline, and they are among the most common offenses in the military.

Usually, short, unauthorized absences are handled by nonjudicial punishment, but this may not be the case when there are aggravating factors, such as closeness in time to a deployment or important exercise or when the offending soldier is higher in rank than a junior enlisted soldier. Courts-martial for AWOL and desertion are relatively uncommon in peacetime, but are usually in the top 10 in offenses prosecuted during wartime. Typically, they are among the easiest cases to prove, because prosecutors only need to present a "paper case," admitting into evidence properly authenticated documents that show the accused soldier was on the rolls of a unit and was reported absent on the dates in question. The question of intent to remain away permanently is the central issue in desertion cases and often is a matter of drawing an inference from bits of evidence; among the factors that typically contribute to that analysis are not only the length of the absence (because a short absence could still result from an intent to remain away permanently), but whether the soldier reintegrated into the civilian community, got a job, changed his name, disposed of his military identification card, and similar factors. AWOL and various failures to report on time are prosecuted under Article 86; missing movement is prosecuted under Article 87; desertion is prosecuted under Article 85.

"About that President..."

No nation protects speech, especially political speech, more than the United States. Obviously, that freedom includes the right to say almost anything about political officials. Not so for soldiers. One of the clearest illustrations that the military is a separate society and that soldiers do not enjoy all Constitutional rights to the same extent as their civilian counterparts is the prohibition in Article 88 against using "contemptuous words" against the president or certain other public officials. It is a crime to use contemptuous language against the president, vice president, secretary of defense or military department (e.g., secretary of the Navy, etc.), and the governor or legislature of the state or territory where he is present.

Although rarely invoked, it illustrates a number of factors unique about the UCMJ, beyond the obvious point that no such law could survive scrutiny in the civilian world. It also applies only to officers, one of the few provisions (conduct unbecoming an officer obviously is another) that applies only to one segment of the military. The theory is that their position as commissioned officers and leaders makes such statements disloyal and undercuts the point that such individuals serve the national interest as exemplified by those who hold these important positions. It serves the broader purpose of reminding commissioned officers of their unique status, the fact that the military is subordinate to political leadership, that personal views must not get in the way of duty performance, and that such criticism can confuse and demoralize subordinates who take an oath to "obey the orders of the officers appointed over me."[1]

A number of limitations and conditions make the invocation of Article 88 a rare event. There is an exception for purely private speech, and the words must be used by the officer in a way that brought them to the attention of the public official in question (for example, in a speech, letter to the editor, or the like, as opposed to a comment in a bar or living room). It only applies to those currently serving in office, not, for example, to former presidents. Though rarely invoked, it provides reinforcement of the principle of civilian supremacy and deters officers from straying into the political realm. It is more likely to be asserted as a basis for nonjudicial punishment or reprimand of an officer.

Fighting the Boss

Assault is punished under the UCMJ similarly to most civilian criminal codes. There is a separate crime, however, for striking or assaulting (raising a weapon or otherwise threatening violence) a superior commissioned officer in the execution of his office. Congress clearly meant to reinforce the respect for military authority by using Article 90 to enact a unique crime of striking or threatening a superior.

This is only a crime when the officer is "in the execution of his office," normally not in dispute because officers are considered to be on duty all the time—but it can be an issue for someone with whom the accused might be unfamiliar. If the accused did not know the identity or status of the person she assaulted, though knowledge can be proved by circumstantial evidence, then there is no crime under this article. It is also a defense if the officer acts in a manner that forfeits the protections of this article (forfeits the "mantle of command"), because the military interest in protecting the officer—and the officer corps—evaporates when the officer behaves in a manner that makes the accused's response understandable if not justified, or at least downgrades it to an assault rather than the aggravating circumstance of assault on a superior commissioned officer. Striking or assaulting a warrant officer, petty officer, or noncommissioned officer in the execution of his office also is a crime (Article 91) and reflects the same concern for good order and discipline as the crime of striking a superior commissioned officer. Reflecting the elevated significance of carrying a commission, however, the crime of striking a commissioned officer in the execution of her office carries a maximum confinement of 10 years, while the same crime committed against a noncommissioned or petty officer carries a maximum of 5 years' confinement.

Disobedience

Article 90 also makes it a crime to disobey a lawful order of a commissioned officer. It goes without saying that such obedience is a core principle of military service and a major reason for a separate code of military justice. Disobedience is so serious that the maximum punishment for this offense during wartime is the death penalty (otherwise, five years' confinement, dishonorable discharge, total forfeiture of pay and allowances). Several concerns relating to obedience in the U.S. military reveal the balance the UCMJ seeks to strike between individual freedom, society's expectations, and good order and discipline in the military.

- *Lawful orders.* Soldiers are not required to obey any order given by any commissioned officer. They must only obey lawful orders. Clearly, a soldier should normally assume that an order is lawful and obey it. The more ordinary the order, and the more obvious the military nature of the order, the clearer it should be that the soldier must obey it. Still, soldiers are trained to disobey unlawful orders—such as orders to commit or conceal a crime. The military takes this so seriously that, not only is obedience to orders a difficult defense to mount, but affirmative disobedience or questioning is expected in appropriate circumstances. Still, such disobedience is and should be the rare event, and the Manual for Courts-Martial provides that an order, especially one tied to military duties, "is disobeyed at the peril of the subordinate." Nevertheless, this requirement for lawfulness does cause commanders to ask questions and seek advice about the lawful limits of their ability to give orders and make policy. Questions about the extent of commanders' authority have grown in recent years as the military has taken increased interest in the off-duty conduct of soldiers when it believes that it can have an impact on performance of duties. It is common in wartime and deployments to limit soldiers' freedoms even more than they are limited in garrison life (for example, barring drinking of alcohol or receipt of otherwise lawful pornography on deployments). In garrison, however, the outer limits of lawfulness are tested by rules that require, for example, the wearing of motorcycle helmets off post, even when there is no civil requirement to do so, or to limit or forbid tattoos and body piercings.
- *Conscience.* Although a soldier should disobey a clearly unlawful order, he may not disobey just because he finds the order abhorrent, ill-advised, or a personal violation of his conscience.
- *Specificity.* The order should be an order to perform or refrain from a specific act. An order or exhortation to "obey the law" and the like is not separately enforceable, because it imposes no new duty—and can otherwise unfairly ratchet up the potential maximum punishment that a soldier is facing for her conduct.
- *Willfulness.* Disobedience must be an intentional act to defy authority. If a soldier is lazy, inefficient, or obtuse, he may face punishment elsewhere under the UCMJ (possibly dereliction of duty or charges under either of the general articles) but, without more, is more likely to face corrective training or administrative sanction.

Disobeying a General Order or Regulation

As discussed above, it is a crime to disobey the lawful order of a superior commissioned officer under Article 90. Article 92 addresses a broader and less personal disobedience in making it a crime to disobey lawful general orders or regulations and other lawful orders that a soldier has a duty to obey. Offenses prosecuted under this article typically involve disobedience of written regulations and orders applicable to an entire military service or a large military unit. A lawful general order must be issued by a general officer, meaning a general in the Army or Air Force or an admiral in the Navy or Coast Guard. One key difference between prosecutions under this article and those under Article 90 is that there is no need to prove that the soldier knew of the lawful general order; it is presumed that soldiers know them, the same concept familiar to the civilian world that ignorance of the law normally is no excuse. And the orders are presumed to be lawful, unless contrary to the Constitution, the law of the United States, or rules set by a superior officer.

Article 92 is a frequently cited article, reflecting the heavily regulated nature of the military. Many military installations have rules such as a prohibition on running while wearing headphones or a requirement that soldiers wear motorcycle helmets. In wartime, it also is common for theater commanders to issue a "General Order No. 1," in which they prohibit a wide range of activities such as drinking alcohol, possessing pornography, retaining war trophies, or visiting local churches. Again, many routine violations of such orders and regulations are handled at nonjudicial punishment, but it is not uncommon for such violations to be added to court-martial charges to depict a wide range of misconduct or to be prosecuted alone if they are considered to be serious violations.

Dereliction of Duty

Many observers consider this to be the most typical military offense—essentially failure to do what you are supposed to do. Dereliction does not have its own article of the UCMJ—it also falls under Article 92 (disobedience of a lawful general order or regulation) and is a "lesser included" offense of such articles, in that a person can be found guilty of dereliction even when there is a technical problem with the proof regarding a lawful order or regulation. Dereliction of duty requires proving that a soldier had a duty and that she wrongfully failed to fulfill it. The issues that surround such cases concern the source and clarity of the duty and the circumstances of failing to perform. A duty can stem from something as clear as a law, rule, regulation, or treaty or have its source in something as indistinct as a custom of the service. The government must prove the source of the duty and then prove that the soldier knew or should have known of the duty (unlike for a lawful general order, in which knowledge is presumed). Then it must be shown that the soldier failed to perform intentionally (willfully) or through negligence or inefficiency. Dereliction is commonly charged, often as an alternative to failure to obey an order or regulation. Although it is sometimes criticized as too vague an offense, the government still must prove each element beyond a reasonable doubt, and the government must clearly establish the existence of a duty as a threshold matter. While soldiers have countless duties, prosecution for dereliction typically is reserved for those that are consequential—and commanders need to take care not to seek to punish soldiers for trivial derelictions, lest the commander create a chilling or intimidating atmosphere in which soldiers do not take initiative or in which they are tempted to cover up mistakes. Finally, dereliction cannot be charged when a soldier is unable to perform; for example, a soldier who tries but fails to qualify with an assigned weapon might find himself separated for inability to perform, but it would not be proper to charge him with dereliction of duty.

Talking Back

Serving as a dutiful subordinate does not mean simply refraining from assaulting the boss. It also is a crime for any soldier—officer or enlisted—to "behave with disrespect" toward her superior commissioned officer (Article 89). Doing or failing to do certain acts or using certain language toward a superior officer in a manner considered disrespectful constitutes a violation of this article. It is no defense to claim that it was done outside the presence or earshot of the officer about whom it was intended, and it is no defense to argue—as in contemptuous words—that the officer was not likely to hear or observe the conduct, although they may be mitigating factors. Violation of this offense can be the obvious disrespectful language or gesture that anyone could think of as well as intentional neglect of military courtesy, such as a salute. As with contemptuous language, disrespect, standing alone, is not likely to result in a court-martial, but it might form the basis for a charge at court-martial in the context of an array of other charges; disposition through nonjudicial punishment is more likely. Again, in the civilian world, a disrespectful subordinate might receive an unfavorable report in a personnel file or be fired; it is unique to the military that disrespect can result in a conviction and jail time.

Insubordination

While disrespect generally involves language or gestures that directly affront a superior officer, insubordination is a separate crime with a different universe of victims: noncommissioned or petty officers rather than commissioned officers. A soldier can commit this offense by disobeying the lawful order of such a person, under the same analysis discussed above for disobeying the order of a superior commissioned officer. A soldier can be insubordinate toward a warrant officer, noncommissioned officer, or petty officer if he uses language or does or fails to do certain acts toward and within the hearing of the victim in a way that is considered to be disrespectful or contemptuous. Again, besides obvious misconduct such as obscene language, insubordination can also encompass a gross and intentional failure to render military courtesy, refusal to speak in circumstances that call for a reply, and similar contemptuous behavior. The prosecution finds itself in such cases having to prove that the custom of a service makes such behavior offensive or insubordinate under the circumstances. Such offenses commonly are addressed by nonjudicial punishment, but they can be the basis for courts-martial if they are egregious cases—or as additional charges when other offenses are brought to court-martial.

Spying

Other than treason, it is unlikely that any other military offense carries the sense of dishonor and breach of soldierly chivalry as much as spying. Spying under Article 106, UCMJ, tracks closely with most citizens' street sense of the crime. Spying punishes anyone who clandestinely collects or attempts to collect valuable information with the intention of passing it to the enemy. The heart of the offense is "lurking," a verb not found elsewhere in the criminal code. Spying requires that someone lurk—act clandestinely—in an effort to obtain information that the person intends to be used against the United States. The offense can only arise during time of war, and, while it typically takes place on a military installation, ship, or the like, it can occur anywhere. It does not matter that the lurker succeed, only that the government can prove the intent to harm the United States.

Spying is unique in its breadth and severity, because it applies to more than soldiers and it carries the punishment of mandatory death. Most provisions of the UCMJ specifically apply to "person[s] subject to this chapter," meaning this chapter of the U.S. Code, meaning service members. Spying applies to "any person," meaning that it can punish not only U.S. civilians but noncitizens as well. In addition, death is mandatory for those convicted of spying—a rare and striking departure from the UCMJ's general practice of not mandating minimum court-martial sentences. Because it is such a grievous offense, it is intentionally narrow in its application. It does not apply to opposing soldiers who wear their nation's uniforms and carry out their operations openly—concealment is permissible, but false pretenses are not. There is also a sort of safe harbor provision in the law, which forbids prosecution of a spy for prior acts once he has rejoined the armed force of which he is a member—a provision that keeps the UCMJ consistent with the 1907 Hague Convention. Finally, although noncitizens and civilians can be punished as spies, someone who lives in occupied territory and passes on information to the other side cannot be tried as a spy as long as the person does not act clandestinely or under false pretenses but merely passes on what she sees. That person may well be liable for prosecution under Article 104 of the UCMJ, which prohibits giving intelligence to or communicating with the enemy (addressed below), which is still a serious offense but which carries different proof requirements and a different theory of criminality.

Espionage

This offense punishes any soldier who provides information to the enemy with the intent that it harm the United States or help a foreign nation. Under some circumstances, the penalty can be death. Espionage, Article 106a of the UCMJ, differs from spying in several important respects: It applies only to soldiers, and it does not require acting clandestinely. This relatively recent offense, added by Congress in 1986, covers conduct by soldiers that might not qualify as treason, spying, or aiding the enemy. It focuses on providing information to the enemy—the Manual for Courts-Martial provides a nonexclusive list that includes code books, sketches, photographs, and blueprints—with the intent or reason to believe it will harm the United States. One case prosecuted during the first Gulf War illustrated the potentially innocuous information that could qualify under this provision, when a U.S. soldier based in Germany gave copies of installation newspapers to someone he believed to be an Iraqi contact, while offering to provide other information as well.[2] Circumstances made clear that the soldier intended to harm the United States, even though the publicly available information had no real operational value. The maximum punishment for the offense is life in prison, but the government can seek the death penalty if it can show that the information passed to the enemy directly concerned nuclear weapons, spacecraft, satellites, war plans, intelligence or codes or major weapons systems or elements of defense strategy.

Mutiny and Sedition

Obedience to orders and compliance by individual soldiers are prerequisites to the effective functioning of a military organization—and even to the civil order. It is well recognized in criminal law that an offense is more likely to happen if more than one person is involved—this is why conspiracy is a crime. These two reasons together make clear why mutiny is a capital offense. If soldiers work together to usurp or override military authority, they can be found guilty of mutiny under Article 94. Mutiny can be accomplished passively—by refusing to carry out orders and military functions—as well as actively or violently. The essence of command is the ability to give orders and have them executed by a structure that reaches from the top of a military organization to its lowest-ranking member. Mutiny is the act of two or more people to usurp such command authority. Sedition also is punishable under Article 94, but it makes criminal the overthrow or destruction of lawful civil authority rather than military authority. Unlike mutiny, sedition cannot be passive, but must constitute revolt or violence; as with mutiny, it requires at least two people. Students of American history might recall the discredited Alien and Sedition Acts of the John Adams presidency. Sedition under the UCMJ differs in many important respects, especially the narrow population to which it applies (we already have established that servicemembers' constitutional protections are not in all instances coextensive with other citizens), its direct tie to good order and discipline, and its narrower construction (the Sedition Act of 1798 made it a crime to publish "false, scandalous, and malicious writing" against the government or government officials). It is rare in the criminal law to require a person to act to prevent someone from committing an offense. A person on the streets can see a crime about to happen—whether a purse-snatching, a murder, or a bank robbery—and is normally free to do nothing, not even to call the police. Although this might not constitute conscientious citizenship, it is generally not unlawful. Members of the military, especially those of senior rank or officers, often have affirmative obligations that are not present in the civilian world. Consequently, it is also a capital crime for a soldier to fail to prevent mutiny or sedition when committed in her presence or when she knew or had reason to believe it was taking place. The law charges her with doing her utmost to prevent or suppress mutiny or sedition—an "utmost" that the Manual for Courts-Martial says can include deadly force under the circumstances. The military is not a democratic institution, but there are avenues through which individuals can raise concerns about their leaders—whether such avenues are fruitful or frustrating, they never extend to usurping or taking over that authority.

Compelling—or Creating Incentives for—Courage in Battle

Military leaders recognize that, in most instances, courage or fearlessness in the face of mortal danger is not natural and that fear is a normal and appropriate response in such circumstances. Fear has salutary effects, including heightened awareness, consciousness of others, and caution. It also can be paralyzing and intimidating, tempting or encouraging a person to shirk or avoid duty that could result in death or terrible injury. Consequently, much military training and culture is geared to rationally overcoming fear—confidence courses, emphases on teamwork, and encouragement to trust one's equipment and to trust one's leaders. The UCMJ tracks and reinforces these instincts, assumptions, and practices. A series of offenses go to the core of the difficulty of soldiering—courage and duty in the face of grave danger in combat. Several offenses are designed to create a final incentive for courage or disincentive toward cowardice; consequently, the maximum punishments for some of these offenses, the death penalty, is solemn recognition of the potential impact of cowardice in battle.

- *Misbehavior before the enemy.* Article 99 makes criminal a service member's conduct that occurs "before or in the presence of the enemy." It applies to a service member who "runs away"; "shamefully abandons" a place, unit, or property that he is pledged to defend; "casts away his arms"; and several other offenses. Another crime under this article is "cowardly conduct." The UCMJ and other military measures (notably the nonstatutory Code of Conduct)[3] are built on the recognition that soldiers *should* experience fear and that it is a natural result of combat. Because fear is normal, service members need to be equipped to deal with that fear. While developing courage in the abstract is noble and aspirational—and often successful—it is also well recognized that the possibility of shame or punishment exists for service members' carrying out their missions in the most dangerous and stressful conditions. Consequently, Article 99 criminalizes a soldier's inability to overcome fear to carry out her military duty. It defines cowardice as "misbehavior motivated by fear" and defines fear as "a natural feeling of apprehension when going into battle," further counseling that being afraid—"mere display of apprehension"—"does not constitute this offense," but rather the "[r]efusal or abandonment of a performance of duty before or in the presence of the enemy as a result of fear."

Article 99 also lists several other manifestations of misbehavior before the enemy, all united around the theme of failing to serve. These include causing "false alarms in any command" (the military equivalent of pulling the fire alarm to evacuate an area and avoid combat), "willfully fail[ing] to do his utmost to encounter, engage, capture or destroy any enemy troops"—emphasizing that passivity can also be a crime—and failing to "afford all practicable relief and assistance to any troops, combatants, vessels" "when engaged in battle."

All of the offenses under Article 99 carry the potential of the death penalty, a stark reinforcement of the fact that good order and discipline are at the heart of the military justice system and that no other juridical mechanism could encourage, enforce, and adjudicate the unique interest in good order and discipline as well as a separate system of military justice. It also highlights the value of the due process and independent defense counsel that are available to accused service members, as the impact of cowardice should be expected to be felt acutely by military commanders—and ultimately military juries.

- *Subordinate compelling surrender.* An enemy force wants to exploit the fact or potential of dissension or fear undermining the effectiveness of a military unit. One way to do this is to take advantage of a soldier who might force someone in her unit, ideally a leader, to surrender to the enemy against his will. Article 100 forbids any soldier to compel a commander of a military unit to surrender. The offense must consist of acts, not just words (commanders are expected to be able to resist words), but, unlike mutiny, there is no requirement for concerted action—that is, a soldier may act alone in committing this offense. The article also forbids surrender by "striking the colors or flag" or similar gesture by someone who does not have authority to make such an offer. Again, these offenses are meant to support commanders in their greatest areas of responsibility—bringing the fight to the enemy in a unified manner. A subordinate who undermines the command in this manner may face the death penalty for this offense.

- *Misconduct as a prisoner.* It is well understood, even by those without military experience, that a person's conduct in captivity can have tremendous ramifications, not just on herself, but on those captured with her, the morale of those who know of her conduct, and potentially on the course of a conflict. Those who resist the temptation to accommodate themselves to enemy interests and propaganda find themselves boosting the courage of their fellows and wearing down their captors—and reinforcing the strategic effort of the war. Conversely, a person who seeks or obtains or simply agrees to favors or special treatment can have a corrosive and potentially fatal effect on comrades and national security. It is on these assumptions that Article 105 makes criminal, while in the hands of the enemy and in time of war, conduct by a captured soldier that is designed to secure favorable treatment and that works to the detriment of others held by the enemy as prisoners. It is a broad charge, in that it makes criminal acts "contrary to law, custom, or regulation" that harm others, and it applies to harm to civilian or military prisoners, heightening the duty of a captured person to care for fellow captives. The harm to fellow prisoners may be such measures as reduced rations or physical punishment—almost anything that makes their lives worse and that reduces hope, thereby potentially creating a spiral of dispirited captives. The offending conduct is as wide as the imagination of the potential collaborator and traditionally includes conduct such as accepting better treatment or food or reporting escape plans or the location of food and ammunition caches.

Article 105 also punishes conduct of a leader who, while in confinement, maltreats those over whom he is in authority. Most often the person is in authority by virtue of his senior military status, and the military chain of command entrusts that person with significant responsibilities for the discipline and morale of other captives. Consequently, abuse of those placed in that trust, whether physical or mental (the crime includes "inflammatory and derogatory words [that produce] mental anguish"), is a tremendous breach of that trust—considered sufficiently grave that this article also carries the maximum punishment of death.

- *Malingering*. A military organization must be able to count on all of its members to be ready for duty at all times. As long as there have been armies, there has been the temptation to find an honorable-seeming way to avoid the risks of battle—and a well-tested route is injuring oneself or feigning injury to avoid combat and the risk of grievous injury or death. Article 115 prohibits malingering, which has two main components: self-injury and feigning injury or illness. Malingering applies to avoiding any kind of service—not just combat or danger.

A predicate for the offense is that the soldier faced certain duty or was aware of a particular prospective assignment. Because she wants to avoid that service, the accused feigns illness or other problems—disablement, mental illness, almost anything that would make her unavailable for duty—in the expectation that she will lawfully be excused from the duty. Similarly, a soldier commits this offense in the manner most commonly understood by the public—by hurting himself, known widely as "shooting himself in the foot." Any intentionally inflicted injury with the intent to avoid such service also constitutes this offense. It does not matter who does the injuring—the soldier avoiding the duty or a confederate she convinces to do so (the confederate could also be guilty as a principal to the offense or as a co-conspirator).

This is a difficult crime to wriggle out of, because the core of the offense is not the injury or disablement that is inflicted or faked—it is the desire to avoid service. Therefore, whether the soldier is really sick or whether his attempt to fake sickness is poorly executed or short-lived will not matter as long as the government can establish the intent to shirk. That intent element, however, is a significant burden for the government, which must be able to establish that the injury was not a result of negligence or recklessness but rather stemmed from the intent to shirk or avoid service. Similarly, a soldier who grazed a toe and needed a Band-Aid but intended to shoot herself in the foot would still be guilty of the offense. In addition, a soldier who is legitimately sick or injured but uses the opportunity to prolong the sickness or disability (for example, rejecting or abusing medicine) can also be guilty of the offense. The extent of the injury might be a factor that would mitigate the sentence, just as the intensity or proximity of dangerous operations might increase the sentence and could also help a judge or jury to evaluate the intent of the accused.

The duty being avoided is not relevant to the offense—he could be avoiding KP because of an overbearing boss, the arduous hours, or the aroma of the garlic—but it is relevant in calculating the potential maximum punishment; logically, the more dangerous the duty being avoided, the greater potential punishment, because the loss of the soldier and the impact on good order and discipline ("if she can get away with it, what am I doing here?") are greatest.

The maximum punishment for this offense again reflects the seriousness of fleeing from difficult duty—it carries the potential of a dishonorable discharge, even for its least serious offense, feigning illness or disablement, which carries a maximum of 1 year's confinement. The maximum confinement triples when the offense occurs during time of war or in a hostile fire pay zone. The maximum sentence for self-injury is 5 years (recognizing the seriousness to the system of self-injury as opposed to feigning—among other impacts, it uses medical resources that otherwise would go to those harmed in honorable fashion), and it doubles to 10 years if in time of war or a hostile fire pay zone.

Releasing Prisoner without Proper Authority

The law of war permits a military force to detain prisoners of war until the end of conflict. Commanders have the authority to release prisoners at any point, however—typically when they decide there is no military value in retaining the prisoner or when the logistical burden of keeping the prisoner outweighs whatever military value the prisoner might be able to contribute if returned to the enemy. That is, however, a commander's decision, and it is a crime under Article 96 for a soldier to release someone without authority or negligently to permit a prisoner to escape. Permitting a prisoner to escape through design (intentionally) or releasing a prisoner without authority carries a maximum punishment of two years' confinement—relatively mild—but also a dishonorable discharge.

"Are You Not People?"—The Court-Martial of Billy Mitchell

One of the most famous and most publicized courts-martial in U.S. history featured a flamboyant and popular rogue juxtaposed against a seemingly stiff, thin-skinned, and unimaginative military bureaucracy and an unpopular "catch-all" provision of the Articles of War that seemed to punish an officer for his far-sightedness as much as for his impolitic nature.

Billy Mitchell cultivated but also earned a reputation as the early-20th-century prophet of air power, having been drawn to the skies since early in his military career, even before he observed Orville Wright conduct a flying demonstration at Fort Myer, just across the Potomac River from Washington, DC, in 1906. The scion of a wealthy, politically prominent Wisconsin family, he nevertheless enlisted in the Army at age 18, was commissioned shortly thereafter, and, by the time the United States joined World War I in spring 1917, 37-year-old Lieutenant Colonel Mitchell was working closely with the British and French in employing the nascent air power in that war, including at *Saint-Mihiel*. He returned home, the first American to win the *Croix de Guerre,* ceaselessly to argue for the recognition and expansion of air power—and not always in a manner that won him friends inside the military.

By 1925, then 45, and having served in a series of positions in which he advocated for air power as a—and in his analysis generally *the*—key source of future combat power, Mitchell publicly expressed his frustration when the Navy dirigible, *Shenandoah,* floated well above the safe altitude of about 3,800 feet and broke apart in the sky somewhere above 6,000 feet.[4] Determining that the commander had recommended against takeoff (and, later, that his widow was pressured by the Navy to absolve it of responsibility), Mitchell, who recently had been returned to his "permanent" rank of colonel after having reached major general, issued a press release on September 5, 1925, in which he said the *Shenandoah* and two other recent accidents were "the direct result of the incompetency, criminal negligence, and almost treasonable administration of our national defense by the Navy and War Departments." Soon he was facing court-martial under Article 96 of the Articles of War, a predecessor to Article 133 of the UCMJ, which provided for court-martial for "all disorders and neglects to the prejudice of good order and military discipline [and] all conduct of a nature to bring discredit upon the military service."

The court-martial was ordered by President Coolidge, and the original panel of 12 general officers was reduced to 9 members (he challenged one officer who had publicly criticized him), all but one West Point graduates and all of them World War I veterans. Congressman Frank R. Reid, a Republican from Illinois in his first term, defended Mitchell at his request and had two major themes: Mitchell was being punished for exercising his First Amendment right of free speech and that he was right—air power was the wave of the future, and the military leadership was leaden, defensive, and inflexible in its contemplation of air power. Several prominent witnesses testified for Mitchell, including Generals Henry "Hap" Arnold, Carl Spaatz, and "Ace of Aces" Eddie Rickenbacker.

The government took the defense's bait in trying to disprove Mitchell's and Reid's assertions of the quality and future of air power, but it also argued that, even if he were right, Mitchell was disloyal in making a public statement of the sort—"almost treasonable" is still harsh criticism from a senior military officer notwithstanding the "almost"—and that military members, especially senior officers in positions such as Mitchell's, did not have the right to make such statements. Some of the testimony involved detailed analysis of whether the Japanese would have the resources or cunning to, as Mitchell had predicted, bring a flotilla of submarines and aircraft to attack Ford's Island in Pearl Harbor. Much of the trial, however, involved questions of character and the right of an officer to criticize his leaders while in uniform. Some of Mitchell's supporters, such as Will Rogers, made appearances in the courtroom to reinforce his man-of-the-people status.

In any event, the government did not have a chance in the public relations war and was pummeled in the courtroom and in the nation's newspapers. At one point, the defense found a way to call Congressman (later New York Mayor) Fiorello

LaGuardia. When the government tried to impeach LaGuardia by holding up a headline that quoted him as having said, "Billy Mitchell is not being tried by a jury of his peers, but by nine beribboned dog robbers of the General Staff," LaGuardia replied, "I did not say 'beribboned.'" He added, perhaps with a hint of mischief, "I want to say that at that time I didn't know that General MacArthur was on this court."

Mitchell himself testified and parried with the prosecutor, Major Allen W. Gullion, who later served as the Judge Advocate General of the Army. In addressing the sensitive issue of the (almost) treason allegation, Mitchell did not retreat. He said one definition of treason was outright war against the United States, but that the other was "betraying of any trust or confidence. . . . I believe that the departments, the system, is almost treasonable . . . in that it does not give a proper place to air power in organizing the defenses of the country. . . . It is a question of the system, and not the individuals, entirely."

At the end of the seven-week trial, Mitchell dramatically announced that, because "[t]he court has refrained from ruling whether the truth in this case constitutes an absolute defense . . . [t]o proceed further with this case would serve not useful purpose. I have therefore directed my counsel to" waive closing argument. Gullion ensured that he could argue regardless, and he displayed a newspaper headline that read, "The people are behind Mitchell," prompting him to ask the panel, "Are you not *people*? You served your country in war and risked your lives . . . I say that you are the real people, the real citizens, and that what you believe is what matters." He called Mitchell not a "George Washington type" but rather "the all-too-familiar charlatan and demagogue type," who, "except for a decided difference in poise and mental powers in Burr's favor, [was] like Aaron Burr." There is no way to know whether Gullion's seeming appeal to vanity and prejudice affected the panel. Mitchell was found guilty of all charges and ordered suspended from rank, command, and duty with forfeiture of all pay and allowances for five years—but he was not dismissed. He was permitted to resign in February 1926. While he continued to speak out as an air power advocate, he never again commanded the worldwide platform that he had enjoyed during the weeks of riveting testimony. He died at age 56 in 1936, and in his death regained his reputation, as President Roosevelt raised him to the rank of major general on the Army Air Corps retired list, and he received numerous official and civic recognitions; Milwaukee's international airport and the Air Force Academy's dining hall are named in his honor, but his conviction by court-martial remains a matter of record.

Beyond the Headlines: The Enduring Issues of Candor, Command Influence, and the General Articles

The Mitchell trial provided a public sensation in its own right—the popular and swashbuckling hero in vivid contrast to the inflexible bureaucracy, a conflict made only more stark by the accuracy of his prophecies, when the Japanese accomplished in 1941 what he had predicted in 1924. It provoked criticism of Article 96 and encouraged controversy over the sweep of the general articles, one that continued for generations—but the articles remain virtually unchanged and in continued use more than 90 years after Mitchell's trial. Mitchell's many supporters argued that he was "punished for telling the truth" and that Article 96 was unconstitutional, making criminal Mitchell's exercise of his First Amendment rights, embittered by a belief in the accuracy of his criticism. Mitchell, a nonlawyer, argued that Article 96 was so broad as to permit trying an officer for "tickling a horse." Finally, the trial also highlighted the subtlety of concerns about command control over the military. There is no suggestion and no proof that the verdict or sentence were preordained; there remained, however, a sense that Mitchell was drummed out for his beliefs and the fact that they stung the establishment that held him in judgment. "Are you not *people*?" seemed a prosecutor's reminder that Mitchell had strayed from the club, perhaps less artful and less cogent than arguing that, even if Mitchell were right, thick headedness of a boss or a bureaucracy did not equate to a subordinate's right to publicly call it treason.

Improperly Caring for Government Property and Personal or Public Property

The U.S. military budget is huge, reflecting the most well-resourced and well-paid military ever known. Such a robust budget cannot excuse, however, recklessness in the treatment of property entrusted to military personnel or the property of others whom they encounter. Consequently, it is a crime to lose or destroy military property and also a crime to destroy or damage private property. These are both rules of prudence and accountability (not stealing from or taking advantage of government largesse in resourcing the military) as well as of individual and unit discipline, military reputation, and compliance with the law of war.

Waste, Spoilage, or Destruction of Property Other than Military Property of the United States

Article 109 punishes waste and spoilage of real property, as well as the destruction or damage of personal property. It is a crime to damage real property, whether done intentionally or recklessly. Examples include burning buildings or piers, tearing down fences, cutting down trees, or harming utilities. In a peacetime environment, this expands the military's ability to hold a soldier accountable for destruction of property as a vandal or malicious actor, or in concert with other crimes such as burglary or house breaking. In time of war, obviously, this has more significant ramifications. Destruction of personal and private property that is not incident to or collateral to military operations can be a war crime. Even when not clearly a war crime—issues of proportionality and avoidability are debatable and context-specific—it can be destructive to the political purpose of a war when soldiers are seen to loot or damage private property. It can reflect poorly on the discipline and goals of a military force. This is a long way from Sherman's March to the Sea, which included scorched-earth tactics along the path from Atlanta to Savannah. While Sherman was not indiscriminate in the context of his times and gave specific orders to minimize destruction in parts to avoid destruction of those who cooperated (not a meaningful distinction in the Law of Armed Conflict that has developed in the subsequent 150 years), such orders as the following would violate current understanding of the law.

Sherman's March—"Devastation" . . . and Relative Restraint

V. To army corps commanders alone is entrusted the power to destroy mills, houses, cotton-gins, &c., and for them this general principle is laid down: In districts and neighborhoods where the army is unmolested no destruction of such property should be permitted; but should guerrillas or bushwhackers molest our march, or should the inhabitants burn bridges, obstruct roads, or otherwise manifest local hostility, then army commanders should order and enforce a devastation more or less relentless according to the measure of such hostility.[5]

It should also be known that Sherman counseled restraint in other portions of the order: "In all foraging, of whatever kind, the parties engaged will refrain from abusive or threatening language, and may, where the officer in command thinks proper, give written certificates of the facts, but no receipts, and they will endeavor to leave with each family a reasonable portion for their maintenance. . . . Soldiers must not enter the dwellings of the inhabitants, or commit any trespass, but during a halt or a camp they may be permitted to gather turnips, potatoes, and other vegetables, and to drive in stock of their camp. To regular foraging parties must be instructed the gathering of provisions and forage at any distance from the road traveled. VI. As for horses, mules, wagons, &c., belonging to the inhabitants, the cavalry and artillery may appropriate freely and without limit, discriminating, however, between the rich, who are usually hostile, and the poor or industrious, usually neutral or friendly. Foraging parties may also take mules or horses to replace the jaded animals of their trains, or to serve as pack-mules for the regiments or brigades." The larger point remains: Tactics once considered harsh but lawful are now expressly prohibited, as a matter of discipline, prudence, and compliance with the evolving Law of Armed Conflict.

A "Sherman necktie" of a railroad tie twisted around a tree would not only be the intimidating calling card of a rampaging military force, but also likely evidence of a crime.

Destruction of personal property also is a violation of Article 109. Unlike waste or spoilage, which can be accomplished through recklessness, destruction of personal property requires intent on part of the soldier charged. This would apply not only to the cotton gins and feed stores of Sherman's era, but also to any property owned by another that the soldier does not have a lawful excuse for damaging or destroying.

The maximum punishment for either offense is a year in jail and a bad-conduct discharge if the value is $500 or less; the punishment is 10 years in confinement and a bad-conduct discharge if the value is greater than $500.

Defining Criminal Conduct in a Unique Society

Sale, Damage, or Destruction of Military Property of the United States

Soldiers are custodians of property bought by the same taxpayers who also furnish their pay, allowances, and health care. While such property exists to serve soldiers in the accomplishment of their missions, it is not their property and must be treated with reasonable care—under no circumstances is it theirs to trade, abuse, keep for personal use, or destroy. Article 108 is designed to reinforce a soldier's sense of accountability for taxpayer property, individuals' and units' sense of discipline, and to guard against greed and self-dealing.

Therefore, a soldier may not sell equipment that he has access to only because he is a soldier—whether this is tents, bullets, or meat slicers. In addition, she is responsible for damage to such property caused by her neglect. It does not mean that property damaged in the hearty and daunting work of soldiering or training is a crime—normal wear and tear is obviously an exception. It does mean, however, that the work or soldiering does not excuse a failure to care for property, because the care of military property and personal equipment is at the heart of unit readiness and good order and discipline. It is one thing, therefore, for a tent to get soaked and muddy in an exercise; it is another for that tent to be stowed in its muddy and moist state. It is one thing to drive a Humvee through gullies and across berms in the course of normal military operations; it is another to fail to conduct preventive maintenance and upkeep and to have the Humvee break down because of that failure. At times, there are issues of whether something constitutes military property (for example, a meal ready to eat issued to a soldier but not intact and not eaten, sold to a surplus store), but most of these questions are obvious and easily solved.

A soldier cannot profit just because he is a soldier (by taking or using government property) and he must take reasonable care, understanding all of the circumstances in which equipment is used, but also understanding that it is entrusted to him by taxpayers who expect careful preservation and protection of it. The maximum punishment for selling, damaging, destroying, or disposing of military property or for willfully suffering its loss or destruction is 1 year in jail and a bad-conduct discharge if the value of the property is less than $500 and 10 years and a dishonorable discharge if the value is over $500. Destroying or losing such property by neglect carries a maximum punishment of 6 months' confinement and 6 months' forfeiture of pay if the value of the property is less than $500 and 1 year's confinement and a bad-conduct discharge if the value is greater than $500.

Sexual Harassment and Other "Cruelty and Maltreatment"

There is always a limit in the military, especially a military in a modern liberal democracy—and even more so in an all-volunteer military drawn from a diverse, contemporary society—on the lawful exercise of authority by those entrusted with the power to issue military orders. Though perhaps made more complex by some of the conditions in modern society, it is not a novel concept that commanders and leaders inhabit positions of immense trust and that abuse of those positions, demonstrated by degrading treatment of those whom they are trusted to lead—of which sexual exploitation is a modern manifestation—is contrary to good order and discipline, greatly rotting the structure on which healthy and lawful command is built and poisoning the effectiveness of a unit and of military operations.

Article 93 is entitled a prohibition against "cruelty and maltreatment" and has its roots in forbidding barbaric, sadistic, or unjust practices. Such practices can result in injury, exploit the person on the receiving end of the order or abuse, and degrade that person's effectiveness—and often the morale and cohesion of those who come to know of the maltreatment in the close-knit environment of a military unit. Examples only run the limit of the imagination, but the clear examples of cruelty or maltreatment are conduct such as forcing someone into harsh weather without the proper protective gear, punching or kicking a subordinate, or denying food and water. The conduct need not be physical, however, and can include conduct intended to abuse, punish, or isolate a subordinate, such as refusing to speak to or respond to a subordinate or directing others to act this way, and it certainly includes patently offensive statements or conduct of a racially or sexually discriminatory nature.

This set of offenses has received renewed attention, and the number of prosecutions and instances of nonjudicial punishment under it have increased, because it also includes sexual harassment. When a leader influences, offers to influence, or threatens the career, pay, or job of another in exchange for sexual favors or is guilty of repeated and unwanted comments of a sexual nature, that conduct is made criminal by this article. There are matters of nuance and degree involved—not every offhand comment or off-color joke is a crime. But there is no "that's just who I am" defense for a military leader. Clearly offensive words, especially when part of a pattern of conduct or when directed against a certain individual or set of individuals, is a crime under Article 93, as is unwelcome touching of a sexual nature. Women constitute about 15 percent of the military services, a percentage that has stayed stable in recent years, and numerous well-publicized sexual scandals, both in the active military and the service academies, have caused significant public and congressional attention. There have also been highly publicized prosecutions of officers charged with sexual maltreatment of subordinates, both in training units—where the impact on good order and future soldiers is especially acute—and among senior leaders of all services. Hazing also has become a concern in recent years, prompting Congressional attention and discussion of whether to amend the UCMJ expressly to prohibit it; such conduct currently would be prosecuted under Article 93.

Cynics and some critics argue that such provisions criminalize supervising by turning aggressive military leaders, whose job is to prepare subordinates for war and lead them in times of stress and danger, into cautious and timid personnel. It is worth remembering, however, that the judgments and actions in question under Article 93 are evaluated by an objective standard, and a jury would be

Defining Criminal Conduct in a Unique Society

asked to evaluate the conduct in terms of the reasonable leader and reasonable subordinate—ruling out those with exquisite sensitivities and generally ruling out mistakes or remarks of a passing, inconsequential nature. Still, this provision—which can also apply to leaders' conduct with civilians, under the circumstances in which civilians are subject to military leaders (consider deployment settings as well as disaster relief)—reinforces the necessary burdens and limitations of leadership. Leaders are expected to be effective leaders within the law, and they should be able to lead effectively without resorting to abuse. There is a long and honorable tradition of "extra training" in the military, which can involve discomfort and carefully managed stress (for example, conducting physical training in the heat of the day for a subordinate who is out of shape or needs motivation); the traditions and practices of the military services place such conduct in context, and it is generally well understood by those—commanders, juries, and judges—who would be called on to determine whether such conduct is criminal.

While *command climate* is a relatively modern term, the concept is not new. Article 93 does not make criminals out of those whose command climate could stand to be improved—leaders, too, are expected to grow and adapt, and imperfect leadership is not a crime. It does criminalize objectively offensive practices that threaten individuals and undermine readiness.

False Official Statements

Combat is too dangerous, too fast moving, and too stressful for leaders to have to doubt the truth of what they are told. A soldier must be able to be trusted to tell the truth, especially about matters that relate to the mission. A soldier's word might not just be what she says under stress—"Did you check the radar?" "Are we clear on the right?"—but statements or representations that she has made in the course of her duties and which a leader might rely on, such as reports that attest that vehicles have been inspected and properly maintained and that munitions are properly loaded. It is not a concept unique to the military that senior personnel rely on the representations of junior personnel in making decisions; it simply carries extra poignancy because of the potentially fatal consequences to soldiers in combat or training and the potential impact on national security when such a representation has been relied on to a leader's or a unit's detriment.

Article 107 prohibits the making of "any false record . . . order, or other official document, knowing it to be false, or makes any other false official statement knowing it to be false." It requires knowledge and intent, so a true mistake cannot be made criminal—though, depending on the nature of the mistake and the reasonable expectations of the individual, it could constitute a dereliction of duty and be punishable under Article 92, discussed above.

Sometimes prosecutions under Article 107 (nonjudicial punishment is a common sanction for this article) center on whether the author or speaker knew the representation was false or whether the representation was consequential—that is, whether it made a difference in an important decision. While the speaker or author must have intended the falsehood, it is no defense to say that it was not important; that is not a matter for that person to evaluate and is no defense to an intended falsehood.

Statements to law enforcement officials also are controversial. Because Article 31 protects soldiers from being questioned without being advised of their rights against self-incrimination, they are never obliged to talk to law enforcement officials—whether in custody or not. Soldiers may not be compelled to talk to any law enforcement official, but if they do talk, they must tell the truth. Because of this, Article 107 sometimes forms the basis for prosecuting those who lied to law enforcement. The "ordinary lie"—denial when facts turn out otherwise—is not likely to garner much in a prosecution under Article 107, and prosecutors rarely will expend resources on it, but it can be actionable, and the doctrine of a noncriminal "exculpatory no" does not excuse such denials. If, however, a suspect tells an elaborate lie that itself consumes investigative resources (I was mugged, raped, drugged; person X committed the offense; various versions of "they went that way"), it may well become the basis of a charge or an additional charge when holding a soldier accountable for other offenses. This vibrant article reinforces the military tradition of honor and accountability, magnified by the unique impact of lying when offering official information. The maximum punishment, recently increased to align itself with a similar offense under the U.S. Code, is five years' confinement and a dishonorable discharge.

Dueling, Malingering

Considered by many observers to be a harmless anachronism, dueling remains in the UCMJ despite periodic suggestions that it be repealed. A soldier can be prosecuted under Article 114 if he "fights or promotes, or is concerned in or connives at fighting a duel" or fails to report his knowledge that a challenge has been sent by one person to another.

The government must prove that the fight was conducted with deadly weapons for private reasons and by prior agreement. The impact on good order and discipline is self-evident—dueling corrodes unity, teamwork, and trust, which are the bulwark of units' effectiveness, and promotion of dueling ("urging or taunting another to challenge or to accept a challenge to duel, acting as a second or as a carrier of a challenge or acceptance") is directly contrary to unity and effectiveness. Though no longer "pistols at 10 paces," the essential crime remains relevant and current in the contemporary military. It is not difficult to conjure a situation in a barracks or on a ship, made easier by availability of weapons and intoxicants, in which trash talk can lead to deadly confrontations.

The General Articles: Conduct Unbecoming and Conduct Contrary to Good Order and Discipline

Two of the more controversial, but also cherished and deeply rooted offenses in the UCMJ enable the military to criminally prosecute soldiers for conduct that is not explicitly covered elsewhere in the UCMJ on the grounds that it is so

Defining Criminal Conduct in a Unique Society

incompatible with service traditions or so harmful to the military's effectiveness and reputation that it should be characterized as a crime. The general articles frequently have been litigated for their vagueness and overbreadth, yet they have been upheld by appellate courts and continue to be used by commanders.

Conduct Unbecoming

Article 133 applies only to commissioned officers and academy cadets, and it simply prohibits "conduct unbecoming an officer and a gentleman." The question, of course, is under what circumstance such conduct should actually constitute a crime for which someone can receive a federal conviction, be deprived of liberty, and lose her military status. The Manual for Courts-Martial provides nonbinding guidance by making clear that this prohibition covers conduct in an official or unofficial capacity—reinforcing the point that appears throughout the UCMJ that there is no private or off-duty conduct that is necessarily beyond the reach of the military, especially for officers. Official behavior or conduct that "seriously compromises" an officer's standing can be prosecuted under Article 133, as can "action of behavior in a private capacity" that dishonors or disgraces the officer and, using the same term as for official misconduct, "seriously compromises" the officer. The Manual for Courts-Martial provides an insight into military culture by acknowledging that an officer (it makes clear that *gentlemen* also means women in this context) is not "expected to meet unrealistically high moral standards, but there is a limit of tolerance . . . below which the personal standards of an officer" or cadet "cannot fall without seriously compromising the person's standing." The Manual provides a nonexclusive list of the types of offenses that commonly can fall under Article 133, including lying, associating with prostitutes, failing to support one's family, and reading another's mail without authorization.

Conduct that is punishable under other articles of the UCMJ (larceny, lying, adultery, etc.) may also be charged under Article 133 as long as the government takes on the burden of proving the additional element of conduct unbecoming. The maximum punishment for the offense is the maximum for the most analogous offense under the UCMJ when applicable (e.g., larceny, drunk driving) and, where not specified, one year's confinement. Dismissal and total forfeiture of pay and allowances are always available as part of the punishment under Article 133.

One of the more famous cases prosecuted under Article 133 involved Captain Howard Levy,[6] an Army dermatologist who refused an order to train Special Forces personnel, made public statements critical of the Vietnam War, and specifically counseled "Negro soldiers" that they should not fight in an unjust war. He also referred to Special Forces personnel as "liars and thieves," "killers of peasants," and "murderers of women and children." Levy was prosecuted under several provisions of the UCMJ, but much of the contentiousness on appeal centered on the statements and exhortations made "while in the performance of his duties" that "wrongfully and dishonorably" were aimed at turning other soldiers against the war and undermining their loyalty and duty to serve. The Supreme Court summarized Levy's statements as "intemperate, defamatory, provoking, disloyal, contemptuous, and disrespectful to Special Forces personnel and to enlisted personnel who were patients or under his supervision." The Court found that Article 133 (and Article 134, discussed below) were not "void for vagueness," a Constitutional concept that determines whether an offense is stated with sufficient specificity to place someone on notice that his conduct might be criminal. In an opinion by Justice Rehnquist, the Court also found that the general articles were not "overbroad," a related Constitutional concept designed to guard against a criminal provision that "sweeps too broadly" in that it endangers or intimidates ("sweeps up") those engaged in lawful conduct by the expansive way in which a prohibition is drafted.

Article 133 remains a commonly charged offense in the military, more often employed in offers of nonjudicial punishment, because many of the more common officer infractions, such as substance abuse, lying, and consensual sexual misconduct, are handled at that level, often followed by an officer's resignation or proceedings that seek his administrative separation from the military. Despite occasional slang to the contrary, there is no such crime as conduct unbecoming a noncommissioned officer, and the only general article available for all members of the military is Article 134.

Article 134—The Multifaceted, Multipurpose General Article

While Article 133 applies only to officers, Article 134 is the general article for all military personnel that covers a range of noncapital offenses not otherwise addressed in the UCMJ. It has three distinct components or clauses: (1) forbidding conduct prejudicial to good order and discipline, (2) forbidding conduct of a nature to bring discredit on the military, and (3) punishing noncapital offenses not otherwise covered in the UCMJ but made criminal by local laws that the federal government assimilates by law. Article 134 is to be used as last resort, when conduct is not specifically addressed elsewhere in the UCMJ. Although it has been the topic of criticism for seeming to be too imprecise and broad and therefore too open for manipulation by the government, the intent, as explained by William Winthrop in his seminal *Military Law and Precedents,* is the opposite— "to prevent the possibility of a failure of justice in the Army" because of a failure to anticipate or specifically codify particular misconduct. Winthrop wrote that it reaches conduct "not certainly or fully designated or described in some other particular article."[7]

- *"all disorders and neglects to the prejudice of good order and discipline."* This portion of Article 134, commonly referred to as clause 1, makes such delicts a crime, but only when the government can prove direct prejudice; it expressly does not cover "acts which are prejudicial only in a remote or indirect sense," borrowing language and guidance that originally appeared in Winthrop's work. This clause is meant to ensure that military members understand that their conduct should not be guided by a strictly legalistic

Defining Criminal Conduct in a Unique Society

approach; that is, this clause is meant to discourage an ethic that says that any conduct not expressly prohibited must be permissible, and to heighten awareness that most any misconduct can be harmful to the mission. Article 134 recognizes that some conduct, not otherwise expressly criminal, can undermine good order and discipline because of its impact on military order. The impact must be "reasonably direct and palpable," and proof in such cases might involve a prosecutor calling a senior leader to address the impact of the conduct in question. This clause also captures violations of military customs, and the Manual for Courts-Martial emphasizes that such customs must be long established to attain the force of law—and the custom must be deeply rooted and its violation consequential enough to be charged as a crime. For example, it might be customary to send a thank you note, but failing to do so is nothing more than a social faux pas, even if intended as an insult or snub; on the other hand, failure to salute or to render military courtesies might constitute a criminal violation under this clause. Good order, in Winthrop's characterization, is the "condition of tranquillity [sic], security and good government—of the military service," the breach of which can be a crime.[8]

- *"all conduct of a nature to bring discredit upon the armed forces."* As with conduct prejudicial to good order and discipline, the prosecution must establish a violation of clause 2 of Article 134 by demonstrating that such conduct "has a tendency to bring the service into disrepute or which tends to lower it in public esteem." Conspicuous misconduct by someone with military identity might cause the military to fall in esteem in the civilian world and be punishable under this clause. Soldiers who have misrepresented their military service or who have engaged in outrageous or embarrassing conduct in civilian communities, including overseas, might find themselves charged under this clause. Scholars and critics argue that this clause permits the enforcement of pique and potentially criminalizes conduct over which an officer is not reasonably on notice. In practice, however, it is most often used to punish officers—most often nonjudicially—for indiscreet conduct or for violations of civil laws that leaders believe have an impact on overall fitness for duty.
- *Typical offenses under clauses 1 and 2.* The Manual for Courts-Martial provides a nonexclusive list of offenses that qualify as violations of clauses 1 and 2. Some are arcane and infrequently used, such as abusing a public animal or breaking quarantine, but others represent codification of offenses rooted in military culture and provide guidance on elements and pleading, among them:
  - *Adultery.* Traditionally a military offense, it has become more controversial as civilian prosecutions have become so infrequent. While the offense remains the same—essentially sexual intercourse with a person not one's spouse—commanders are specifically instructed to dispose of it at the lowest possible level (when it is the only offense, this is most often via nonjudicial punishment or official reprimand) and to evaluate all factors, including its notoriety and impact on a military organization.
  - *Bad debts.* Dishonorably failing to pay debts as well as dishonorably failing to maintain sufficient funds to cover checks are both offenses under 134, consistent with the position that a soldier should be fiscally responsible. Article 123(a), however, is the most appropriate "bad checks" offense when the prosecution is able to establish intent, and that offense also serves as a reminder of the preemption doctrine that counsels prosecutors to charge service members under the enumerated articles of the UCMJ when the conduct qualifies for one of those offenses, and only to use Article 134 when those provisions are unable or do not adequately capture the essential criminality of the conduct.

- *Drunk on duty.* Various offenses relating to incapacitation of alcohol appear under Article 134, drunk on duty being perhaps the most serious, but also disorderly conduct and drinking liquor with a prisoner. These offenses are not serious simply or solely because they involve consumption of alcohol but because otherwise lawful conduct, taken to excess, imperils a soldier's ability to perform her mission.
- *Fraternization.* This complicated offense is listed as one of the Article 134 offenses in recognition of its long tradition in the U.S. military (and most other militaries) that discourages or prohibits relationships of undue familiarity between officers and enlisted soldiers. Essentially, such relationships must remain professional and generally not social or intimate. The military services have their own regulations and traditions that inform the permissible contours of such relationships, and testimony on such particulars is likely to be the part of a prosecution for such an offense.
- *"crimes and offenses not capital, of which persons subject to this chapter may be guilty."* Clause 3 violations represent gap filling by the UCMJ, an attempt to ensure that service members do not escape responsibility for ordinary laws that are common in civilian communities but that might not be specifically addressed in the UCMJ or other federal laws. Therefore, the Assimilative Crimes Act applies local laws to most military installations (where there is exclusive or concurrent federal jurisdiction), ensuring that measures such as traffic violations and other measures typical of states and municipalities, are available to the federal government. This relieves the federal government from passing a host of largely duplicative laws and ensures that those that are sensibly adapted to local conditions and customs (speed limits and the like) are best defined and addressed at that level.

Notes

1. 10 U.S. Code 502.

2. Specialist Albert T. Sombolay pleaded guilty to several offenses, including espionage, in a court-martial held in Germany in 1991. Among other facts, he admitted to having contacted Jordanian officials and sought to communicate with Iraqi officials as well, through their Belgian embassy, during the Gulf War of 1991.

3. The Code of Conduct, published as Executive Order 10653 by President Eisenhower in 1955, was designed to provide guidance for U.S. soldiers who were captured as prisoners of war. Sometimes misunderstood as being part of the UCMJ or itself being binding, it is not law and not punitive; rather, it is a source of guidance and reinforcement for those facing the unique stresses and pressures of being confined by enemy forces. Its six articles, revised slightly over the years, are: "(I) I am an American, fighting in the forces which guard my country and our way of life. I am prepared to give my life in their defense. (II) I will never surrender of my own free will. If in command, I will never surrender the members of my command while they still have the means to resist. (III) If I am captured I will continue to resist by all means available. I will make every effort to escape and to aid others to escape. I will accept neither parole nor special favors from the enemy. (IV) If I become a prisoner of war, I will keep faith with my fellow prisoners. I will give no information or take part in any action which might be harmful to my comrades. If I am senior, I will take command. If not, I will obey the lawful orders of those appointed over me and will back them up in every way. (V) When questioned, should I become a prisoner of war, I am required to give name, rank, service number, and date of birth. I will evade answer-

Defining Criminal Conduct in a Unique Society

ing further questions to the utmost of my ability. I will make no oral or written statements disloyal to my country and its allies or harmful to their cause. (VI) I will never forget that I am an American, fighting for freedom, responsible for my actions, and dedicated to the principles which made my country free. I will trust in my God and in the United States of America." It could, of course, be used to describe a military custom and ethic in support of a violation of Articles 133 or 134, discussed at the end of this chapter. Nevertheless, misconduct as a prisoner is intentionally codified in Article 99 and elsewhere, making these the best sources for charging such violations.

4. The *Shenandoah* had taken off from the same Lakehurst location from which the ill-fated *Hindenburg* would launch 12 years later.

5. General William T. Sherman Special Field Orders, No.120, November 9, 1864. William Tecumseh Sherman, *Memoirs of General William T. Sherman*, vol 2 (New York, 1875), pp. 651–53. See also http://www.sewanee.edu/faculty/Willis/Civil_War/documents/Sherman120.html last visited October 17, 2009.

6. 417 U.S. 733 (1974).

7. William Winthrop, *Military Law and Precedents* (1896; second edition reprinted 1920) at 720.

8. Winthrop at 723.

CHAPTER 6

Basics of the Military Justice System: The Trial and Appellate Processes

If the participants in a court-martial wore civilian clothes, even an experienced criminal attorney would have trouble distinguishing it from a civilian criminal trial. The similarities are far more numerous than the differences, and most of the differences are either artifacts of earlier versions of the military trial process or unique terminology or procedure tied to national security or military operations.

Rules of Evidence

One of the great changes in the history of military justice (for historical treatment, see chapter 7) occurred in 1980, when the military adopted the Military Rules of Evidence. They are based on the Federal Rules of Evidence and are virtual carbon copies of the Federal Rules in most important respects—which makes a military trial very similar to a civilian criminal trial in most ways. Matters that most people would associate with the comprehensive set of rules governing criminal trials in the civilian world are identical in the military—matters such as privileges, self-incrimination, litigating issues of illegal searches, hearsay, impeachment of witnesses, and many others. They deviate from the Federal Rules in several specific instances in which clauses have been added to address military concerns that do not have a civilian equivalent.

Intrusions without Probable Cause: Inspections and Urinalysis

One area in which the military differs markedly from the civilian world is the unique provision in the Military Rules of Evidence that permits inspections and inventories of military units, vessels, and installations. Military Rule of Evidence 313(b) permits commanders to schedule—though they need not publicize them in advance—shakedowns of barracks, ships, and work spaces. The rule permits leaders to examine all or part of a unit, vessel, or the like as long as it is tied to "security, military fitness, or good order and discipline." Its nonexclusive list of purposes includes ensuring a unit is properly equipped, ready, clean and sanitary, and "that personnel are present, fit, and ready for duty."[1] It can also aim at contraband and unlawful weapons.

As long as the commander can tie the intrusion to military readiness, then any criminal fruits of the intrusion can also be used for criminal purposes. In all ordinary respects, these inspections look like searches—they involve military officials going through soldiers' possessions without consent—but they stand on distinctly different Constitutional footing, because the distinguishing factor justifying the intrusion is the military's need to ensure the readiness of a unit. Besides searching places and things, the rule also permits inspections of persons, most notably through compulsory urinalyses. Because the soldier also must be fit if he is considered to be mission-ready, and because being under the influence of illegal drugs is presumed to make a soldier unfit for duty, a urinalysis not based on probable cause is lawful because its primary purpose is to ensure readiness. However, as mentioned, the results can also be used for disciplinary purposes. The military's right to make criminal use of mandatory urinalyses was vigorously litigated in the 1980s, but in a series of cases, the military appellate courts upheld the right to require urine samples as long as the entire unit was tested (unit sweep) or the test was truly random (leaders must be able to point to a scheme that is truly random, such as all whose social security number end with a certain digit)—which would comply with Rule 313(b)'s requirement that the inspection's "primary purpose [was not] for use in a trial by court-martial or in another disciplinary proceeding." Such factors remain the topic of litigation from time to time—whether, for example, a commander cloaks her intent to test a particular individual by constructing randomness criteria that happen to include someone she suspects—but the military's essential right to test soldiers at any time in the interests of readiness is well established.

No Polygraphs

Very few criminal courts admit polygraphs under any circumstances, but the military provided the Supreme Court the opportunity to test the concept of a complete bar to the use of polygraph evidence when it introduced a rule to that effect in 1998. In an eight-to-one ruling, the Court found, in *United States v. Scheffer*,[2] that Military Rule of Evidence 707[3] was properly promulgated and that its prohibition on the introduction of polygraph results in courts-martial did not violate a soldier's (or anyone else's, as the case was only incidentally military) Sixth Amendment right to present a defense.[4] The Court relied heavily on a jurisdiction's right to set rules for admissibility of evidence, as long as they were not arbitrary or disproportionate to the interests they were intended to serve—in this case, to save courts the time and diversion of resources necessary to litigate the admissibility of polygraphs, given their questionable reliability. The issue continues to be litigated occasionally on trial and appeal in the military courts, as proponents of admitting polygraph evidence have asserted that language in the *Scheffer* opinion left the door open to reconsidering the absolute ban if a compelling set of facts were presented.

National Security

In some circumstances, such as espionage or other cases of disloyalty, the government obtains very reliable evidence in manners that it would prefer not to expose in open court. This often sets up a clash between a desire to hold someone accountable in open court and a need to protect national security. Anyone facing trial in a military court, just as in a civilian court, has the Sixth Amendment right to confront accusers, which means a right to examine evidence and to test it in open court through cross-examination of the sponsors of the evidence. It also includes the right to examine evidence in advance of trial, and the military further accentuates this by Article 46 of the UCMJ, which promises "equal opportunity to obtain witnesses and other evidence." On the other hand, the government believes it should not have to choose between bringing a criminal case and exposing sensitive technology or practices. In those circumstances, Military Rule of Evidence 505 provides the prosecution with the opportunity to make a presentation to a military judge, privately (in camera) and with no defense counsel present (ex parte) in which it offers a declaration from the organization that obtained the national security information (for example, a wiretap or a tip from a sensitive source) and offers a means by which the evidence will be made available to a court without exposing the manner in which it was collected. The judge has the right to reject the government's proffer or to approve the government's recommended course of action or to require some other course of action. Common ways of managing such classified information include masking certain parts of documents; substituting generic or anonymous descriptions for sources, people, or places; and authorizing the introduction of summaries of classified information. In addition, Rule 505, which is patterned closely after the Classified Information Procedures Act, a federal statute that governs the use of classified information in federal courts, also provides a process by which the defense can seek to introduce classified information, a process intended to balance legitimate interests in case preparation and presentation with the government's interest in not disclosing essential national security information—or being "graymailed" by the threat of such disclosures.

Right to Counsel

All accused soldiers have the right to no-cost, independent military defense counsel. The right to counsel normally attaches when a soldier is read his Article 31 rights or when he is charged with an offense. A right to a military defense lawyer is broader than the right to a public defender in the civilian world in several respects. The soldier has the right to counsel regardless of income—all receive the no-cost lawyer. Every military accused receives a no-cost appellate lawyer to represent her throughout the entire military appellate process—a right not provided in all instances by civilian public defenders. In addition, the military accused has the right to an attorney at a wide range of administrative proceedings—essentially, any time the military seeks to take adverse action against him. For example, soldiers facing nonjudicial punishment (except for those facing summarized nonjudicial punishment) have the right to counsel for consultation, and soldiers facing administrative separations also have the right to military counsel throughout that process. The development of the independent military trial defense services is treated in greater detail in chapter 7.

The Case on the Merits

Presentation of the Case

Trials in military courts proceed according to the same sequence as most any criminal court: arraignment of the accused; litigation of pretrial motions; selection of trial forum; entry of plea; opening statements;[5] presentation of the government's case,; presentation of defense case, if any;[6] government and defense rebuttal, if any; closing argument by the government; defense closing argument; and government rebuttal argument. Before the case goes to the panel, the military judge will give instructions on the law and procedure. It has become more common to instruct the members on the law (elements of the offenses, possible defenses, legal burdens) before closing argument, and then to instruct on procedures (voting requirements, confidentiality, factors relating to deliberations) after argument and before closing the court. Judges orally instruct the panel and may also provide their instructions in writing, a once-rare practice that has become more common, encouraged by technology that makes it easier to tailor and print them. The panel fills out a findings worksheet on which it records its verdict, and which the military judge reviews before the president of the court publishes it by announcing it in open court.

Government Appeals

Since 1984, the prosecution has had the authority to appeal significant evidentiary rulings of a trial judge that could have an impact on the government's ability to continue to prosecute a case. Article 66, as amended in 1983, and Rule for Courts-Martial 908 explain the process by which the government may appeal trial rulings that exclude evidence that is substantial proof of a material fact or that direct disclosure of classified information that the government believes is too risky. While the government may not appeal a ruling that is or amounts to a finding of not guilty, this rule provides the government with the opportunity to seek interlocutory relief when a judge excludes evidence, commonly a confession or physical evidence, on grounds that the government considers to be erroneous.

Although Congress contemplated that the mechanism would be used relatively infrequently—trial judges merit deference and finality in most instances—it approved this procedure, common in civilian courts, so that the government had a timely mechanism available in which to contest significant rulings that had significant impact on their cases. It is considered to be more just and efficient than waiting for an issue to be addressed on appeal or forcing the government to forego or curtail its prosecution, based on an erroneous ruling that, corrected later, would not give the government a realistic opportunity to litigate the case in as timely and vigorous manner. Rule for Courts-Martial 908 contains strict notice, filing, and response requirements to ensure cases continue to progress in a timely manner.

Trier of Fact

The default position for a court-martial is a trial by officer members (jurors). As noted earlier, the number of members varies according to the level of court-martial, and enlisted soldiers can insist on trial with at least one-third enlisted members. Any accused may request trial by judge alone in lieu of members, and that request will be granted in all cases except for cases involving the death penalty, which must be heard by members. Whatever forum the accused chooses for the merits of the trial also governs the sentencing phase.

Choice of forum is a major decision for an accused soldier to make; she makes the decision in consultation with her counsel, but it is one of the trial decisions (including how to plead) that she must make personally. There is considerable conventional wisdom in the ranks and among military justice practitioners about which forum is most advantageous under what circumstances. Many believe that military offenses, especially the most common offenses such as disrespect or disobedience, are best tried by enlisted panels, because they are most likely to understand, if not forgive, the conduct by the soldier on trial. At the same time, it is generally accepted that highly technical or legal defenses that might turn on a fine point of interpretation, should be tried by a military judge. For example, in a situation in which an accused is charged with disobeying a lawful order and there is no question that he disobeyed it but a question about its lawfulness, many defense counsel would take such a case to a judge. The sentencing ramifications of this decision are discussed in the next section, reinforcing the significance of the decision, because the military is one of few jurisdictions in which the trier of fact is also the sentencing authority.

The military judge, as discussed in chapters 2 and 7, is a relatively recent creation, having come into existence in 1969. Judges must be judge advocates, members in good standing of a state bar, selected by a service judge advocate general. They often have significant experience as trial and defense counsel, but there is no requirement that they have practiced in courts-martial recently, extensively, or ever. Some of the services offer tenure to judges, protecting them against transfer for three years, but it is not a statutory requirement, more a policy statement

The Trial and Appellate Processes

meant to reinforce the services' commitment to independent trial and appellate judges. All trial judges are required to attend a three-week course offered by the Army and pass an examination before they are certified to sit as judges.

The Sentencing Phase of Trial

Courts-martial, like most civilian trials, are bifurcated proceedings. After a judge or panel finds guilt on at least one charge, a second phase of trial is convened to determine an appropriate sentence. As in civilian jurisdictions, the prosecution has the opportunity to present evidence in aggravation, and the defense has the opportunity to present evidence in support of a lesser sentence. There are some distinct differences in the military system, though there remains a broad similarity in that a proceeding is convened to determine an appropriate sentence.

No Guidelines—Wide Discretion

The greatest difference is that, except for a handful of serious crimes, there are no mandatory sentencing guidelines in the military. Every convicted soldier is subject to the maximum punishment provided in the Manual for Courts-Martial, but the sentencing authority has complete discretion, except in a few cases of mandatory sentences.[7] This reinforces the concept of individualized treatment—theoretically, each soldier receives a sentence tailored to her offense, experience, and potential—but critics point to the fact that soldiers convicted of the exact same offense can receive greatly disparate sentences as evidence of too much unpredictability and capriciousness in the system.

Sentencing Authority

In the civilian world, it has become increasingly common for judges to sentence individuals after they are found guilty by juries. Soldiers do not have this option—the forum that the accused chooses for the trial on the merits also determines the sentence. As discussed in the preceding section, the accused and counsel consider various factors in deciding which is the optimal forum in a particular case. Complicating the decision is the fact that the ideal forum on the merits might not be ideal if it comes to a sentencing case. For example, many counselors believe that enlisted panels hold the greatest potential for a finding of not guilty on certain (especially military) offenses but also the greatest potential to hit an accused hardest with a significant sentence if convicted. On the other hand, all-officer panels might be more exacting on the merits for an accused (holding the government to its proof but finding guilt if the evidence supports it) but more open to a moderate sentence. Many believe that officer panels are more inclined to give weight to factors such as psychiatric testimony and stories about rough upbringings or life obstacles, whereas enlisted juries might consider these to be circumstances that an accused should have been able to overcome because many of them have overcome them. Most accused's select panels for the merits, but the great majority who plead guilty choose military judges. This is partly because the government frequently insists on a judge alone proceeding as a condition of a negotiated pretrial agreement and also because military judges' sentences generally are more predictable than sentences from officer or mixed panels, especially on the more common offenses. In any event, there is much conventional wisdom among practitioners and enough variables and distinctions in particular cases to thwart the certitude of the most experienced practitioner.

Government Case

The Manual for Courts-Martial places definite limits on the scope of evidence that the prosecution may present during the sentencing phase. The prosecution is permitted to present evidence in aggravation and on the rehabilitative potential of the accused. Unlike many civilian jurisdictions, military prosecutors do not produce and admit any sort of presentencing report, variations of which are common in civilian courts, and which often include hearsay and allegations of misconduct that have not been adjudicated, much less proven beyond a reasonable doubt. The broad concern for good order and discipline again is balanced by the system's need to seek justice and temper command authority in this area. The sentencing rules are designed, in part, to ensure that sentencing decisions do not reflect the interests of a particular command but the broader interests of the military and of society.

Aggravation

The Manual provides that the evidence in aggravation is limited to that "directly relating to or resulting from the offenses."[8] While that includes a wide range of analysis, including the impact on victims, society, and the military, the impacts must be tied to the offense. To keep the government from characterizing every infraction as carrying potential strategic impact ("for want of a nail..."), the Manual provides that the government's mission impact evidence must be "of significant adverse impact on the mission, discipline, or efficiency of the command directly and immediately resulting from the accused's offense." The extent to which the evidence directly relates is often a matter of contention at trial, and judges generally rule in favor of the accused in this area. Evidence in aggravation ordinarily will include at least calling victims of crimes against person or property and, when appropriate, those able to testify about the impact on individuals or units or military missions. Much of this depends on the creativity and aggressiveness of the prosecution, the ability of the defense to seek to limit it within the rules, and the predilections and judgments of the military judge.

Rehabilitative Potential

A soldier's rehabilitative potential is a key concern during sentencing. Because the sentencing authority may effectively fire the accused by discharging him, the

The Trial and Appellate Processes   97

question of his potential is central to the sentencing phase and distinct from the question of a punitive discharge. The government may present such evidence, but the way it is presented and the conclusions that can be drawn from it have been matters of great contention since the 1980s. Military courts wrestled with this issue in a series of cases in which they repeatedly found that evidence on rehabilitative potential was too loosely presented, and it became a code for recommending to the sentencing authority whether the accused should receive a punitive discharge—in that testimony regarding a lack of rehabilitative potential was a coded message that the soldier should receive a punitive discharge or dismissal. The Manual has been amended to codify several of the decisions of the military appellate courts that limit and make explicit the grounds and scope of such evidence of rehabilitative potential. Often shorthanded by practitioners as "*Horner-Ohrt*" issues, in reference to two key cases that form the basis for restrictions on the prosecution in this area,[9] they reflect the struggle between a process meant to sentence a particular accused for a particular offense and the complications that arise from the availability of discharge from the service as one of the available sentencing sanctions. The Manual for Courts-Martial provides that a witness's opinion about an accused's rehabilitative potential must be based on knowledge of the accused's character, duty performance, and determination to be rehabilitated. The witness must base the opinion on "relevant information and knowledge" about the accused, and the opinion may not be based principally on the severity or nature of the offense—that is, the opinion must be based more on knowledge of the accused soldier, and not an opinion that mainly characterizes the severity of the offense or speculates on the impact of the crime. This is an intended limitation that ensures that those with fleeting exposure to the accused or those who might know her mainly as an offender are not given the opportunity unduly to affect a panel's judgment about an appropriate sentence.

These limitations on the government's sentencing case are based on three factors unique to the military justice system: (1) the availability of a punitive discharge as part of a court-martial sentence, (2) concern regarding command over-reaching, and (3) the goal of individualized justice as demonstrated by the absence of sentencing guidelines. The decision on discharge is supposed to be made independent of an assessment of the accused's rehabilitative potential (i.e., it is considered to be an appropriate judgment to find that an accused possesses rehabilitative potential but must receive a punitive discharge because of the severity of the offense and other sentencing factors)—that is why the term is defined so broadly in the Manual for Courts-Martial and includes the phrase "potential to be restored, through vocational, correctional, or therapeutic training or other corrective measures to a useful and constructive place in society."[10] The Rule for Courts-Martial also sets the standard for a witness's ability to state an opinion about rehabilitative potential, requiring that the witness "possess sufficient information and knowledge about the accused to offer a rationally-based opinion that is helpful to the sentencing authority."[11] All together, the rule regarding rehabilitative potential, especially with its restrictive foundational requirements, discourages the government from putting on such evidence. Clearly, a person could have potential "to be restored . . . to a useful and constructive place in society" but still merit discharge from the military. Because discharges at courts-martial are *punitive* discharges and not administrative measures (administrative discharges are available outside the court-martial setting; see chapter 8), it is considered a separate element of punishment, not a way to administratively remove someone from the military in addition to the traditional elements of a sentence. This concept was the subject of much contention for years; it is not intuitively understood throughout the military but is another reflection of the concept that courts-martial are mainly instruments of justice and that the decision about whether to adjudge a discharge should be based on the gravity of the offense and be intended as *punishment* rather than on an evaluation of the accused's skills as a military member. In practice, prosecutors still are likely to seek and call witnesses who can assess an accused's rehabilitative potential. Most have learned, however, to seek specific conclusions and not to appear to be speaking in code, such as "no potential for further service," that courts will interpret to be a vote for a punitive discharge—when witnesses are not permitted to make recommendations regarding any particular form of punishment. It is not clear whether the court-directed distinctions that have been codified in the Manual are intelligible to or important to military juries when evaluating whether to adjudge a punitive discharge as part of a sentence. The decision of whether to adjudge a punitive discharge is seriously contested in a relatively small number of cases, and the decision of whether to adjudge a bad-conduct discharge versus a dishonorable discharge also is a matter of contention in some cases, though relatively rarely the focus of counsel on either side.

Defense Case—Extenuation and Mitigation

The defense cannot be in a position, legally or by the inference of its presentation, of continuing to litigate the case on the merits. The defense case traditionally focuses on two broad areas: extenuation and mitigation. As on the merits, the defense is not required to put on a case at all—though it is almost certainly ineffective assistance of counsel not to do so. At a minimum, the defense may contest, limit, or refute information that the government presented during its sentencing case and present material in extenuation and mitigation of the offense. Extenuation and mitigation are not uniquely military terms, though they are used most comprehensively (commonly referred to as "E&M") in military jurisdictions. Extenuation generally relates to the offense, while mitigation relates to the accused.

Extenuation is anything that helps explain the offense but does not constitute an actual defense. For example, it may be a defense to some assaults that an accused was provoked or defending himself. Should that fail as a defense—or should there have been some provocation but not to the level of constituting a legal defense—the accused and his counsel might decide to call this information and perspective to the attention of the judge or panel. It may be done through calling witnesses, presenting documents, or calling the accused. This area can

The Trial and Appellate Processes

come closest to impeaching the verdict, and it is important in the case of a guilty plea not to do so or appear to be doing so, because the military judge retains the authority to reopen the plea inquiry. If a panel has found the accused guilty, then the extenuation is most effective if it is presented in the vein of explaining the circumstances without offering it as a legal excuse.

Mitigation is information that should reduce (mitigate) the sentence because of something about the accused that is generally not related to the offense but related to her, her background, service, or upbringing. For example, the circumstances in which the accused was raised might be relevant to placing an offense in context (even on matters as sensitive as domestic violence, as well as substance abuse, violence, and the like). In addition, the accused's good reputation for all of the traits that the military especially values—honesty, selflessness, valor, loyalty, etc.—and her good acts, whether as a service member, volunteer, or in the community, are tremendously important in deciding a sentence tailored to *this* soldier for *this* offense. It is common for defense counsel to call family members, military leaders, clergy, and coaches who are or were important in the accused's life to shine a favorable light that the defense will argue shows something about the accused that should complicate the sentencing authority's analysis—and, ultimately, moderate the sentence.

The accused is not required to testify at all. If he does take the stand, he has the option of making a sworn or unsworn statement and may present the unsworn statement in several manners. The key difference between sworn and unsworn statements is the vulnerability to cross-examination. If the accused gives a sworn statement, it is the same as any other testimony—and subjects him to cross-examination. Unsworn statements are not subject to cross-examination, though the government may present evidence to rebut information contained in that statement. The protection against cross-examination is an attractive feature of the unsworn statement for many defense counsel and their clients. They balance this advantage against their analysis of whether a judge or panel would give greater weight to a sworn statement and the accused's bearing the risk of answering questions from the judge or panel. The conventional wisdom is to give an unsworn statement, but defense counsel sometimes find the government to be unprepared to effectively cross-examine an accused who testifies under oath during sentencing—or find them disinclined to do so, uncertain about how to take advantage of it consistent with the theme of the government case. The accused has a third option: presenting information through counsel. The accused's counsel may make an unsworn statement on the accused's behalf ("he wants you to know. . ."). This permits counsel to keep an accused off the witness stand if the accused is so volatile that even a well-prepared unsworn statement carries risks, and it also permits an articulate defense counsel to explain and emphasize concerns that the accused might not be able to express as well or that might appear self-serving or less credible if she did so. Finally, the government may seek to refute statements of fact contained in unsworn statements, even though it may not cross-examine the accused. For example, if the accused says that he attended rehabilitation sessions but in fact he had not, the government could present evidence or witnesses to contradict the claim. A vague statement such as "I feel I have served well" will generally not be seen to have opened the door to the extent of permitting the government to bring in evidence of subpar duty performance.

Rules Relaxed

The rules of evidence are relaxed for matters in extenuation and mitigation. This means that various evidentiary substitutes that might be inadmissible on the merits or that would require the laying of demanding foundations for their admission may be admitted for the defense during the sentencing phase with less scrutiny. This relaxation is sometimes misunderstood, as when the government seeks to invoke it on its own behalf, but the rule clearly states that a judge may relax them "with respect to matters in extenuation or mitigation."[12] This can also work to the government's advantage, as prosecutors can express a willingness to admit an evidentiary substitute to spare the cost and logistical difficulty of producing defense witnesses for the sentencing phase. Usually, it means deviating from the strict foundational requirements that counsel must meet to establish the authenticity of evidence. During sentencing, judges are expected to be less exacting when admitting "letters, affidavits, certificates of military and civil officers, and other writings of similar authenticity and reliability."[13] This rule avoids protracted and distracting debates on the authenticity of something like a transcript, a certificate of accomplishment, or a letter of support.

Sentencing Factors

Sentencing authorities are expected to take into account all of the evidence admitted in both the findings and sentencing phases of trial. They normally are instructed to evaluate that evidence in light of four factors:[14]

- *Rehabilitation of the accused.* The sentencing authority should consider not just whether the accused can be rehabilitated, but what components of a sentence could contribute to her rehabilitation. Rehabilitation is a goal of the sentence process for all accused and must be considered in all cases, including those that might result in sentences of life in prison or death. Elements of a sentence commonly considered to be punitive, such as confinement, can also contribute to rehabilitation by removing an accused from negative influences (though some criticize the environment of confinement facilities as providing opportunities for some criminals to perfect their crafts, hardening them) and providing the opportunity for "enforced contemplation."
- *Specific deterrence.* Sometimes referred to as "disabling" the accused, this orients a panel to a fundamental purpose of sentencing—ensuring or reducing the risk that the accused will reoffend. In crimes of violence, this logically takes the form of confinement, but deterrence also means administering a sentence of sufficient and appropriate severity that the accused will not reoffend, not simply because he might be locked up for a period of time, but because (since nearly all convicted soldiers go free at some point) the sentence

stings sufficiently to remove or reduce the temptation to reoffend. This area obviously calls to the fore the need to balance justice with sufficient mercy that the accused will not harden further and that fellow service members will find the sentence to be appropriate and just.
- *General deterrence.* This sentencing factor considers the impact of the sentence on service members other than the accused. Although general deterrence is a long-validated sentencing criterion, appellate courts repeatedly counsel against making "send a message" arguments the exclusive or central focus of the government's case, because it undercuts the individual impact of sentence, which is an especially significant component of military justice, further reinforced by the lack of sentencing guidelines and near absence of mandatory minimum sentences. Nevertheless, it is appropriate for panels and judges to consider the impact on others who might learn of a sentence when crafting an appropriate sentence. Some judges try to reinforce the deterrent element of sentencing by encouraging—or in the case of some commanders, requiring—attendance by rank and file at the sentencing proceeding or announcement of the sentence.
- *Social retribution.* While rehabilitation is a proper consideration, so is sheer punishment—not revenge but retribution. It is appropriate for a panel to exact a cost from the convicted soldier, and, while this is conventionally accomplished through confinement and other restrictions on liberty as well as financial penalties and loss of rank, the punitive discharge, a unique component of the military justice system, can also contribute to that retribution by adjudicating what the Judge's Benchbook characterizes as the "ineradicable stigma" of a punitive discharge. As with all factors, retribution should not receive undue weight, but, in the context of the other sentencing factors, it is a reminder to sentencing authorities that it is appropriate for them to express the ire and disapproval of the community through the sentences they impose.

Available Punishments

The sentencing authority determines the appropriate sentence in each case, limited only by the sentence provided for each offense in the Manual for Courts-Martial or the jurisdictional limit of the court. When the panel is the sentencing authority, it follows the same voting procedures as when it votes on the merits. Two-thirds of the members must agree on a sentence, except that three-quarters must agree on a sentence of 10 or more years' confinement. (Capital sentences require unanimity and are addressed separately.) Panels are instructed to vote on the lowest sentence first and to stop voting as soon as they reach the two-thirds or three-fourths requirement.

No Punishment

Except in the rare circumstances in which a certain punishment is mandatory (e.g., life in prison for premeditated murder, death for treason), a court-martial has no obligation to adjudge any sentence at all. While rare, it is not unheard of for a panel to adjudge no punishment—it is a way for a panel to send a message that it assessed a conviction because the accused was technically guilty of an offense but that the members (or military judge) believe that the case might have been inappropriately placed at that level of court-martial, or there is serious question about the leadership to which the soldier was exposed, or questions about the conduct of others involved with investigating or prosecuting the case, or simply that they deem the conviction alone to constitute sufficient punishment.

Reprimand

A reprimand may be adjudged as part of almost every sentence. It does not preclude other punishment. Typically the reprimand is published in the convening authority's action, the official document that publishes the result and sentence of the court-martial as approved by the convening authority. Although of no direct consequence in the military or civilian worlds in that it carries no concrete consequences such as loss of privileges, it provides an opportunity for the command, through the convening authority who formally issues it, to characterize the disgrace, significance, or impact of the crime. There is no appeal of a reprimand issued as part of a punishment, unlike a reprimand administratively issued, to which some due process rebuttal rights generally attach (see chapter 8). In addition, although a judge or panel recommends the sentence of reprimand, it is the convening authority who determines its wording (in practice, normally drafted by her legal staff), and she must personally sign and issue it.

Forfeitures

Forfeitures are available for virtually every offense. At a general court-martial, forfeiture of all pay and allowances (commonly shorthanded as "total forfeitures") is available for almost every offense. At a special court-martial, forfeiture of two-thirds pay per month is available for almost every offense. When total forfeitures are adjudged, it encompasses both pay and allowances, but only pay may be ordered forfeited when less than total forfeitures are enacted. Pay is a soldier's salary per month and can include additional pay for factors or qualifications such as serving in a hazardous deployed environment, serving in airborne slot, language proficiency, professional pay for physicians and other specialists, and numerous other reasons; allowances are other entitlements paid to a soldier for a variety of reasons. All receive a housing allowance (unless they live in military quarters, in which case the military retains the allowance in exchange for no-cost housing), and soldiers may receive allowances for a host of other reasons, including cost-of-living adjustments for living overseas or in high-cost areas in the United States. If a judge or jury wants to adjudge forfeitures for a period in which the accused will not be in confinement, then it may not adjudge forfeiture of more than two-thirds pay. This is in recognition that punishment should not cause additional trouble, such as extreme financial straits; consequently, a soldier not in confinement must be permitted at least one-third of his pay so that he can meet basic expenses. Because a sentencing authority is not required to adjudge any forfeitures at all, in some circumstances they will take effect for administrative purposes.

Forfeitures by Operation of Law

Because forfeitures are not necessarily required as an element of any court-martial sentence, it has not been uncommon for those serving confinement, including long-term confinement, to draw pay while confined. As a result of some publicized instances of such arrangements in the 1990s, Congress changed the law so that it now provides that individuals serving confinement who have a punitive discharge or those who are serving sentences of more than six months, regardless of whether they received a discharge, shall forfeit pay or pay and allowances (if general court-martial) while they are confined. This is an administrative consequence of confinement, codified in Article 58(b), UCMJ, meaning that it does not constitute punishment and does not interfere with the sentencing authority's or convening authority's discretion. It simply means that while in prison for more than six months—or any length of time with a punitive discharge—the individual will not be paid.

Fine

A judge or jury may adjudge a fine as part of a court-martial sentence even when there is no issue of unjust enrichment by the accused soldier. In practice, however, fines are most common in cases in which the accused has made some sort of financial gain or stolen from or defrauded the government. The Manual for Courts-Martial also contains the authority to impose a condition on the fine such that if it is not paid within a certain period of time, then additional confinement will be imposed. That additional time cannot exceed the maximum punishment authorized for that offense, and, in the case of a special court-martial, the fine combined with the forfeitures cannot exceed the two-thirds limitation of a special court-martial. Because of the administrative complexities involved with adjudging that confinement (a hearing at which the government must prove that the accused is able to pay), it is uncommon.

In civilian courts, it is not uncommon for judges to order that a convict make restitution to victims of larcenies or frauds. There is no such provision in the military; therefore, sentencing authorities may not include such orders or contingencies in their sentences. Sometimes, creative defense counsel or prosecutors will seek to include restitution as a condition of a pretrial agreement (for example, a commitment to make good all bad checks or make restitution to a defrauded victim by the date of trial) in exchange for sentencing leniency, and, as long as such provisions are clearly stated, military courts generally will enforce them.

Confinement

Convicted soldiers may be confined for a maximum of one year at special courts-martial, and for general courts-martial, the length of time authorized in the Manual for Courts-Martial. Confinement is normally in a military confinement facility, but that is not a requirement.

Hard Labor without Confinement

This uniquely military punishment may be adjudged at any level of court-martial but only for enlisted soldiers. It permits a soldier to perform her regular duties and then requires her to perform other—often fatiguing—duties after her normal duties conclude for the day. Courts may adjudge hard labor without confinement at a rate of one and a half times the rate authorized for confinement (e.g., if the maximum punishment were one year's confinement, the soldier could be adjudged 18 months' hard labor without confinement), though most often it is used for much shorter periods of time. Typically, hard labor without confinement is adjudged for soldiers whose conduct is not considered serious enough to warrant confinement but for whom the judge or panel believe significant punishment is still necessary, or the sentencing authority might think that hard labor without confinement—logically imposed in the absence of a punitive discharge—provides the service member the opportunity to "soldier back" from the stigma of a court-martial by showing dedication and reliability during the stressful period of hard labor. Adjudging hard labor without confinement does not preclude adjudging a punitive discharge, but it is unusual to combine the two, because hard labor without confinement generally is geared to a soldier whom the judge or jury thinks worthy of retention in the military after serving the sentence. The hard labor to be performed need not be constructive or meaningful in any way (in contrast to the administrative rules governing corrective training, which require that it have a constructive purpose tied to the deficiency), so it can include such demeaning or futile tasks as repeatedly digging and refilling the same hole, cleaning a latrine with a toothbrush, or cutting the grass with nail clippers. Most commanders, however, assign tasks similar to those assigned to soldiers serving extra duty as part of nonjudicial punishment, most often tasks that need to be accomplished for the unit (cleaning, organizing, and the like) but that are not often done thoroughly or regularly because of the press of business. Although the sentencing authority adjudges hard labor without confinement, it is up to the accused's commander to determine the details such as the schedule and the duties to be performed.

Punitive Discharges

Courts-martial have the option of adjudging discharges as part of the punishment of the court, hence their characterization as *punitive* discharges. Different discharges are available, depending on the level of the court and the status of the accused. Because a punitive discharge is a separate element of a court-martial sentence, it is never required—though it would be anomalous, for example, to sentence a soldier to significant confinement and not also adjudge a punitive discharge, it would be lawful to do so. Any punitive discharge removes most privileges associated with military or veteran status, including most benefits administered by the Department of Veterans Affairs, such as education and home loans as well as the privilege of being buried in a national cemetery. A dishonorable discharge removes a few rights and privileges that are not excluded by a

The Trial and Appellate Processes

bad-conduct discharge. All punitive discharges carry an "ineradicable stigma" and must be considered to be punishment in and of themselves.

Bad-Conduct Discharge

This is the lesser of the two punitive discharges that may be adjudged against enlisted personnel. It may be adjudged by general courts-martial as well as special courts-martial unless the special court-martial convening authority expressly excludes the possibility of a bad-conduct discharge when he convenes the court. Generally, the bad-conduct discharge ("BCD") is considered appropriate for a serious but isolated incident of criminal misconduct or for a series of relatively minor violations of the law.

Dishonorable Discharge

This is the more severe of the two punitive discharges that may be adjudged against enlisted personnel. Generally, the dishonorable discharge ("DD") should be judged for only the most serious offenses that warrant separation under the conditions of dishonor. It is common for those who receive significant sentences of confinement also to receive a dishonorable discharge. Generally, those with shorter sentences receive bad-conduct discharges, but in circumstances in which the judge or panel is particularly disgusted with the accused's conduct, especially breaches of trust by senior leaders, a dishonorable discharge might be adjudged with comparatively little confinement.

Dismissal

This is the only punitive discharge available for commissioned officers and for service academy cadets and midshipmen. It may be adjudged for any offense of which a commissioned officer is found guilty.

Death

As in many areas of military practice, death penalty procedures and practices have evolved along with civilian practices and in compliance with Supreme Court rulings, starting with the military's application of *Furman v. Georgia* in *United States v. Matthews*[15] in 1983. A soldier may not be sentenced to death in the military unless several events occur:

- The convening authority expressly refers the case as a capital trial.
- The government pleads and proves at least one aggravating factor beyond a reasonable doubt.
- A panel of at least 12 members unanimously finds the accused guilty of a capital offense.
- After hearing all the evidence during the sentencing phase of the case, the panel unanimously finds at least one aggravating factor beyond a reasonable doubt.
- The panel unanimously concludes that mitigating factors do not significantly outweigh the aggravating factors.

President Reagan reinstituted the military death penalty in 1984, and numerous death sentences were imposed in the following years, but protracted litigation occurred in each case. In late 2008, President Bush approved the death sentence of Ronald Gray, which would make him the first service member executed since President Kennedy permitted the execution of Private John A. Bennett in 1961, but it and several other capital cases remained in litigation at the end of 2009. It has proven difficult for the military to bring a capital case to the point of execution, several cases having repeatedly worked their way through the military appellate courts with *Gray* the only case having reached the president for action in a quarter century of post-*Furman* capital practice. Critics and observers offer a host of theories for this. The most common are that military capital cases are sufficiently infrequent—in some years, there are no capital cases tried in the military—that the military has not developed a sufficient base of expertise and routine practices, meaning that each case travels a nearly unique path; and that lessons learned are generic or insufficiently specific to guide practitioners. Implicit in this concern is recognition that military counsel lack significant experience in capital cases. This factor, however, applies to both prosecutors and defense counsel, and therefore the quality of advocacy, standing alone, is not a sufficient explanation. Regardless, military capital practice no longer suffers from many of the criticisms that had plagued it earlier, in that it requires unanimity at all stages of trial by a minimum 12-person panel. Critics still argue, however, that there is no cadre of "death-qualified" military defense counsel, putting military accused to the option of hiring expensive civilian attorneys or trusting military defense counsel who might be trying their first capital case.

Some offenses, including treason, carry the penalty of mandatory death, but the most common crime for potential application of the death penalty is murder, for which it is discretionary. The military also carries unique protections in the capital area, forbidding admission of deposition testimony in a capital case (meant to ensure defense opportunity to confront a witness in person), and forbidding an accused from pleading guilty in a capital case, though it is permitted in federal court. In addition, a military accused may not plead guilty to a capital offense and may not elect to be tried judge alone in a capital case.

Mandatory Life

Several offenses carry a mandatory minimum penalty of life in prison, the most common of them being premeditated murder.

Life without Parole

The military has a comparatively liberal corrections system, in which confined soldiers are eligible for parole after a minimum of one year or one-third of their punishment; all are eligible at 10 years. This system caused public concern during the 1990s after a notorious case in which a paroled soldier committed additional

The Trial and Appellate Processes

crimes in the civilian community. As a consequence, Congress amended the UCMJ in 1999 to provide for life without parole for some offenses that previously carried life in prison or the possibility of a death sentence. This sanction remains a matter of study and concern, because even prisoners serving such a sentence remain eligible for clemency, which means that their sentences could be reduced to a term of years by Secretarial authority, which would then make them eligible for consideration for parole.

Effective Dates for Sentences

Most sentences take effect as soon as they are adjudged, but some must wait for the convening authority's action (discussed later in this chapter). A sentence to confinement takes effect immediately unless the convening authority takes action to postpone it. Sentences to forfeitures take effect 14 days after trial, unless convening authority action occurs sooner (nearly never in practice). Sentences to fines and reductions in grade do not take effect until convening authority action. Punitive discharges do not take effect until the case completes the first level of appellate review by the service courts of criminal appeals.

Pleas and Pleading Guilty

Entering a Plea

An accused may plead guilty or not guilty to any offense or combination of offenses. It is common for military judges to permit the accused to refrain from entering a plea upon arraignment, but it must be entered before trial. The decision whether to plead guilty or not guilty—or some combination—is a decision exclusively within the province of the accused, though obviously made in consultation with her attorney.

Pleading Guilty

An accused soldier may plead guilty at court-martial but must participate in a detailed inquiry conducted by the military judge before the judge will accept the plea of guilty. This is another area in which the military justice system seeks to protect soldiers from the pressures, perceived or otherwise, of operating in the military system. A soldier who pleads guilty must respond in open court to a series of questions from the military judge designed to ascertain that he is pleading guilty because he is truly guilty and not for any improper reason. He is permitted to plead guilty out of self-interest—for example, to attempt to limit his punishment—but must affirm his guilt on each element of each offense to which he pleads guilty and must tell the judge in his own words why he is guilty. Counsel may not speak for the accused during this colloquy, though the accused is free to consult with counsel throughout the process.

Pretrial Agreements

An accused may enter into a pretrial agreement—plea bargain—in which she agrees to plead guilty to certain offenses in exchange for promises from the government, most commonly a limitation on her sentence. Counsel may bargain to drop or reduce any of the charges, and on all potential punishments. It is common for the government to alter charges and to agree to sentence caps, especially limitations on confinement and reductions in rank. The parties also may bargain to refer a case to a lower level of court and most other terms, as long as the military judge finds that the terms are clearly understood and enforceable. The special attraction of plea bargaining in the military is that the accused receives the better of the bargain she has struck or the sentence adjudged by the judge or jury—who do not become aware of the terms of the bargain when they deliberate and adjudge a sentence. More than 50 percent of courts-martial result in guilty pleas, and most guilty pleas involve pretrial agreements.

Care *Inquiry*

There are many manifestations of the military's near-paternalism in the military justice system—mechanisms, rules, and protections designed to minimize the pressure, real or apparent, on soldiers accused or suspected of criminal offenses. The extensive inquiry that military judges conduct with accused soldiers attempting to plead guilty is one example. Commonly referred to as the *Care* inquiry, because it is based on the case of United States v. *Care*,[16] in which the Court of Military Appeals incorporated a major Supreme Court decision, its formal term is the *providence inquiry,* because its purpose is for the judge to determine the providence (essentially the wisdom or prudence) of the plea.

In many civilian courts, an accused can plead guilty to a crime with few (and, in some instances, no) words out of his mouth, merely some affirmation that his lawyer speaks accurately for him in admitting the crime and that he understands the offense and the rights he gives up by pleading guilty. In the military, it is considered critical that the inquiry be more extensive. Although it is conducted in the presence of and with the assistance of counsel, each accused ultimately must admit to the elements of every offense to which she intends to plead guilty. Before making those admissions, however, the judge will advise her that she must freely waive three key rights before the guilty plea can be accepted:

- The right to trial by court-martial on the facts and to force the government to prove the case beyond a reasonable doubt. the offense beyond a reasonable doubt.
- The right to confront witnesses against her in open court.
- The right against self-incrimination.

The military judge will advise the accused of each of these rights, the accused's absolute right to insist on all three of them, and the consequences of his relinquishing them. The accused will have to state on the record that he waives each of them, and the judge must be satisfied that the waiver is knowing, intelligent, and voluntary. After talking theoretically about waiving those rights, the judge will then talk about each of the offenses to which the accused intends to plead guilty. For example, the elements of simple assault are that: (1) the accused attempted or offered to do bodily harm to a certain person, and (2) the attempt or offer was done with unlawful force of violence.

After explaining and discussing the elements, the judge also will explore any of the possible defenses available under the circumstances. For example, in an assault case, self-defense might be an issue. If the judge hears anything in the accused's replies to the questions on the elements (or in the written stipulation of fact that often accompanies a pretrial agreement and guilty plea) that might suggest self defense, she likely will read or adapt the jury instruction on self-defense and explore it with the accused. In most circumstances, the defense counsel will have anticipated the issue and prepared the accused for this colloquy, and the issue will be settled. The parties often refer to "protecting the record," and exhaustive raising and disposing of potential defenses during the *Care* inquiry is one illustration of protecting the record. Obviously in more sensitive or complex cases, the potential defenses (such as, consent in a sexual assault case or provocation in a murder or manslaughter) will require significant attention.

It is common but not required that a stipulation of fact accompany a pretrial agreement. The main purpose of the stipulation of fact is to commit both parties to a version of the facts, providing supporting evidence for the *Care* inquiry and often a guide for the judge's questioning of the accused in open court; it is entered into evidence as a prosecution exhibit. The stipulation of fact normally is signed by the prosecutor, the defense counsel, and the accused, and often—but it is not a requirement, and practices vary—it accompanies the pretrial agreement for consideration by the convening authority when deciding whether to approve a proposed pretrial agreement. The judge will refer to the stipulation of fact and ensure that all parties affirm its contents before he enters it into evidence; if an accused seeks to deviate from it in court, it may provide grounds for canceling the pretrial agreement.

The stipulation also provides a guideline for the accused when the judge asks the accused to "tell me in your own words" about the offense—again, a requirement not typical in civilian courts and a significant challenge to the defense team, especially for embarrassing offenses and especially when the accused's family members or crime victims are present. It is an indispensable part of the inquiry, however, given the high burden of ensuring that the plea is voluntary and that it is based in fact. As with the more structured portions of the inquiry, it is not uncommon for issues to arise, especially potential defenses. Again, judges will instruct the accused on those possible defenses and may also re-advise her of her right to plead not guilty if she believes that her description of what she did does not comport with the judge's description of the crime. It is common for judges to recess the inquiry so that the accused and his counsel can confer; this is not considered to be inappropriate "coaching" as much as it is ensuring that the accused makes the critical decision to plead guilty fully aware of the consequences and is able to communicate confidentially with his counsel throughout the process.

By the end of the inquiry, the judge must be satisfied that the plea is voluntary and that it is supported by admissible evidence. It can be a relatively time-consuming process, but it is long validated by years of practice and custom. Counsel often will comment, accurately, that it is faster to prove some offenses than it is to go through the providence inquiry for the same offense—for example, pleading guilty to absence without leave requires entering two self-authenticating official documents showing that the accused was absent and then returned; in the absence of objection by the defense, that can take virtually no time, and if the defense presents no case, conviction is swift.

Inquiry into the Terms of the Pretrial Agreement

When the judge has concluded the portion of the inquiry during which she explains the accused's rights, the elements, and defenses, she will then ask—formally, because she likely has been told informally—whether there is a pretrial agreement. She will then examine the agreement that sets out the accused's plea and talk to him about the terms, the affirmation of the offenses to which he is pleading guilty of any adjustments to the charged offenses. As part of this portion of the inquiry, the government may be asked to acknowledge certain conditions to which it agreed, including dismissal of certain charges. If the sentence portion of the trial is to be conducted by a panel—an infrequent occurrence because most prosecutors will insist on a judge-alone trial as a condition of a pretrial agreement—the panel will be instructed that the accused has been found guilty, and the defense has the option of having the judge advise whether the accused has pled guilty.

- *Statements made during the providence inquiry.* Because the accused has waived her right against self-incrimination as part of the plea of guilty, she incriminates herself during the inquiry. If the *Care* inquiry reveals the plea to be improvident—that is, if the judge "busts the plea" and enters a plea of not guilty—the government is barred from using the statements in a future trial.[17] In the process of giving details about the offenses—the "in your own words" portion—the accused may provide details that make the offenses seem more aggravated. The government has the right to present those portions of the plea inquiry, either through a witness or a portion of the transcript; a careful and alert defense counsel prepares an accused to minimize this possibility and intercedes to the extent possible when he sees this problem developing.
- *Pronouncing guilt.* The *Care* court advised in 1969, "The record must also demonstrate the military trial judge . . . personally addressed the accused, advised him that his plea waives his right against self-incrimination, his right to a trial of the facts by a court-martial, and his right to be confronted by the witnesses against him; and that he waives such rights by his plea."[18] Once the military judge is satisfied, she will then pronounce the accused guilty, at which point the findings stage of the trial is ended and the sentencing portion proceeds.
- *Withdrawal.* Once the accused is found guilty, he may not withdraw from the guilty plea. There is a strong policy against withdrawing without a good reason, because the

principle of finality, which appears in many settings in the law, is important for criminal convictions so that all parties, including society, accept and depend on the results of the criminal process; therefore, mere regrets, or a recognition that a person is now a felon is not a good enough reason to withdraw from a guilty plea for which the basis was adequately explored in open court in the presence of counsel.
- *No Alford pleas.* There are only two options under the UCMJ: plead guilty or plead not guilty. Other forms of pleas that are common in the civilian world, in which an accused admits responsibility in some manner but does not expressly plead guilty to an offense, are not available in the military. Many jurisdictions permit *Alford* pleas, which are based on a 1970 Supreme Court decision.[19] In an *Alford* plea, an accused does not admit a particular act and is permitted to maintain that she is not guilty, but she does admit that there is sufficient evidence with which the prosecution could convince a finder of fact to find her guilty. Many jurisdictions also permit a no-contest or nolo contendere plea. Such a plea does not involve even the tacit acknowledgement of responsibility that accompanies or is inferred from an *Alford* plea, and in many places does not qualify in the eyes of the law as a conviction.[20] The military does not recognize or permit such pleas for several reasons, chiefly that they could be seen as the products of duress and do not serve the clarity of responsibility that a verdict of guilty or not guilty provides. (In military commissions, however, addressed in chapter 9, such pleas are permitted.)
- *Policy—why bother?* The reasons for permitting pretrial agreements are similar to those in civilian jurisdictions: judicial economy coupled with an inducement to plead guilty both to limit one's sentence and to encourage others to plead guilty. One of the purposes of adopting the Military Rules of Evidence in 1984 was to encourage maximum disclosure of information to the defense (a similar purpose of the Federal Rules to which they are identical in most respects; see later in this chapter for a more detailed treatment). When faced with a comprehensive and fair sense of the case against them, it is generally thought, a negotiated plea of guilty is more likely. This is borne out in part by the high percentage of guilty pleas in military practice, about 70 percent at the general court-martial level; though it may seem high to many observers, it is lower than the greater than 90 percent level of guilty pleas in federal felony courts.
- *"Naked pleas."* A service member may plead guilty at any time to any noncapital offense. He owes no notice to the government and need not bargain with the government for any sort of sentence limitation. If she pleads guilty, she will undergo the providence inquiry discussed earlier in this chapter, and the military judge will accept the plea if he decides that it is provident. At this point, the sentencing phase of the trial would begin. The government has an interest in the sentencing authority's knowing as much as it can about the circumstances of the offense. Because there is no negotiated plea in this situation, there would be no stipulation of fact in which both parties set out the agreed version of the background and circumstances of the offense. Consequently, the government may present in its sentencing portion of the case any evidence that would have been relevant on the merits. This can result in a mini-trial in some circumstances, but it is the most efficient way for the government to ensure that the judge or sentencing panel knows enough of the facts on which to base its judgments. Because there are no presentencing reports in the military, in contrast to federal courts and many civilian courts, the prosecution is responsible for presenting the facts to the sentencing authority in open court. It also means that, unlike with presentencing reports that can carry significant amounts of hearsay and do not carry any evidentiary threshold (the information in them need not be proven beyond a reasonable doubt), the defense may contest any of this evidence as it is presented in court.

The rest of the sentencing proceeding in a nonnegotiated plea continues as in any other sentencing hearing, with the government presenting sentencing in aggravation and relating to the accused's rehabilitative potential and the defense presenting any information it chooses in extenuation and mitigation. In practice, the factual information about the case often is mixed with aggravation evidence, in that a victim need not be called twice during the sentencing phase but might present evidence ordinarily admitted in the merits stage of the case that helps establish the factual basis for the offense while also providing impact evidence.

The dynamic of a nonnegotiated plea often works in favor of the defense, in that it can catch the government in a situation in which it is not fully prepared for trial, especially because the sentencing phase in military trials normally follows immediately upon the verdict on the merits. It is most common in judge-alone cases, and defense counsel count on it to temper a judge's likely sentence, because they seek credit for pleading guilty without the protection of a pretrial agreement, meaning that a judge realizes that whatever sentence she imposes is the sentence an accused actually will serve. Sometimes, in cases involving pretrial agreements, judges feel free to impose a relatively high sentence as a way to emphasize the accused's criminality, confident that only any seemingly harsh sentence would be tempered by the terms of a negotiated pretrial agreement.

Post-Trial Procedures

As similar as a military trial is to a civilian trial, especially the merits phase of a case, the post-trial process diverges greatly—generally to the benefit of the accused, because the system provides unique authority for court-martial convening authorities to alter the conviction and sentence in ways that would make civilians envious. All convictions, even at the summary court-martial, receive some level of review, and the level of review increases as the level of sentence increases. This is an area in which protections for soldiers on trial and the concept of command control converge. The convening authority has tremendous and unreviewable discretion to take action that benefits the accused after trial.

Production and Authentication of the Record of Trial

The government must produce a verbatim transcript of any court-martial that adjudges a sentence of one year's confinement or a punitive discharge. After it is produced, the military judge must authenticate the record and certify its accuracy, after providing the trial counsel the opportunity to review it. Often the judge also gives the defense the opportunity to review the record, but this is not required. Summarized records of trial must be produced for lesser sentences. Authentication of the record often takes a considerable period of time, which can be a source of contention, because the post-trial process cannot proceed until authentication occurs, and some defense counsel will argue, especially for their clients who received relatively short sentences to confinement or forfeitures, that

The Trial and Appellate Processes 113

they are unable to obtain substantial sentence relief because they will have served some or all of their punishments before clemency becomes available.

Opportunities Clemency and Other Relief

The defense has several opportunities to seek relief for the accused soldier, starting immediately after trial, even before production of an authenticated record of trial. A convening authority also may grant relief on his own even without or contrary to a request from the defense or the accused.

- *Deferral of confinement, forfeitures, or reductions in grade.* An accused may immediately petition the convening authority to defer a sentence to confinement. Because this is a post-trial matter that is a result of a judicial process that applied the standard of proof beyond a reasonable doubt in finding him guilty, the burden of proof shifts to the accused to demonstrate that his and the community's interests in deferring an element of the sentence outweigh the community's interest in imposing the punishment.[21] The convening authority should consider factors such as the likelihood that the accused might flee or intimidate witnesses, the nature of the offense, the impact on the victim, and the military's need for the soldier. The convening authority need not state the reason for her decision but must put it in writing. The broad discretion that the convening authority enjoys to defer the sentence is rooted, as are so many aspects of justice and discipline, in the system's function as a tool of the command. Deferral of any portion of an accused's sentence should be viewed less as a matter of clemency—pure mercy—and more as a recognition that a commander is entrusted with the authority to determine that the military's need for a particular soldier outweighs the need to immediately send the soldier to jail, reduce him in rank, or take his pay.
- *Waiving forfeitures to care for dependents.* In recognition of the fact that forfeitures can have an impact beyond the soldier who is punished, especially on her family and those who depend on her, the law permits a convening authority to waive certain forfeitures so that a convicted service member still has the means to care for dependents.[22] The only forfeitures that may be waived, however, are those that occur "by operation of law," not those expressly adjudged by a court. Forfeitures imposed by operation of law are those that are mandated because of confinement, as opposed to those adjudged by a court-martial. The convening authority may waive these forfeitures for up to six months and direct that they be paid to individuals who qualify as the soldier's dependents under federal law. These liberalized rules have come into effect since the 1990s, a recognition of the fact that the career military of recent generations has a far higher percentage of married soldiers as well as dual military couples and that forfeitures in some instances bring great hardship to innocent family members.
- *Judge advocate post-trial review.* After the record of trial is authenticated, the staff judge advocate (SJA) is required to evaluate the case before presenting it to the convening authority, who must decide whether to approve the findings and sentence and whether to modify either in favor of the accused. Rule for Courts-Martial 1107 requires the SJA to inform the convening authority of the findings and sentence (a formality in most cases, as he ordinarily but unofficially will have learned of it close in time to the verdict), any clemency recommendations from the sentencing authority, a summary of the accused's service record, information on pretrial restraint, and any terms of a pretrial agreement (which the convening authority or her predecessor would have approved). The SJA must then make a recommendation to the convening authority regarding the

sentence. The post-trial review was an extensive document, the requirements for which were trimmed considerably in 1984 changes to the Manual for Courts-Martial, enabling counsel and decision makers to concentrate on issues that are of consequence after the trial (for discussion of the historical background, see chapter 7), rather than drafting extensive summaries of testimony that (a) are contained in the record of trial, (b) were rarely read, and (c) the drafting of which drained resources. The SJA is not required to address possible legal errors in his review, but is expected to do so when they affect his recommendation. He is not obliged to address the defense requests for clemency (discussed below), but he may do so in his advice to the convening authority, recommending how much weight, if any, to give to the matters and pointing out factors such as whether the information was provided in court before the sentence was adjudged. If, however, the SJA includes "new matter," typically negative information regarding the accused that was not presented in court, he must serve that information on the accused and her counsel and provide them an additional 10 days to respond before the convening authority takes action.[23]

- *Defense submission of matters in support of clemency.* After the defense counsel and the accused receive the authenticated record of trial and the SJA has completed his review of the case, the defense has about a month in which to prepare a request to the convening authority that he exercise clemency in the case. Even if the convening authority already has limited the sentence by signing a pretrial agreement—and even if the result of trial is more favorable than the terms of the pretrial agreement, the accused has the right to seek clemency. It is most common for the defense to raise key matters it may have emphasized at trial as well as any additional information generated since the trial, such as the accused's post-trial cooperation with the government or the disposition of cases of other persons connected with an offense. They may also seek clemency recommendations from the judge or panel members who heard the case.
- *Convening authority's action.* After she receives the recommendation of her staff judge advocate and considers all of the materials submitted by the accused, the convening authority must take action on the findings and sentence. She may approve the findings and sentence as adjudged or alter any parts of the findings or sentence as long as she does not make them harsher.[24] She may disapprove any findings or reduce any of the findings to less serious offenses. It is not uncommon, for example, for a convening authority to conclude, often on the advice of her legal advisor, that a certain offense was not proved beyond a reasonable doubt and might be in jeopardy on appeal. She might, under these circumstances, reduce the offense to a lesser offense or disapprove the findings. Should she disapprove or reduce any findings, she might also choose to reduce the sentence, though she would not be required to do so. She may also reduce any element of the sentence regardless of whether she has altered any of the findings. She need not state any reason for altering any aspect of the findings or sentence, and her decision is unreviewable. A convening authority literally could set free an individual who was sentenced to death. This plenary authority has two main functions:
  - *Protect the soldier.* While a conviction or sentence might be legally defensible, there are also circumstances in which the findings and sentence, while lawful, might not be just, either because a co-accused received a greatly different sentence from a different sentencing authority, or facts about the offense or the soldier came to light since the trial in a way that makes the findings unjust or the sentence disproportionate. By empowering the convening authority to alter the findings or sentence at this stage, it brings justice to the accused sooner and with more certainty than going through the appellate process.

- *Military effectiveness.* A convening authority is considered to be the official best qualified to determine the needs of the military, one of the main reasons that commanders retain such significant quasi-judicial roles as convening authorities in the military justice system. Consequently, he can decide, notwithstanding the findings and sentence of the court, that the military needs this soldier to serve now—which would permit him to suspend or disapprove any parts of the sentence. It also can work the other way by sending a soldier back to duty when the soldier may have committed an offense in the hope or expectation of being confined or removed from duties. Returning a soldier to duty in those circumstances—especially to hazardous or unpleasant duty—can have a greater deterrent impact than the sentence of the court. Regardless, it is the convening authority whom the system entrusts with making that judgment, and he may make such a judgment irrespective of and even contrary to the requests or preferences of an accused or his defense counsel.

The Appellate Process

The system's concerns—Congress's concerns—about ensuring scrupulous justice extend into the appellate process. The structure of the military appellate courts generally parallel most civilian jurisdictions, with an initial appeal "as of right" tied to a certain amount of punishment, then a discretionary appeal by the highest court in the jurisdiction, after which there is the opportunity to seek review by the U.S. Supreme Court. Military appellate courts have broader authority than their civilian counterparts, an expansive grant of jurisdiction designed to ensure, at the final stage of the process, independence from command control. Cases that did not meet the sentence threshold for review by the courts still receive review by legal officials before they are final.

Launching an Appeal

After the convening authority takes action on a case, it is launched into the review and appellate process. The path ahead and procedures available to a convicted soldier (who still is called the "accused" in military parlance throughout the process) are determined by the sentence received.

Military Review

Article 66 of the UCMJ designates a court of criminal appeals (called courts of military review until a name change in 1994) for each of the military services. One of the major changes of the 1968 Military Justice Act was the conversion of the Boards of Review into traditional appellate courts. After the convening authority takes action on a case that meets the threshold of Article 66, the record automatically is sent to the appropriate service court of criminal appeal. The court automatically hears all capital sentences and any case in which a soldier receives a punitive discharge or a sentence of confinement of one year or more. Just as at trial, the soldier is represented by a military lawyer free of charge on appeal (this is an attorney who exclusively handles appeals and is normally not the soldier's trial defense attorney), and each service also has a staff of appellate attorneys who represent the government (as with prosecutor and defense counsel positions, these are due course assignments of military officers). While review is automatic for qualifying cases, an accused has the right, except in capital cases, to waive or withdraw an appeal. Although it may seem counterintuitive to do so—given that courts never can increase the findings or sentence—some accuseds choose to do so either because they are satisfied with or resigned to the verdict or because obtaining a final conviction and discharge certificate enables them to transition more quickly to civilian life.

The most distinctive feature of the service courts of criminal appeal is that Article 66 gives them authority to evaluate the legal sufficiency of a case, not only legal error. Most civilian criminal appellate courts do not have the authority to look behind the record and evaluate whether the lower court properly evaluated the evidence, but Article 66 permits them only to affirm findings and sentences that the court "finds correct in law and fact."[25] It permits them to evaluate "the credibility of witnesses and determine controverted questions of fact." This unusual authority stems from the military's concern that soldiers be protected against command control at all stages of the judicial process. Military appellate courts, then, have freer reign than their civilian counterparts, who are normally limited to evaluating whether legal error has occurred; civilian courts, unlike military courts, generally have to affirm a case in which there is no legal error even when they believe that a jury's findings were not sufficiently supported by the evidence. The military courts' broader authority is further supplemented by their ability to remand cases to the trial courts for additional findings.

The service courts of criminal appeals commonly are composed of senior judge advocates, but Article 66 permits them to be composed of officers or civilian attorneys. The independence of the military members is protected by Article 66's requirement that members of the court not be in each other's rating chains; the services are free to institute tenure protections by regulation, but not all have done so.

The service courts issue published and unpublished opinions, with only the former having precedential value, and then only in the service of the issuing court (appellate counsel frequently will cite the opinions of other service courts, but they are not bound by them). This is similar to civilian jurisdictions in that an opinion by the Delaware Supreme Court, of course, has no precedential value in New Jersey but might be cited as support for a proposition of law. The potential for divergent interpretations by different service courts of criminal appeal is one of the reasons for the existence of a higher military appellate court whose rules bind all the services.

The issue of the service courts' jurisdiction to hear matters other than completed cases reached the Supreme Court in 2009. In *United States v. Denedo*,[26] the Court held that military courts of criminal appeal do have the authority to entertain writs of *coram nobis*, which are petitions seeking to overturn trial rulings that are claimed to be fundamentally in error. The Court held that these writs are part and parcel of Article 66's broad authority for these courts to review issues of law and fact at court-martial. The Court also made clear that the authority to

The Trial and Appellate Processes

entertain writs of *coram nobis* did not mean that the military courts had authority to issue other writs; those writs are controlled by congressional discretion under the All Writs Act, whereas *coram nobis* is inherent in the review authority rooted in Article 66.

Civilian Review

One of the major changes brought about by the enactment of the UCMJ was the establishment of a top military appellate court composed exclusively of civilians. The Court of Appeals for the Armed Forces, known as the Court of Military Appeals from 1951 to 1994, is the final court for most military convictions. Except for capital cases, which it must hear, it has a discretionary docket. It generally receives hundreds of petitions a year and produces about 80 to 100 written opinions per year. Its five civilian members sit for 15-year terms, and the chief judge position rotates every five years. There must always be no more than three members from either major political party,[27] meaning that presidents have routinely had to nominate judges from the other political party.

Like the service courts of criminal appeals, it has unusual features and authority. Cases can reach it in the routine manner of appeals from the service courts, and it may choose which of the appeals to accept. It also must review cases certified to it by the judge advocate general of any of the armed services. This unique authority of the judge advocate general in this area is meant to encourage and ensure that the courts tackle difficult issues that it might not do in light of its largely discretionary docket. Certification performs a function similar to that of the Supreme Court when it chooses to reconcile different interpretations of the law by circuit courts of appeal.

Supreme Court Review

After a decision by the Court of Appeals for the Armed Forces, an accused may petition the U.S. Supreme Court for review of a case via a writ of certiorari, the mechanism by which most cases reach the Supreme Court. Although several military cases have reached the Court over the years, most of them did so through writs of habeas corpus; it is only since 1984 that military members have been able to employ the conventional course of seeking certiorari. The Court has taken cases infrequently in the 25 years since then, accepting nine during that period, and therefore seems to have done so for specific purposes.[28] As discussed in chapter 7, the Supreme Court effectively overturned *O'Callahan* and *Relford* when it ruled in 1986 that military jurisdiction was not dependent on the location of the offense or any other constellation of factors; military jurisdiction applied worldwide for any person subject to the UCMJ. In 1994, the Court affirmed the issue of the independence of the military judiciary in *Weiss v. United States*.[29] In that case, the Court took the occasion to provide an update on the quality of military justice, pointedly contrasting the state of military justice, especially its vulnerability to unlawful command influence, with the picture painted by Justice Douglas in *O'Callahan* (see discussion in chapter 7). The Court rejected the arguments that military judges "needed another appointment pursuant to the Appointments Clause before assuming their judicial duties." That clause, in Article II of the Constitution (the portion defining the authority of the executive), requires the president to appoint all officers of the United States—and the Court unanimously found that a military judge's appointment as a military officer was sufficient to cover his judicial duties. The Court rejected the argument "that the position of military judge is so different from other positions to which an officer may be assigned that either Congress has, by implication, required a second appointment, or the Appointments Clause, by constitutional command, requires one."[30] Justice Ginsburg, among the more liberal members of the Court, used her short concurrence to reassert the point "that men and women in the Armed Forces do not leave constitutional safeguards and judicial protection behind when they enter military service." She highlighted the progress that many critics had seen in the military justice system, one that she characterized as "notably more sensitive to due process concerns than the one prevailing through most of our country's history, when military justice was done without any requirement that legally trained officers preside or even participate as judges."

Most of the times that the Court has taken a military case, it has been to make a distinct point about an important feature of the military justice system. On one occasion, however, the Court used a military case to address an issue, the admissibility of polygraphs in criminal proceedings, that transcends military practice. In *United States v. Scheffer*,[31] the Court found by a substantial majority that it was appropriate for a criminal jurisdiction, in this case the military, to bar admissibility of polygraphs under most circumstances. The military had promulgated a rule barring the admissibility of polygraphs, and the Court ruled that this was an appropriate exercise of authority, consistent with the Sixth Amendment.

Legal Review of Lesser Sentences: Article 69, UCMJ

If an accused is convicted by courts-martial but does not receive a sentence of sufficient severity to entitle her to review by the military appellate courts, there is still a requirement that the case be reviewed for legal sufficiency. Article 69 requires the judge advocate general of each service to set up a process by which convictions that do not meet the punishment minimums of Article 66 can be reviewed.

The judge advocate general is required to review all general court-martial convictions that do not result in a sentence that meets the Article 66 minimums (a punitive discharge or one year's confinement), unless the accused waives or withdraws that appeal. The scope of review under Article 69 is not as broad as the review by the appellate courts, partly because the stakes are lower—the accused will not have received a discharge and will have received relatively little jail time—and therefore the due process is accordingly lower. The review, then, permits the judge advocate general (in practice, relying on the advice he receives from a judge advocate or civilian attorney who reviews the case for him) to modify the findings or sentence only in a case in which the "findings or sentence is found to be

The Trial and Appellate Processes

unsupported in law." It expands the authority to examine the sentence, however, to permit reassessment of it if "the sentence is [not] appropriate."

Cases other than general courts-martial do not receive automatic review under Article 69. Soldiers who were tried by any level of court-martial and who received sentences that do not trigger the Article 66 threshold, however, may submit matters for review by Article 69 any time up to two years after their sentence was imposed. They may seek review for any of these reasons: "newly discovered evidence, fraud on the court, lack of jurisdiction over the accused or the defense, error prejudicial to the substantial rights of the accused, or the appropriateness of the sentence." This broad range of legal and equitable grounds leaves a wide band of discretion for judge advocate generals to alter the results of courts-martial. In practice, the military services have legal staffs that review all Article 69 appeals, which then work their way through the military bureaucracy. While relief is granted in a relatively small number of cases, as is the case in military and civilian appellate courts, the services do grant relief from time to time on findings or sentence, especially when they detect any scent of unlawful command influence or the sentence seems well disproportionate to the offense.

Military Corrections

Because military justice is fundamentally a function of good order and discipline, its functions logically extend into the corrections process. The military has had a corrections system for more than 100 years (see the discussion of the beginning of military corrections in chapter 2) and a system of military corrections facilities for several generations. The military corrections system continues to operate independently of the U.S. Bureau of Prisons. The Army, as the executive agent for the Department of Defense, has overall responsibility for the system, though the system includes subordinate facilities operated by the Navy, Marine Corps, and Army, in addition to the Army-run United States Disciplinary Barracks.

The rules governing which prisoners are housed at which confinement facilities are matters of regulation and policy, which change occasionally as the total population of confined soldiers and their characteristics—the major offense for which they are confined, age, and prior military rank—fluctuate. For many years, all officers were confined at the United States Disciplinary Barracks at Fort Leavenworth, Kansas, along with enlisted soldiers who met a certain punishment minimum, which has varied from one to five years of confinement, reflecting that the decision was more a matter of space management than a measure of the seriousness of the offense.

In recent years, the corrections system has experimented with different tiers of confinement, as well as with the practice of seeking to concentrate certain types of offenders—such as sex offenders or those needing alcohol of drug abuse counseling, treatment, and rehabilitation—at specific facilities so that treatment resources and opportunities could efficiently be concentrated at certain locations. One fact that has not changed for many years, however, is that nearly no inmates at military confinement facilities are restored to duty. At different times in the past, the system provided organizations such as a retraining brigade that provided the opportunity for some prisoners who had received punitive discharges to work their way back to the military. The retraining unit, as well as the United States Army Correction Activity and one of its predecessors, the Retraining Brigade, have been closed since the 1980s, so there is no realistic possibility that service members who receive punitive discharges have any reasonable likelihood of returning to military duty. Though the military confinement system has a rehabilitation mission set by statute and regulation, the military generally interprets it as a mission to prepare inmates for their return to civilian life as opposed to providing an opportunity to return to military duty.[32]

Notes

1. Military Rule of Evidence 313(b) defines an inspection as an "examination . . . conducted as an incident of command, the primary purpose of which is to determine and to ensure the security, military fitness, or good order and discipline of the unit, organization, installation, vessel, aircraft, or vehicle."

2. 523 U.S. 303 (1998).

3. Military Rule of Evidence 707(a) provides, "Notwithstanding any other provision of law, the results of a polygraph examination, the opinion of a polygraph examiner, or any reference to an offer to take, failure to take, or taking of a polygraph examination, shall not be admitted into evidence."

4. The Sixth Amendment of the United States Constitution provides, in part, "In all criminal prosecution, the accused shall enjoy the right to . . . be informed of the nature and cause of the accusation; to be confronted with the witnesses against him . . . and to have the Assistance of Counsel for his defence."

5. Defense has the option of making its opening statement after the government's or after the government rests and before the defense presents its case, if any.

6. The defense never is required to present any evidence of any kind in a criminal case. It may simply contest the government's evidence through cross-examination and argument or do absolutely nothing and argue that the government has failed to meet its burden of proof, which can never shift to the defense.

7. Premeditated murder carries a mandatory minimum sentence of life in prison, and treason carries the mandatory sentence of death.

8. Rule for Court-Martial 1001 provides, in part, "The trial counsel may present evidence as to any aggravating circumstances directly relating to or resulting from the offenses of which the accused has been found guilty. Evidence in aggravation includes, but is not limited to, evidence of financial, social, psychological, and medical impact on or cost to any person or entity who was the victim of an offense committed by the accused and evidence of significant adverse impact on the mission, discipline, or efficiency of the command directly and immediately resulting from the accused's offense."

9. See generally *United States v. Horner*, 22 M.J. 294 (1986) and *United States v. Ohrt*, 28 M.J. 301 (C.M.A. 1989).

10. R.C.M. 1001(b)(5).

11. The rule continues: "Relevant information and knowledge include, but are not limited to, information and knowledge about the accused's character, performance of duty,

The Trial and Appellate Processes

moral fiber, determination to be rehabilitated, and nature and severity of the offense or offenses." R.C.M. 1001(b)(5)(B). This language also comes from post–*Horner-Ohrt* case law.

12. R.C.M.1001(c)(3).

13. R.C.M. 1001(b)(3).

14. R.C.M. 1001(g) considers these to be the "generally accepted sentencing philosophies."

15. 16 M.J. 354 (C.M.A. 1983).

16. 18 C.M.A. 535, 40 C.M.R. 247 (C.M.A. 1969).

17. The statement could be used to impeach an accused if, in a later proceeding, she testifies contrary to what she said under oath in the providence inquiry.

18. *Care,* 18 C.M.A. at 541, 40 C.M.R. at 253 (citing *Boykin,* 395 U.S. at 239).

19. *North Carolina v. Alford,* 400 U.S. 25 (1970).

20. For purposes such as civil disabilities, prior convictions, and habitual offender statutes.

21. R.C.M. 1101(c)(3).

22. It is less a matter of her providing for her dependents, because she is in confinement and not performing military duties, than it is the system's desire to ameliorate the sometimes harsh impact on family members, especially when they are wholly unconnected to—or victims of—the accused's crimes.

23. R.C.M. 1107(b)(3)(A)(iii).

24. R.C.M. 1107(d)(1).

25. Article 66(c) permits these courts to "weigh the evidence, judge the credibility of witnesses, and determine controverted questions of fact." Article 66 also tells the reviewing courts to recognize "that the trial court saw and heard the witnesses," but it is still unusual authority for an appellate court and an additional source of legal protection generally unavailable to those convicted in the civilian world.

26. 556 U.S. (June 8, 2009).

27. Most of these requirements appear in Article 142, UCMJ.

28. The solicitor general sought certiorari three times in the first 25 years that cert was available for military cases, whereas the defense sought it in about 250 cases. The solicitor general is the official in the Justice Department who determines which cases the government seeks to bring before the Court; therefore, military officials seeking review of a case from the government's perspective must obtain his support to do so.

29. 501 U.S. 163 (1994).

30. The Court noted that, for some military positions, such as chief of staff of the army or chief of naval operations, Congress had specifically provided for an additional appointment—but not for a large range of military jobs, including the deputies of such officials and, since institution of the position in 1968, military judges. A history-rich concurring opinion by Justice Souter provides detailed treatment of the issue.

31. 523 U.S. 303 (1998). This case is discussed earlier in this chapter in the discussion of the Military Rules of Evidence.

32. Department of Defense Instruction 1325.7 sets broad policy for military corrections. It sets the Army as executive agent for corrections for all services, and greater detail for governance of military confinement is contained in Army Regulation 190–47.

CHAPTER 7

Implementing the Uniform Code of Military Justice: A Generation of Change

Both of the two great changes to the military justice system of the last half of the 20th century occurred just before or during periods of great operational stress for the military. The Uniform Code of Military Justice (UCMJ), passed by Congress in May 1950 was promptly signed into law by President Truman on June 25, 1950, just weeks before the start of the Korean War. The Manual for Courts-Martial, an executive order that provides the procedures and evidentiary rules that implement the UCMJ, was published on May 31, 1951. The pattern by which change and ferment in military justice correlated to major armed conflicts repeated itself in the next decade, as the Military Justice Act of 1968, which also implemented landmark changes, was passed during the bloodiest year of the Vietnam War.[1]

Impetus for the UCMJ: World War II Experience

There were about 1.8 million courts-martial during a war in which about 8 million Americans served in uniform. That ratio is unfathomable in the contemporary military justice system, in which there might be one court-martial for every 200 to 250 service members in any given year, not one in four. The intensive experience of what was then our longest war, prosecuted in two overseas theaters (though some of the courts-martial were in the United States for stateside troops), solidified and challenged many judgments and assumptions about the military justice system. By the end of the war, there was a broad consensus that substantial reform was necessary, especially in the area of command control. But, as we have seen, reform is a recurring theme in military justice, and a consensus also was emerging that uniformity was desirable as well, which would involve the Navy's abandonment of the Articles for the Government of the Navy, its independent military justice system.

The Desertion and Execution of Eddie Slovik

The most famous, and perhaps most controversial, military execution occurred in the bitter cold depths of World War II, when Private Eddie Slovik was executed by firing squad on a January morning in 1945. Slovik, sentenced by a court-martial to death for desertion, was denied clemency by General Dwight D. Eisenhower and was the only U.S. soldier executed for desertion during World War II.

Slovik's case has been controversial ever since, because it is inseparable from observers' views of soldiers' duty, the fairness of the military justice system, the concept of deterrence, and the stress of combat.

Eddie Slovik was born in Detroit, dropped out of high school, and was in and out of jail for crimes such as petty theft and breaking and entering. In April 1942, when he was 22 years old, Slovik was paroled for the second time and classified 4-F by the military, meaning he would not be drafted for the war that was raging in Europe and in the Pacific. By the end of that year, he had met and married his wife, Antoinette, but late in 1943, the Army reclassified him as 1-A, placing him in the prime category of American men eligible for the draft.

By all accounts, Slovik was a simple man and, notwithstanding his criminal record, relatively harmless—a follower. He had a close and clinging relationship to Antoinette, reflected in the hundreds of letters he wrote to her as soon as he entered the military at the end of 1943. In August 1944, having completed basic training in Texas, Slovik was shipped to France, where he was to join the 28th Infantry Division, then engaged in fierce fighting in the Hurtgen Forest, a couple of months after the D-Day landings in Normandy. En route to the unit, he and a buddy became separated—it's not clear to what extent they engineered the separation—and joined a Canadian unit for about six weeks. As soon as Slovik joined his assigned unit (he was not punished for the separation) on October 8, he told his commander he was too scared to fight and asked to be sent to a unit that would not have to fight. The next day, Slovik gave a note to officials saying he was going to refuse to fight. After refusing the chance to withdraw the note, Slovik wrote still another note that said he would not fight and would face the consequences. In his handwritten note, he said, "I'LL RUN AWAY AGAIN IF I HAVE TO GO OUT THEIR" [sic]. After being arrested and put in the stockade, the unit's judge advocate (military lawyer) gave him still another chance to recant and return to the fighting unit. Again, Slovik refused.

In short order, Slovik was charged with desertion, and his trial was held on November 11, 1944, before a panel of nine officers. The trial was completed in less than two hours, and Slovik was unanimously sentenced to death, a decision approved by the division commander 16 days later. General Eisenhower, the theater commander, took initial action, approving the findings and sentence on December 23. After giving Slovik the chance to submit matters on his behalf and after a review by a team of lawyers, Eisenhower approved the sentence on January 23, 1945, and Slovik was executed on January 30.

The case provides insight into the mindset of leaders and soldiers at the time and highlights some of the changes in military and U.S. criminal law in the years since:

Deterrence. By almost any account, Slovik was a harmless man in that he seemed unlikely to hurt anyone. His petty criminal record involved no violence, and he seemed a man of low education, low initiative, and heavy dependence on his wife. He was not a leader in the sense that he was likely to motivate others to do anything—including desert from the Army—but he was also impervious to a sense of duty to his country or to other soldiers. From the Army's perspective, desertion was a great problem, and the Army was in a bloody slog through Europe that required thousands of young Americans to risk their lives. No one knew that we were months from turning the corner in the war, and leaders had the challenge to lead, motivate, and care for other soldiers who were as scared as Slovik. This must have been a key consideration by leaders from Slovik's platoon leader up to General Eisenhower—and the fact that Slovik actually was executed could have had the intended effect of deterring other possible desertions.

Equity. There were 21,049 soldiers charged with desertion during World War II. Many critics of the Slovik trial have emphasized the fact that only one was executed. The president of the court-martial, Colonel Guy Williams, has said that the panel recognized the gravity of the case, however, and took three votes—all unanimous—though it only had to vote once. He also has said, however, that he didn't think "a single member of that court actually believed that Slovik would ever be shot. I know I didn't believe it."

Capital cases. It is inconceivable today that a capital case would go from charging to trial in 23 days—much less that the soldier's defense counsel would be a nonlawyer, that the case would take a half day, and that there would be no case in sentencing. Today's capital cases not only require unanimous verdicts but are heavily resourced, typically by a team of experienced military defense counsel who will receive significant resources—various experts and investigators—as they assemble their cases. Obtaining those resources is sometimes a matter of contention and litigation, but modern capital cases are extraordinarily resource-intensive for both parties.

Clemency. The Uniform Code of Military Justice has a process by which convicted soldiers and their attorneys have the right to submit matters to the convening authority (the general who ordered the court into existence) after the record of trial is produced and before the convening authority makes his decision whether to approve the findings and sentence in the hopes of obtaining clemency if not outright reversal of a conviction or sentence (see chapter 6 for details about this process). In Slovik's case, he submitted a letter to General Eisenhower replete with misspellings that testify to its being his own communication, unaided by a defense counsel or other advisor. There is no evidence that Eisenhower read the note, in which Slovik says he is "humbley sorry" and begs not to be executed "for the sake of my wife and my dear mother back home," though his staff appears to have done so.

"New matter"—executed for petty theft? The short sentencing phase of Slovik's trial made no mention of his civilian convictions for petty theft. The post-trial summary, however, prepared by the judge advocate for the command, highlighted the earlier convictions (five juvenile adjudications and two later convictions for embezzlement and joy riding) and used them to emphasize Slovik's apparent incorrigibility. Regardless, such a unilateral characterization would be unlawful today. The staff judge advocate has the authority to include what the Rules for Courts-Martial consider "new

> matter" (generally, negative material that was not presented at trial) in his post-trial review of the case, but he must provide that information to the defense, which must have the opportunity to comment on it. Slovik had no such right in this case, and he did not have legal counsel at this stage, prompting his lament that he was to be executed "for bread I stole when I was 12 years old."
>
> *Justice and the perception of justice.* Slovik's supporters argue that the case was a gross injustice—by its swiftness and its solitary nature as well as his seemingly pathetic personality. It is harder to discern the perception of justice by other soldiers at the time—whether they found it disconcerting or unfair in its seeming summary nature or whether they thought it proper that a determined deserter, given more than one opportunity to rejoin a fighting unit, was brought to justice for his adamant refusal to do so.
>
> Slovik's case has been debated for years in and outside of the military; the topic of critical articles, books, and movies; and all recognize the tragic aspects of the case regardless of their views on Slovik's courage or the equity of the system. The letters between Slovik, who never saw material success in life, and his stronger and more determined wife, are poignant and reflective of his occasional despair (she met him when she ghost-wrote a letter supporting Slovik's parole from one of his civilian convictions on behalf of her father, who agreed to hire Slovik). In one of his final notes to Antoinette, Slovik wrote, "Everything happens to me. I've never had a streak of luck in my life. The only luck I had in my life was when I married you. I knew it wouldn't last because I was too happy. I knew they would not let me be happy."

Vanguard of Reform: The Elston Act of 1948

While the Military Justice Act of 1950 is rightly considered to be the most significant omnibus piece of military justice legislation in U.S. history, the less-noticed reforms of 1948 set the table for the 1950 act in two important ways: (1) The Elston Act gathered data and perspective on the World War II experience close in time to the war, and (2) it tackled some of the most significant reforms and sparked discussion of the others, meaning that the "battlefield was prepared" for the debates and changes that led to the 1950 act. The Elston Act, named for Representative Charles H. Elston, a Cincinnati-area Republican who served seven terms in Congress, was the result of extensive hearings held in 1947 by Elston's subcommittee of the House Military Activities Committee. The subcommittee heard testimony from the expected military and civilian leaders with involvement in military justice, as well as senior representatives of several veterans' organizations, and included statements filed by General Eisenhower, among others. Of the many topics of debate, the most persistent concerns were in four areas: (1) unlawful command influence, (2) qualifications and independence of counsel and the law members who performed judge-like roles, (3) meaningful protections for soldiers during the investigative process, and (4) a need for some sort of appellate process, especially after cases that resulted in significant punishment.

These concerns were at the core of the major reforms that included the Elston Act. While military leaders and the Senate Armed Services Committee opposed the legislation, mainly on the grounds that its provisions regarding command control were too stringent and that it still did not solve the lack of uniformity within the Navy, the Elston Act was passed as a rider to a Selective Service bill in 1948 and signed by President Truman. The major changes included these:

- Requiring appellate review for any case in which a punitive discharge was adjudged (dishonorable discharge, bad-conduct discharge, or dismissal of an officer). No longer was a minimum period of confinement the only trigger for appellate review, in recognition of the significant stigma that attached to a punitive discharge.
- Every case that adjudged a bad-conduct discharge would require production of a verbatim record of trial. This change was consistent with the new requirement for appellate review of such cases.
- Boards of review[2] were given authority to consider the factual merits of a case and not just legal sufficiency, giving the boards broader authority than the standard for most civilian appellate courts.
- Unlawful command influence in the administration of military justice was expressly prohibited. Although a legal prohibition does not necessarily guarantee a cultural change, it was the most dramatic step to address what many had come to view as excessive and largely unconstrained freedom of commanders to control the military justice system in ways that could corrupt rather than enhance or dignify the administration of justice.
- Specific warnings must be given to soldiers suspected of offenses before having to answer questions about those offenses. This requirement, later codified in Article 31, UCMJ, was supported by the attachment of an exclusionary rule to violations of the warnings requirement, meaning that the government risked forfeiting the use of illegally obtained admissions in proceedings against accused soldiers—all of these changes well predating the Supreme Court's *Miranda* decision of 1964.[3]
- Expanding authority for the law member and minimum legal qualifications for those serving in that role. This was still another step toward transforming the law member from a specialized adjunct member of the panel to an independent military judge, though it would be 20 years before that transformation was completed. The Elston changes nearly made the decisions of the law member binding on the other members of the panel, but the member's authority was still not as conclusive as that of a conventional trial judge.
- Requiring an independent pretrial investigation before a case can be sent to a general court-martial. This landmark requirement, later codified in Article 32, UCMJ, ensured that an officer who was not in the accused's chain of command evaluated the evidence before it was presented to the convening authority, had to decide whether to refer it to trial at all and whether to send it to a general court-martial in particular. Besides the requirement for this independent investigation—critics and skeptics observed (and still do) that the investigating officer is still somewhere in the general's command, though not in the chain of those charged with making formal decisions on the charges—it included substantial rights for the accused, including the right to be present at all proceedings and to be represented by defense counsel at the proceedings.
- Minimum qualifications for counsel at courts-martial. Again, this represented the continued professionalization of military legal personnel, though it would be years before prosecutors and defense counsel had to be members of the bar, longer before protec-

tions for the independence of military defense counsel were instituted, and still longer before independent military defense services were created.
- Introducing the opportunity for enlisted members facing courts-martial to insist that enlisted members serve on their panels. The key attraction of this provision was to curb the perception or reality that officers might not comprehend the concerns or pressures that led to the conduct of the accused who were enlisted soldiers. Guaranteeing an enlisted accused's right to have enlisted members on the panel reflected a consensus that such a demographic concession, for which there is no equivalent in civilian practice, was essential to ensuring justice and the appearance of justice.

Major Changes in the Articles of War

Because many of the most significant changes were enacted in the Elston Act, and because they barely had been implemented by the time of the debates over what became the UCMJ, the subsequent testimony and debates included some fresh discussion of the concerns raised in the 1947 hearings that led to the 1948 act (especially those concerning unlawful command influence), but the comprehensiveness of the Elston reforms enabled the drafters of the 1950 act to concentrate on two fundamental changes to military justice: (1) true uniformity, by drawing the Navy under the ambit of the UCMJ, discarding its independent justice system, and (2) introducing the opportunity for review of courts-martial convictions by a single, exclusively civilian court of review, the Court of Military Appeals.

The Navy had resisted prior attempts to persuade it to join in a unified justice system, arguing that the unique concerns of shipboard life and leadership—its remoteness, communication challenges, and close quarters—justified the need for special rules, especially those that truncated due process (for example, not extending the right to refuse nonjudicial punishment and insist on court-martial) or provided for summary punishment. James V. Forrestal, the first secretary of defense (the War Department having become the Department of Defense in 1947) was interested in a unified code, inspired not only by the long-standing concerns about command influence and appellate review, but also by a belief that a uniform code would reinforce the unifying ideals behind the new structure of the Department of Defense. In 1948, he appointed a committee, headed by the esteemed professor Edmund M. Morgan, Jr., of Harvard Law School, who had contributed significantly to the post–World War I debates about military justice. Within a year, Morgan and his small committee, which included a representative from each armed service, had produced the "Morgan Draft," which the Department of Defense submitted to Congress in February 1949. The House and Senate Armed Services Committees held hearings in early 1949, followed by floor debates. Morgan's testimony highlighted both the central themes of the reform—stronger appellate process and reduced opportunity for what was termed *command control* (the current term, *unlawful command influence*, developed in later years)—but also engaged in detailed, substantive discussions of procedural rights and definitions of crimes. Regarding command control, Morgan told the House, "We have tried to prevent court-martials from being an instrumentality of and agency to express the will of the commander."⁴ Still, Morgan emphasized, the goal was not to strip commanders of their authority and responsibility for good order and discipline. "Because of the military nature of a court martial, we have left the convening of the courts, the reference [referral] of the charges, and the appointment of members to the commander."⁵ Regarding unity, Morgan stated, "There will be the same law and the same procedures for all personnel in the armed services." He continued: "The object is to make sure not only that justice can be done . . . but that there be no disparities between the services."⁶ While this was a major change, and many anticipated resistance from the Navy, it had evolved largely into a consensus by the time of the hearings. Navy advocates did mention that there was a need to understand some of the peculiarities of shipboard life in ensuring procedural flexibility, but they seemed to recognize that a single system was inevitable. To emphasize both uniformity and the fact that the UCMJ was similar to most civilian criminal codes, Morgan promised, "A civilian lawyer will have no difficulty in conducting any case at any stage of the proceeding."⁷

Congress decided, after hearing testimony and considering the Morgan Report, that unity was essential to rebuilding and maintaining public faith in the military justice system. Further, the new UCMJ provided the opportunity for the services to publish their own rules in certain areas, including nonjudicial punishment (the Navy still foreclosed the sailor's option to demand trial by court-martial when nonjudicial punishment was offered in a ship that was underway), while the overall structure of the system, its offenses, and the rights of soldiers and expectations of commanders were the same for the first time. There were relatively few changes to substantive offenses, and most of the changes reflected the experience of the recent war. For example, Morgan introduced the committee's recommendation for the new offense of missing movement, characterizing it as "an aggravated type of absence." He explained that "the experience of World War II indicates that a large number of military personnel who were legitimately on leave or who left without permission returned after their unit or ship had sailed or moved,"⁸ and the particular codification of this offense was aimed at deterring conduct that did not seem to be adequately sanctioned under the existing codes.

A Court of Military Appeals (senior, civilian-only military appellate court) had been suggested in one form or another for generations—most recently and most ardently by General Ansell in the post–World War I debates and discussions. The UCMJ established for the first time a court of three civilians (never more than two of the same political party) that would hear all death cases and certain other appeals, while mainly having a discretionary docket—it could hear cases from the service boards of review that it chose. The terms of the judges initially were staggered to ensure that vacancies did not all occur simultaneously, but the term for members of the court ultimately was set at 15 years. The court is a creature of Congress and therefore referred to as an Article I court to distinguish it from the ordinary federal courts, which are referred to as Article III courts, because they fall under the judicial branch. Congress has created other courts for limited

Implementing the Uniform Code of Military Justice

purposes (for example, bankruptcy and immigration courts) that also are Article I creations, and therefore establish their own rules and procedures, generally tied to their specific functions. Although it is given that Article I courts comply with the judgments of the Supreme Court in cases that reach it from their jurisdictions, it has not always been a settled matter—and in some areas remains a matter of debate—that the Supreme Court's interpretation of the law in related areas necessarily binds the Article I court. For example, the Supreme Court routinely makes rulings in criminal cases that reach it through appeals from the federal and state courts, and it is not always obvious that those judgments bind the military, especially in areas of procedure that are not obviously Constitutional judgments. The Court of Military Appeals took little time in establishing its independence and causing consternation among those seeking a period of stability following the World War II experience and who wanted the opportunity to implement the new UCMJ. The court—which Rhode Island Senator Theodore F. Greene, a friend of Judge Quinn, one of the original Court of Military Appeals judges, wanted to rename the Supreme Court of Military Appeals—was renamed the Court of Appeals for the Armed Forces by the same 1994 statutory change that also expanded its membership to five and renamed the service courts of military review as the courts of criminal appeals. The early years of the court are described later in this chapter.

Comprehensive Review and Midcourse Corrections: The Powell Report of 1960—Fairness, Decentralization, Simplicity, and Stability

Recognizing the literal baptism by fire of the UCMJ, which came into force nearly contemporaneously with the first shots of the Korean War, and reacting to continuing criticism of the military justice system—including sweeping legislation recommended by the American Legion that would have set primary jurisdiction over peacetime offenses with civilian authorities and authorized fines and imprisonment for convictions for unlawful command influence—Secretary of the Army Wilber M. Brucker, in 1959, ordered a study of the first eight years' experience with the UCMJ. While finding the system to be functional in most respects, the report, which came to be known as the Powell Report after Lieutenant General Herbert B. Powell, who chaired the committee that drafted the report, spent little time with positive reinforcement and focused on areas in greatest need of change, especially the need for clarity in the area of unlawful command influence. It made some recommendations that were so radical (such as removing the convening authority's power to select panels and act on findings and sentence after trial) that they never have been seriously contemplated by Congress or the president since. While the Powell Report was an Army report, and Air Force and Navy leaders gave it scant attention, its detailed statistical, legal, and policy analyses contributed to the debate that brought about statutory and regulatory changes, especially regarding nonjudicial punishment, and it remained relevant in the debates surrounding the Military Justice Act of 1968. Before presenting its findings and recommendations, the special committee settled on what it considered to be the requisites of the military justice system. Although some seem to be statements of the obvious, they represent a post-UCMJ, late Eisenhower-administration affirmation of the military establishment's reasons for a system of justice and the principles and assumptions that guided it. The report suggested that an effective system of military justice:

1. [M]ust support the mission of the armed forces both in war and in peace, at home and abroad. It must contribute to the maintenance of armed forces in instant readiness. . . . It must operate efficiently in the event of rapid and large-scale mobilization [and] under conditions of major conventional or nuclear warfare.
2. [M]ust provide for the rehabilitation of usable military manpower.
3. [M]ust foster good order and discipline at all times and places.
4. [M]ust protect the military community against offenses to persons and property at times and places where civilian courts are not available.
5. [M]ust provide a commander with the authority needed to discharge efficiently his responsibility in connection with [military justice].
6. [M]ust provide practical checks and balances to assure protection of the rights of individuals and prevent abuse of punitive powers.
7. [S]hould promote the confidence of military personnel and the general public in the overall fairness of the system.
8. [S]hould set an example of efficient and enlightened disposition of criminal charges within the framework of American legal principles.[9]

Most of the principles reflected or asserted the long-developed balance between command authority and soldier and public faith in the essential justice of the military criminal process, but the fourth principle is notable in reflecting the post–World War II military's continued wrestling with the extent to which the UCMJ should apply to military personnel for offenses that could be addressed by the civilian justice system—a discussion that presaged the "service connection" debate (discussed in chapter 2) that generated nearly 20 years of controversy and uncertainty, launched by the *O'Callahan* decision of 1969 and settled in most respects by the *Solorio* decision of 1986. In 1959, however, the main focus was on military crimes, and, at the time, most courts-martial were for military offenses.

The Powell Committee did not concern itself with an academic or theoretical analysis of the UCMJ but focused on the experience of the preceding eight years. It consisted of nine general officers, one of whom was a judge advocate, and it analyzed data produced by the 915,369 Army courts-martial from 1951 to 1959, finding, among other things, that the rate of courts-martial had been cut almost exactly in half (113 per 1,000 troops in 1953 to 66.2 per 1,000 in 1959). It consulted senior leaders at all levels and surveyed all 96 general court-martial convening authorities in the Army. Although it was careful to say it only drew conclusions about the Army's experience, the committee suggested four principles that applied to all of the armed services and that it said should characterize

Implementing the Uniform Code of Military Justice

all of the experiences with the UCMJ: "fairness, decentralization, simplicity, and stability."

The committee's most notable findings and recommendations were in these key areas, reflecting the enduring concerns of the military justice system:

- *Command responsibility.* The report found that the UCMJ's provisions that were intended to prohibit unlawful command influence did not "unduly" dampen "proper execution of command responsibility." It found "little evidence of any intentional effort to influence . . . courts-martial or . . . judicial functions." It did find, however, that the "dividing line between . . . command responsibilities and illegal command influence" was not well understood, a shortcoming that led to unclear "instruction in disciplinary matters," especially "in the Army school system for officers who are potential commanders of battalion and higher units." In a related observation, the committee found that "the offense of conduct unbecoming an officer and gentleman has lost some of its meaning" and recommended that dismissal be mandatory punishment at court-martial for this offense, a change that was never adopted or seriously proposed.
- *Trial efficiency.* One of the committee's solutions for "slow and cumbersome" general courts-martial was to permit out-of-court sessions in which the law member would address legal questions and to permit the law member to rule conclusively on such matters—a peek ahead to the Military Justice Act of 1968 and a reflection of the shortcomings and frustrations that most felt inhered in the limited role of the law member. The committee also found that not all cases required panels and recommended that the UCMJ be changed "to permit a law officer alone to sit as a general court-martial" in certain circumstances.
- *Sentences and confinement.* The report recommended that the secretary of the Army be given the authority to "order military persons to their homes pending appellate review of sentences to punitive separation" when they were not serving sentences of confinement, because their "presence on a military post . . . impairs morale and discipline." The committee also believed that the "prestige of honorable officers and noncommissioned officers is damaged" by permitting them to be confined or reduced without reduction in rank or dismissal from the service. It recommended automatic discharge or reduction in such circumstances. The committee also commended the Army for "a superior system for screening, rehabilitating and restoring prisoners in confinement" and recommended a program to transfer youthful prisoners to the federal system "for further treatment as youthful offenders."
- *New crimes and jurisdiction.* The committee recommended terminating UCMJ jurisdiction over retirees and making several other changes to the punitive articles, including adding a presumption of desertion for those who were absent without leave more than six months in peacetime or 30 days in wartime; defining "general orders" and the authority to issue them (and therefore the authority to penalize their violation); adding a bad check statute, and providing that statements made in line of duty were official statements that, if proved false, could be prosecuted.
- *Company punishment under Article 15.* The committee found that these relatively new procedures still were too cumbersome, which discouraged commanders from using this intentionally less formal and more efficient mechanism for disposing of minor misconduct. It called for radical change. Finding that current proposals for strengthening Article 15 authority were inadequate, and citing the fact of 50,000 summary and special courts-martial

in 1959, the committee recommended abolition of both levels of courts-martial coupled with strengthened nonjudicial punishment authority. It also found, in an argument that has gained currency over time, that the impact of nonjudicial punishment on officers' careers was too great and recommended that rules be changed to moderate its impact.

- *Pretrial investigations.* The committee found Article 32 pretrial investigations to be too time consuming and concluded that in "complicated cases better pretrial investigations and better trials will result if the investigation is conducted by a trial counsel and the accused is represented by a defense counsel." While representation by a defense counsel at Article 32 investigations has become the standard, there never has been much support for requiring a prosecutor to conduct the investigation. Article 32 contemplates a disinterested party conducting the investigation, and, while the trial counsel is not a member of the command, she advises the commander and would either have an interest in the case as prosecutor or be disqualified because of her prior participation. In either event, there has been little support for such a change, though it is not uncommon for judge advocates, typically those not currently serving on a prosecution staff, to serve as Article 32 investigating officers in complicated cases.
- *Post-trial and appellate processes.* The committee was thoroughly dissatisfied with the entire post-trial process, finding that the requirement that the convening authority take action on the findings and sentence of every case he convened[10] was time consuming and superfluous. It criticized the focus of most post-trial litigation as involving issues that "had no direct bearing on the guilt or innocence of the accused or whether he had received a fair trial." The report recommended removing the convening authority's power to approve findings and sentences and retaining only the authority to grant clemency. It called for ending the staff judge advocate review, an exhaustive and time-intensive process by which the staff judge advocate summarized the record of trial and analyzed significant legal issues stemming from the trial before presenting the case to the convening authority for action. It then recommended that boards of review—the service-specific review courts that were the first rung of the appellate ladder—only address "correctness in law and fact" rather than seek and examine issues that the committee found to be extraneous or formalistic. It also criticized the scope of the appellate process, finding that some "cases are reversed because of errors of law that do not materially prejudice the substantial rights of the accused." The committee believed that such actions reduced the stability of the law, meaning that leaders and lawyers could not predict and rely on the law. This may also have reflected that the committee was composed almost entirely of nonlawyers, who may have had less patience with what appeared to be technical points of law that may have seemed to be impediments to good order and discipline. The committee called for increasing the size of the Court of Military Appeals from three to five[11] in the belief that there would be fewer fractured opinions and a more predictable and coherent course of development in military law. The committee recommended that the two additional seats be made available for members with military experience, reflecting a belief that the court did not fully appreciate some of the unique stresses and circumstances of military life.

The Court of Military Appeals Asserts Itself

President Truman appointed the first three members of the new court in June 1951, naming Robert E. Quinn, former Democratic governor of Rhode Island who long had an interest in military justice matters; George W. Latimer, a Republican state supreme court justice from Utah; and Paul W. Brosman, dean of Tulane University Law School. The Court of Military Appeals (informally abbreviated as COMA and denoted in official decisions as CMA) was well aware of its pioneer role as well as the fact that Congress trusted it to address—and, as necessary, redress—concerns about command influence. It also recognized that the extent of its authority would only be settled over time; it was an open question whether the court could interpret the Constitution as it applied to soldiers or whether that was strictly a function of the Article III courts. The Powell Committee singled out the court for criticism, focusing on the split that had developed among Judges Quinn and Latimer and the court's newest member, former Republican Senator Homer Ferguson of Michigan.[12]

The committee found that judicial interpretations of Article 31, which contained the military's unique protection against self-incrimination, and the rules on searches "impeded" the "[m]aintenance of good order and discipline." The committee's attention to and criticism of COMA was noteworthy in that it implicitly endorsed the independence of the still-new, exclusively civilian court, but reflected commanders' frustrations with the exact nature of their authority to question suspects. In one case, the court, in one of the 2–1 decisions that came to characterize its early years, found that ordering a suspect to produce a handwriting sample was protected by Article 31's protection against self-incrimination. The majority found that the handwriting exemplar was a "statement" and therefore could not be compelled—a line of thinking rejected by the Supreme Court in later years (not military cases) on the grounds that producing a handwriting exemplar, like a blood sample, did not implicate self-incrimination concerns, because, though it could incriminate the suspect, it was not a statement; rather, it was a neutral exposition of a physical characteristic.[13] The report also found that judicial interpretations concerning commanders' authority to order searches were not clear and did not appear to satisfy the needs of the military service and seemed to undermine or unduly limit—in many leaders' views—a commander's sense of near plenary authority and responsibility in his unit. The report was not an indictment of military lawyers, however, as its recommended remedy for the "lack flexibility and . . . excessive time" required for Article 32 pretrial investigations was to have them conducted by a prosecutor and have the accused represented by a defense counsel.

Military Justice Matures

Removing Civilians from the Ambit of the Military—and Reconsidering

It is beyond discussion in the 21st century that the UCMJ applies to those in uniform. The idea of trying civilians, however, grew to seem foreign in the later years of the 20th century. In fact, the unavailability of the UCMJ to try civilians is a relatively recent—post-UCMJ, Warren Court—development, and it is not absolute. In 1957, the Supreme Court ruled in *Reid v. Covert*[14] that civilians accompanying the armed forces overseas (typically family members) were not subject to the UCMJ. A few years later, the Supreme Court extended that to all offenses committed by civilians.[15] As discussed in detail in chapter 2, a series of dramatic or highly publicized instances of misconduct by civilians affiliated with the military overseas, either family members or civilian military contractors, drew increased attention to the potential jurisdictional gap for conduct overseas, resulting in amending the UCMJ to apply to civilians in some circumstances. Some of the concern was rooted in misconduct by family members in host countries, but the greater concern was with ensuring that civilian employees and contractors, whose role in the battlefield has increased greatly both because of the shrinking military and the nature of modern war, did not escape liability for their conduct simply because they were overseas and the UCMJ did not apply.

Multiple Lenses: Choosing from among Nonjudicial Punishment, Courts-Martial, and Administrative Separations

As discussed earlier, the clamor for introduction of nonjudicial punishment finally bore fruit—and, by some practitioners' and critics' analysis, was too fruitful. The introduction of a more robust and flexible Article 15 in 1962 quickly proved to accomplish what most drafters desired—a marked decrease in the number of courts-martial. This came on the heels of a trend toward increasing popularity of administrative separations as an alternative disciplinary and force management tool for commanders. Such separations had the benefit or attraction of carrying comparatively little due process (see details about the process in chapter 8) while providing commanders the opportunity quickly to separate soldiers they considered to be substandard in conduct or performance. The most prominent critic of the administrative separation process was Major General Reginald C. Harmon, the first judge advocate general of the Air Force, who served from 1948 to 1960. In a famous 1962 speech, he criticized commanders for relying too heavily on administrative separations, suggesting that they were attracted to the limited due process available and were failing to use courts-martial, meaning that serious conduct was not being addressed and that, in some instances, service members did not have the opportunity adequately to defend themselves.

This concern persisted over the decades and remains a concern of commanders and practitioners today. Air Force statistics showed a ratio of nonjudicial punishment to courts-martial of 4 to 1 in 1964, 12 to 1 by 1973, and 17 to 1 by 1983.[16] The other services have shown similar trends, though the trend was less pronounced in the Marine Corps. The ratio of administrative separations to courts-martial is anywhere from 5 to 1 to 10 to 1, but further statistical analysis is required, because many discharges are not alternatives to courts-martial. Administrative separations can, in rare circumstances, receive the review of federal district courts, but that route carries extremely low probabilities of success; for all intents and purposes, an administrative separation is conclusive once the internal review required by service regulations have been completed.

Revising the UCMJ: Military Justice Act of 1968

Continuing the accident by which major changes to the military justice system occurred during periods of military conflict, President Lyndon B. Johnson signed the Military Justice Act of 1968 on October 24, 1968, which brought courts-martial more closely in line with civilian trials. Most of the changes approved in 1968 had been debated at least 40 years earlier during the post–World War I hearings and the controversies that preceded enactment of the Articles of War of 1920. The 1968 act was a culmination of these discussions and the various reports and analyses that had accumulated since implementation of the UCMJ 17 years earlier. Senator Sam Ervin of North Carolina, a member of the Judiciary Committee but not the Armed Services Committee, took increasing interest in military justice and held hearings in 1962 on the Constitutional rights of military personnel, in which he focused on command control of courts-martial, the right to legally trained defense counsel, differences in military justice among the services, and the effectiveness of military due process.[17] Ervin paid close attention to the controversy regarding administrative discharges and the opportunity for inequity they represented, in part because they could be used to circumvent the harsher outcomes (federal conviction, confinement, punitive discharge) of a court-martial; in part because of the correspondingly lesser due process (only in some circumstances did it include the right to a hearing before a board); and in part because of the potential for inequity among similarly situated service members, some of whom received punishment and some of whom faced administrative sanctions. His wide-ranging interests, represented at some point in the pendency of 18 different military justice–related bills, included single-officer courts-martial and the establishment of a Navy Judge Advocate General Corps. A new set of bills appeared in 1966, accompanied by a new set of hearings and additional scrutiny of administrative discharges. A consolidated set of bills appeared again in 1967, and finally consensus on key—and the least radical—provisions emerged in 1968, as Congress finally passed the bill in October. These were the major changes:

- *Introduction of the military judge, removal of the law member.* After years of debate, the recommendations of most practitioners and many commanders and other nonlawyers with experience in military justice, the position of law member—the awkward hybrid that was part trial judge, part juror, and insufficiently either to satisfy anyone—was eliminated in favor of the military judge, who assumed the attributes of most any criminal trial court judge.
- *Judge-alone trials.* Many of the studies and criticisms of the system had long advocated that once a trial judge was inserted into the process, an accused should have the opportunity to be tried by judge alone. The 1968 act also introduced this concept, designed

not only to ensure justice because of the legally trained officer running the court, but alleviating the burden on commanders to provide panel members for such courts—which also removed a deterrent to convening them.
- *Changing special courts-martial.* The act required that a judge preside at virtually all special courts-martial and that a defense counsel be appointed for every accused soldier tried at this level of court. This recognized that this misdemeanor-level court still carried significant consequences to those who faced justice in this forum.
- *Renaming boards of review.* They were now to be called Courts of Military Review. Although they had essentially the same authority, this reflected the continuing desire to harmonize military practice with civilian terms and concepts, especially where it was thought that the terms could be better understood (it was easier to understand what a court of review did) and the courts and their work enhanced in prestige.

Notwithstanding Ervin's considerable attention to the administrative discharge process in the 1968 act, there was insufficient consensus to support statutory action.

The Son Thang Trials: Military Justice during the Vietnam Era

Two years after the My Lai killings, a group of five Marines on a night patrol near the village of Son Thang, South Vietnam, killed 16 women and children. A fellow Marine had recently been killed by suspected Viet Cong in this Viet Cong–dominated area west of Da Nang, and the young Marines (an 18-year-old, two 19-year-olds, a 20-year-old, and a 21-year-old) were edgy, agitated, and entrusted with significant responsibility for independent operations.

In *Son Thang, An American War Crime,* Gary Solis, who served as a Marine judge advocate in Vietnam, and later as professor of law at several institutions including West Point, portrayed the tensions and mindset that led to the incident and the controversial investigation and courts-martial that followed.

Solis is neither cynical nor blinkered in his assessment of Vietnam and the justice process. He writes, "A U.S. serviceman standing by while an ally tortures a prisoner is itself an offense punishable under both the customary laws of war and U.S. military law. . . . But in U.S. infantry units in South Vietnam, such acts were not unusual. Generals will deny it, colonels and majors may doubt it, but any captain or lieutenant and any enlisted infantryman who was there will confirm it. That's just the way it was. Not in every unit, not in the best-led units, but in most." He plumbs the atmosphere in such small units, especially at that point in an unpopular war, a unit Solis characterizes as a "prototype of disunity," more likely to misinterpret, perhaps conveniently, its lieutenant's direction that, "I want you to pay these little bastards back." In the process, he raises questions about the functionality and purpose of a unique military justice system operating halfway around the world under austere conditions.

In addition, Solis examines a scenario not unique to Vietnam or to Son Thang, but especially poignant in this situation in light of the loss of life and the haziness of the circumstances, which include contradictions (eyewitness testimony by biased and stressed individuals, a disinclination to credit statements by villagers), investigative

Implementing the Uniform Code of Military Justice 137

> lapses, and legal judgments (such as granting immunity to a key witness that was premature in Solis's view, and weakened the investigation).
>
> Solis's book is considered a classic, because he tells a gripping story and draws compelling—and both enduring and prescient—lessons for the conduct of military operations in circumstances in which the enemy is ill defined and when young, stressed service members must make judgments about lawful operations. Besides telling the story of the trials and their inconsistent outcomes, Solis opens a window into military justice during the Vietnam era—including review of one of the convictions by a military staffer for the Secretary of the Navy, James H. Webb, who would become a Pulitzer Prize–winning novelist and U.S. senator. Most significantly, he poses a set of questions that are no less relevant in Iraq and beyond than they were in Vietnam. While characterizing the trials as "reminders of humanity's aspiration to do justice," he calls the trials a failure because the offenses were poorly investigated, inexperienced advocates were assigned to the trials on both sides, and no one above the "killer team" was held accountable at court-martial. Solis believes that the trial proved too complex for the expeditionary environment of Vietnam—even after the peak of the long war—and that factors such as poor law libraries and inefficient forensic support made it more difficult to bring justice. Beyond the legal analysis, however, Solis offered the most provocative observations for those who served, asking without answering how to inculcate ethics in those whom the military receives from the society it defends. "We must train our warriors as best we can, not only in the use of arms, but in the morality of their use. That training cannot be accomplished by the military alone."

More "Civilianization"—Military Rules of Evidence and the 1984 Manual

In the late 1970s, a decision was made to analyze the rules of evidence that applied at courts-martial and to harmonize them to the extent possible with the Federal Rules of Evidence. Promulgated in 1980, the Military Rules of Evidence are patterned after and, in most respects, are identical to the Federal Rules, which had been published in 1975; they deviate only where the drafters determined that factors unique to the military require them to do so (see chapter 6 for a detailed discussion of the rules). The adoption of the Military Rules accomplished the goal of further legitimizing the military justice system by grounding it when possible on established federal practices and also ensured that military courts were more accessible to nonmilitary practitioners, because the rules did not deviate so substantially that a practitioner familiar with federal criminal practice could not, with study, operate in military courts. Emphasizing the desire to conform to civilian practice except where deviations are grounded in military needs, Military Rule of Evidence 1102(a) now provides that changes to the Federal Rules of Evidence automatically shall apply to the military 18 months after the effective date of the change unless the president decides to the contrary.

The Military Justice Act of 1983, which did not change the military legal landscape to the same extent as the 1968 act, reflected the continued maturity of the military justice system. The change that drew the greatest attention was extension of the Supreme Court's jurisdiction to hear cases from the Court of Military Appeals (now the Court of Appeals for the Armed Forces) by grant of certiorari. Although military cases had reached the court before, they had to follow an extraordinary writ process, which meant that service members did not have the same due course opportunity to petition the court for review. The Court grants certiorari sparingly, but it elected to review nine military cases in the first 25 years that this right was in place. Another major change implemented in the 1984 Manual for Courts-Martial promulgated by President Reagan, was the streamlining of the post-trial review process. To this point, post-trial reviews were exhaustive recountings and analyses of the trial process, including dense summarizations of the record, a practice that was considered to be a necessary grounding for the post-trial recommendation that the staff judge advocate was required to make to the convening authority. That recommendation had to be presented to the convening authority, who had to decide whether to approve the findings and sentence or what modifications to make. The post-trial review, commonly drafted by an officer who did not prosecute the case, took an enormous amount of time to write and, some tacitly recognized, was not necessarily read or consulted in a manner that justified that amount of time and detail. Drafters determined that it was excessive if not superfluous, especially in light of the verbatim record of trial that was required for cases with serious sentences and the extent of appellate review that had become available. The 1984 Manual for Courts-Martial, then, simplified the post-trial review by eliminating the extensive summary of the trial, only requiring the staff judge advocate to provide legal conclusions on several key matters about the case. Rather than the summaries and analysis previously mandated, it was expected that the staff judge advocate and the convening authority could consult the record of trial when there was a need for detail about the case. Drafters also hoped that the changes would speed up post-trial processing, typically slow in the military services and a matter of such concern that the appellate courts have granted sentencing relief to accused soldiers because of the length of time it takes to finalize their convictions.

The other major change in the 1983 act, which took effect in 1984, was a provision that permitted the government to appeal certain rulings by military trial judges. The appeals were limited to (1) rulings that amounted to a finding of not guilty, (2) rulings that deprived the government of critical evidence that constituted substantial proof of a material fact, and (3) judicial orders to disclose classified information or judicial refusals to impose protective orders concerning classified information. The rule explicitly—and obviously—precludes the government from appealing a ruling that is or amounts to a finding of not guilty. The government makes regular use of this appeal right and, as expected, does not prevail in the majority of instances, but it is both a rule of justice and efficiency, intended to correct erroneous rulings close in time and to remove error or affirm critical rulings while the case is being litigated, rather than in an attenuated and less satisfactory manner much later on appeal.

Implementing the Uniform Code of Military Justice

Restructured Manual for Courts-Martial. The 1984 Manual, substantively similar to the 1969 model but for incorporating the legislative changes Congress enacted in 1983, was transformed from a practitioner's standpoint, with the introduction of the Rules for Courts-Martial, which separated the procedural provisions of the manual from the Military Rules of Evidence, making it easier to consult and cite. The 1984 structure proved popular and remains in effect. The Manual now is published every several years, incorporating interim changes made since the prior iteration, but is not on a strict publication schedule. It is published in paperbound editions only (earlier, it had been published in a binder with changes issued loose leaf); practitioners need to be sure they are citing the most current edition of the rules and punishments but can always double-check their citations through automated legal research.

Self-Analysis, Operational Flexibility

The UCMJ's effectiveness in operational settings remained a matter of serious debate through the Vietnam War and beyond. General William Westmoreland, who commanded U.S. forces in Vietnam from 1964 to 1968, coauthored an article in the *Harvard Journal of Law and Public Policy* with General George Prugh, judge advocate general of the Army, in which they wrote, "It is our conclusion that the Uniform Code of Military Justice is not capable of performing its intended role in times of military stress. It is presently too slow, too cumbersome, too uncertain, indecisive, and lacking in the power to reinforce accomplishments of the military mission, to deter misconduct, or even to rehabilitate."[18] The criticism by these two esteemed senior leaders reflected and enlivened a debate that continued in the academic and military legal communities for years. Although there was no major conflict between the end of the Vietnam War in 1975 and the first Gulf War in 1991 (and no sustained conflict until the Afghanistan engagement that began in 2001, followed in 2003 by the war in Iraq), many thousands of service members remained stationed overseas, primarily in Europe and Southeast Asia. The extended deployment to Bosnia that started in 1995 and the long conflicts in Southwest Asia saw the routine forward positioning of military judges and defense counsel, along with the prosecutors habitually associated with operational units. Courts were held in locations ranging from tents in the Balkans to the captured palaces of Saddam Hussein, and the concerns of commanders and counsel centered on timeliness of military justice actions, security for witnesses and participants in the justice process, and, as always, the impact on military operations when providing sufficient due process to ensure justice. The concerns expressed by Generals Westmoreland and Prugh have never gone away, and they arise occasionally in professional writing, seminars, and commanders' conferences. All said, there is a broad, though not universal, consensus that the UCMJ is essentially workable in wartime and that it worked adequately in the wars in Iraq and Afghanistan, even though the steady increase in due process rights for accused soldiers, combined with communications technology, has provided some leverage for the accused and defense counsel to increase the costs and risks to the government in conducting fair and timely prosecutions in deployed environments.

William O. Douglas Throws in a Wrench: *O'Callahan v. Parker* and the Requirement for Service Connection

As discussed in chapter 2, concerns regarding the reach of military justice—the extent to which it encompassed soldiers' off-duty conduct and whether it reached civilians at all—concerned the courts from the 1960s until well into the 1980s. The Supreme Court's 1969 *O'Callahan* decision requiring that the military establish a service connection as a predicate to court-martial threw military justice into turmoil; it was the most disruptive decision regarding military justice that the Court ever issued. *O'Callahan* was followed as quickly as the Court could find an opportunity to clarify itself, by 1971's decision in *Relford v. Commandant*, which tried to provide some structure to the *O'Callahan* analysis by suggesting a nonbinding and nonexclusive list of 12 factors that courts-martial should consider in evaluating whether the government had established the required service connection. Military trial courts were consumed with jurisdictional motions, and the military appellate courts labored to calibrate their opinions to the guidance they tried to divine from the *O'Callahan* and *Relford* opinions.

While that issue continued to roil military practice, military courts began to look at characteristics of soldier misconduct in determining whether or under what circumstances the military had jurisdiction over an offense. Drug use was a key area. Initially, the controversy concerned off-post conduct, but the issue became more complex as technology and military practice made it possible to conduct reliable urinalysis testing—which could demonstrate that a service member used illegal drugs, but, of course, it could not show where or under what circumstances. In 1980, the Court of Military Appeal took a major step toward clarity, as well as a broad assertion of military jurisdiction, when it held that "the gravity and immediacy of the threat to military personnel and installations posed by the drug traffic and . . . abuse convince us that very few drug involvements of a service person will not be 'service connected.'"[19] The unanimous court held that all drug use by service members, regardless of where or when the activity occurred, could be prosecuted under the UCMJ because the influence of drugs can persist beyond the period in which the person is high or obviously under the influence. This opinion was significant, because the military's highest court, which had tended toward decisions that critics and commanders found to be liberal and expansive of service member rights, made a clear ruling that expanded military jurisdiction, encompassing a persistent area of service member conduct. It was grounded in the court's belief that the effect of illegal drug use could never be contained to the location where it occurred, and it would have an impact on a soldier's fitness and readiness to perform duties regardless of its timing and location.

Unlawful Command Influence

As long as there is a military justice system, there will be concerns about unlawful command influence. The key part of the term is the adjective, because the military justice system is built on the *lawful* influence and involvement of commanders—it is only when it becomes unlawful, sapping the system of its independence and justice, that it becomes harmful and, in some circumstances, unlawful. Long condemned as the "mortal enemy of military justice," unlawful command influence has remained the most sensitive concern of senior leaders, military appellate courts, and judge advocates. A consensus has grown since the latter years of the 20th century that the worst of command influence has been rooted out of the system, in part by law and regulation, but perhaps as much by cultural changes that have made most senior leaders and their legal advisors acutely aware of the potential for and consequences of unlawful influence. There have not been systemic, widely publicized instances of unlawful command influence since the controversies that arose from the Army's Third Armored Division in the 1980s, a series of cases in which military appellate courts found that a division commander acted improperly when he publicly questioned how his subordinates could recommend courts-martial and then testify on behalf of an accused soldier.[20] Many unlawful influence cases are tied to leaders' comments, because those comments can be seen to chill their subordinates in the exercise of their military justice duties (for example, encouraging them to alter their recommendations in the hope of gaining or maintaining the favor of a boss) or responsibilities (deterring service members from assisting or testifying in favor of another unit member or subordinate). Courts have a range of corrective measures available, ranging from ordering retractions or rescinding improper policies to, in the most egregious cases, ordering substantial sentence relief or even invalidating convictions. Courts sometimes will disqualify a convening authority from taking further action on a case, ordering that the case be transferred to a different convening authority, but courts also have permanently disqualified convening authorities, a less common sanction reserved for the most egregious cases. As leaders and their legal advisors have increased their sensitivity to the potential for unlawful influence, they often will have taken corrective measures themselves—retracting or clarifying statements, briefing soldiers on the fact that they are expected to exercise their independence and that they will not face adverse consequences for cooperating in a soldier's defense—so that appellate courts often are in the position of determining whether the self-correction was timely and sufficient enough to moot the need for relief on appeal.

In practice, allegations of unlawful influence capture the attention of trial judges and commanders, and, once the defense makes a colorable showing, then the government must disprove the influence beyond a reasonable doubt. The standard for granting relief is whether someone with military justice responsibilities acted in an inappropriate manner because of actual or perceived command pressure, affecting the case in question, but, in some rare instances, courts will find "apparent command influence." This doctrine permits finding that, even though there was no actual impact on a case, the perception of injustice, to someone knowing all the facts, would still be so outrageous as to warrant relief; while this doctrine is sparingly applied, it reflects the seriousness of the charge and its potential not only to affect the case being litigated but the confidence of the rank and file as well as the public in the integrity of the military justice system. Critics and some defense counsel believe that unlawful influence has only become more sophisticated and undetectable and that the decline in military justice actions in general has made junior leaders more susceptible to unlawful influence than ever—even unwitting influence—because they are less experienced in military justice and therefore less confident in their judgments. Some also believe that command focus on certain crimes, perhaps drugs or sex crimes, can create an atmosphere in which leaders are chilled in their exercise of discretion in favor of an accused because of the belief that the military as an institution has singled out certain crimes for special emphasis.[20]

The Army's Judge Advocate Legal Center and School has long published the "Ten Commandments of Unlawful Command Influence," a document that has circulated widely among leaders and lawyers of all military services as a thumbnail guide and discussion tool on the sensitive issue. The Commandments:

I: The commander may not order a subordinate to dispose of a case in a certain way.
II: The commander must not have an inflexible policy on disposition or punishment.
III: The commander, if accuser, may not refer the case.
IV: The commander may neither select nor remove court members in order to obtain a particular result in a particular trial.
V: No outside pressures may be placed on the judge or court members to arrive at a particular decision.
VI: Witnesses may not be intimidated or discouraged from testifying.
VII: The court decides punishment. an accused may not be punished before trial.
VIII: Recognize that subordinates and staff may "commit" command influence that will be attributed to the commander, regardless of his knowledge or intentions.
IX: The commander may not have an inflexible attitude towards clemency.
X: If a mistake is made, raise the issue immediately.[21]

Independent Defense Services

Besides honest and vigilant legal advisors, the next best bulwark against unlawful command influence is a competent and independent defense counsel. For most of the history of military justice, prosecutors and defense counsel have been fungible creatures, literally a prosecutor in one case and a defense counsel in the next—a practice that stemmed from a belief that an honest and prepared counsel (who, for most of U.S. military history, did not even have to be lawyers) was essential to justice and that those serving in either role would do their ethical best. As the military became acutely sensitive to claims of command influence

Implementing the Uniform Code of Military Justice

and as military practice became more complex and sophisticated, criticism from the outside—bar associations, politicians, and some veterans' organizations—grew, to the point that the military found it increasingly difficult to defend the practice of not providing dedicated, full-time defense counsel to accused service members.

Not all of the services made the changes at the same time and in the same manner, but all services now have an independent body of defense counsel drawn from the ranks of uniformed judge advocates who will serve for a period of time exclusively as defense counsel and who will, except for their leader, report only to defense counsel and receive professional ratings or fitness reports from those in the defense counsel supervisory chain. The Army led the way in the transformation, as its experiment with the independent Trial Defense Service was made formal in 1980. Although some of the details vary among the services, all have a chief defense counsel, a colonel or captain (O-6) who supervises all of their defense counsel. While the chief defense counsel must report to a non–defense counsel, that officer typically reports to a senior judge advocate (an officer of flag rank in that service) who is obliged to supervise and assist in the defense function and has no supervisory responsibility over prosecutors. Most services and most critics generally agree that the independent defense services have been successful, because they have permitted counsel to concentrate exclusively on the skills and techniques that are best suited to defending accused soldiers, and they have enhanced soldiers' trust in their military counsel, because the accused knows that she can trust the defense counsel, who has no ties to the command that is court-martialing her.

Unlike in the civilian world, all military accused have the services of a military defense counsel; there is no means-testing as there is for a public defender in the civilian world. The services have their own policies on when they extend the right to defense counsel, but anyone who has had his Article 31 rights read to him will be provided with a defense counsel; obviously, formal charging warrants the assignment of defense counsel. The services also generally provide the right to consult defense counsel when service members receive nonjudicial punishment charges and, in most instances, when they are recommended for involuntary administrative separation. The services organize and distribute their defense counsel in different manners, with the Army generally assigning defense counsel to most every installation while the Air Force places its counsel into regional offices and dispatches them to various bases. The Navy generally will have defense counsel aboard ship, but on shore they tend to concentrate their counsel in a manner closer to the Air Force than the Army model.

Some critics believe that true independence only will come with independent budgets for defense counsel and perhaps a command of some sort that further reinforces defense structural independence from the prosecution function. It is a common practice for judge advocates to serve as defense counsel once or twice in their careers, and there is little residual belief that aggressive work as a defense counsel has negative career implications—most leaders recognize and reinforce the work of ethical and well-prepared defense counsel, and the services generally believe that a tour as a defense counsel is important soldier service that also provides practitioners with a valuable perspective on military justice.

Why a Military Justice System in the 21st Century

By most measures, the military justice system in the United States is stronger than ever—confirmed in its robust jurisdiction, generally trusted by the rank and file, and broadly respected by national leaders and most critics. After a period in the 1980s in which court-martial rates declined significantly, they rose for several years, reaching a new plateau that was higher than the low point of the early 1990s but well below the historic norms of the 1960s through 1980s. Although there has been much speculation about the reasons for the decline—reasons posited include the decline of the drug problem through sustained compulsory urinalysis; the professionalization of the force, tied in part to the all-volunteer military; and a rough parallel to the decline in the crime rates in many metropolitan areas—there has been no credible study of the dynamic. Besides the lower rate, there was a notable shift away from military crimes so that, by the 1980s, the great majority of courts-martial were for nonmilitary offenses. The wars in Southwest Asia brought some of the military crimes back to the fore, especially absences from duty and disrespect, but the military continued to try far more sex crimes than it had in the past (some sexual offenses perhaps reflecting the sustained presence of women in the military, albeit a minority of the force; some perhaps reflecting the greater number of married soldiers, including those with stepchildren, giving rise to a persistent problem with child abuse cases), but far fewer crimes of violence (perhaps reflecting the volunteer force, the fact that far more service members were married—not infrequently to other service members—or the fact that arresting the drug problem reduced a major source of conflict). The UCMJ is changed in minor ways by almost every Congress, perhaps adding a new offense or inserting a procedural change, and the manual is changed regularly, often by increasing a maximum punishment (accomplished for several sexual offenses and attempted murder between 1990 and 2005). The manual also changes by operation of law, when the Supreme Court issues a ruling, which prompted the psychotherapist privilege,[22] or the Federal Rules of Evidence change, as they have in several areas, especially regarding the government's added flexibility in prosecuting sex offenses,[23] but the changes generally are less frequent and certainly less extensive than they were during periods of greater ferment.

Military justice certainly has its critics, but it has been hard to maintain a sustained, thematic emphasis on shortcomings in the system. Consequently, most contemporary criticism attacks the concept of a separate military justice system or uses the occasion of highly publicized courts-martial less to attack a particular feature of the military justice system than to attack policies that critics consider to be unpopular, such as the continued criminalization of adultery or homosexual conduct. Critics once had a standing list of perennial, systemic concerns about military justice, typically led by unlawful command influence and including other asserted shortcomings such as inadequate or insufficiently independent defense counsel. Mainstream critics of military justice in the 21st century generally tend to focus on these concerns:[24]

- *Why a system at all?* The sophistication and portability of the federal criminal system, and the clear trend to greater federalization of crimes in general and of extraterritorial crimes in particular, makes the asserted need for the UCMJ's worldwide reach an anachronism, critics say. Proponents argue that the UCMJ is proven in its flexibility, including in multiple conflicts from its inception in 1951 through the Afghan and Iraqi wars, and the occasional federal extraterritorial case does not mean that routine worldwide reach by the Department of Justice is realistic. The criticism is not only aimed at the worldwide applicability of the UCMJ but also rests on the belief that local jurisdictions that border military installations should be able to handle most offenses, and certainly most offenses that occur off the installation. Regardless, most proponents argue that a system run by civilians could not take into account the unique perspectives and demands of military life—and that such an understanding runs as much in favor of an accused as it does the prosecution.
- *Command control.* If a separate system must persist, critics argue that the command should be removed from it, or the extent of command involvement should be curtailed. Rather than commanders as convening authorities, some reformers argue for a version of a legal command by which a senior judge advocate would have district attorney–like powers to bring charges. Critics argue that this analog to proven civilian practices will keep the justice system in house but remove the potentially corrupting influence of rank and command—and liberate commanders to prepare for operations and not be consumed by disciplinary concerns. Proponents of the system argue that such a change would undermine the central reason for being—the reinforcement of good order and discipline that is best managed by those who are responsible for the good order and discipline and welfare of the men and women who are serving their country, and that it is essential to their effectiveness as a fighting force. While some defenders of the system have been open to some alterations of command control, such as random selection of panel members, most believe that commanders should retain their central role and that structural and cultural impediments to unlawful command influence should be vigilantly enforced.
- *Nonunanimous verdicts, other arcane procedures.* While system proponents argue that nonunanimous verdicts help an accused, because the first vote counts, critics insist that unanimity is the Constitutional gold standard that the military should apply. Other features of the system, such as the broad right to inspection contained in Military Rule of Evidence 312, continue to draw critics based on the belief that service members, who place themselves in harm's way, should not have fewer protections than their civilian counterparts.[25]

Almost any critic of military justice finds the opportunity to quote the sentiment, often attributed to Georges Clemenceau, France's World War I leader, that "military justice is to justice what military music is to music." It can be said of Clemenceau, whose frame of reference was the notorious Dreyfus trial of 1895, that he predated the Uniform Code of Military Justice and never listened to John Philip Sousa.[26]

Notes

1. U.S. forces suffered 14,595 deaths in 1968 and more than 87,000 wounded; there were about 9,400 U.S. combat deaths in 1967 and 1969.

2. Later to become courts of military review and then later to become courts of criminal appeals—discussed in chapter 6.

3. The Court had applied the exclusionary rule to illegally obtained evidence in 1961 in *Mapp v. Ohio,* 367 U.S. 643(1961).

4. Hearings before a Subcommittee of the Committee on Armed Services House of Representatives, Eighty-First Congress, First Session on H. R. 2498 (hereinafter House Hearings) at 606.

5. House Hearings at 606.

6. House Hearings at 600.

7. Id.

8. House Hearings at 605.

9. *The Committee on the Uniform Code of Military Justice Good Order and Discipline in the Army,* report to Secretary of the Army Wilber M. Brucker, submitted January 18, 1960.

10. Successors in command take action on those cases convened by their predecessors, because the alternative would be unworkable and inconsistent with the principal of command authority.

11. A change implemented years later, in 1994.

12. Judge Brosman died in December 1955, and Ferguson took his seat in April 1957.

13. See, for example, *Schmerber v. California,* 384 U.S. 757 (1966).

14. 354 U.S. 1 (1957) (plurality opinion).

15. *Kinsella v. United States,* ex rel. Singleton, 361 U.S. 234 (1960).

16. See a discussion of this issue in James B. Jacobs, *Socio-Legal Foundations of Civil-Military Relations* (Transaction Publishers, 1986), 12–13.

17. William T. Generous, Jr., *Swords and Scales* (1973), see generally pp. 187–89.

18. George S. Prugh and William C. Westmoreland, Judges in Command: The Judicialized Code of Military Conduct in Combat, *Harvard Journal Law & Pub. Policy* (1980). For an excellent and comprehensive treatment of military operations in Vietnam, with a mainly Army focus, see Frederich L. Borch III, *Judge Advocates in Vietnam: Army Lawyers in Southeast Asia 1959–1985* (CGSC Press, 2003).

19. *United States v. Trottier,* 9 M.J. 337, at 340, 351 (C.M.A. 1980).

20. See *United States v. Thomas,* 22 M.J. 388 (C.M.A. 1986), *cert. denied,* 479 U.S. 1085 (1997).

21. This argument arose, among other times, during the Aberdeen Proving Ground sex scandal of 1996–1997, in which several Army officers and noncommissioned officers at that training installation were found to have had improper, often sexual, relationships with trainees. One of the issues concerned statements by the Army leadership, including the secretary of the Army, about zero tolerance for such behavior—and whether such statements constituted unlawful influence because of their potential impact on those involved in the justice process. Ultimately, none of those convicted obtained sentence relief based on claims of unlawful influence.

22. The commandments well precede the author's service as an Army judge advocate, but he did alter the eighth commandment when serving as the head of the criminal law department at that institution.

23. Military Rule of Evidence 513.

24. See Military Rule of Evidence 413, which permits the prosecution to introduce, in a sexual assault case, evidence of prior sexual offenses under some circumstances. Military Rule of Evidence 414 is a similar provision for child molestation cases. Both of these rules are nearly identical to their counterparts in the Federal Rules of Evidence.

25. One of the better works that sets out some criticisms and suggested reforms from a wide range of perspectives is *Evolving Military Justice* edited by Eugene R. Fidell and Dwight H. Sullivan (U.S. Naval Institute Press, 2002).

26. The former is certain, while the latter is a surmise, even though they were near contemporaries, Clemenceau having died in 1929, while Sousa died in 1932.

CHAPTER 8

There's More to Military Justice than Courts-Martial: Nonjudicial Punishment and Administrative Separations

> Nonjudicial punishment provides commanders with an essential and prompt means of maintaining good order and discipline and also promotes positive behavior changes in servicemembers without the stigma of a court-martial conviction.[1]

Nonjudicial Punishment

Although courts-martial are the mechanism most Americans associate with military justice, full-scale prosecutions are the least common encounters with the military justice system. Most military personnel are far more likely to face discipline in some other realm, most commonly nonjudicial punishment, than they ever would through courts-martial. Nonjudicial punishment, a disciplinary mechanism with no civilian equivalent, enables commanders swiftly to impose sanctions against soldiers for violations of the Uniform Code of Military Justice (UCMJ) in a manner that is far speedier—with less stigma but also less due process—than courts-martial. Since the turn of the 20th century, there had been a growing consensus, as discussed in chapter 2, that there were too many courts-martial and that there was a need for a mechanism to adjudicate minor misconduct in an efficient manner that reinforced a commander's authority, set an example to others, stung the soldier enough to serve as a deterrent—but did not end his career or sap his morale. Nonjudicial punishment (NJP) creates a record of discipline internal to the military—and for young soldiers a record that disappears after a time—that is not a federal conviction and does not follow the service member in any direct sense after she leaves the military.[2] NJP has become the bread and butter of military discipline, heavily employed in all of the services as a means of addressing minor offenses. In the Army, for example, there were about 2,000 courts-martial per year between 1996 and 2006, while there were more than 40,000 instances of nonjudicial punishment each year.[3] The authority to impose NJP comes from

Article 15 of the UCMJ; as a result, the punishment mechanism is referred to as Article 15 in the Army and Air Force (as in "he received an Article 15 for that offense"), while in the Navy and Coast Guard it is referred to as captain's mast or just mast, and the Marines commonly refer to it simply as NJP. Because it is such a commonly used mechanism, exercised almost every day in almost every military unit and vessel, it is important to understand its purpose, the range of punishments available, the procedures that govern NJP, and its consequences for recipients. Article 15 UCMJ is the statutory source of the mechanism, further explained in Part V of the Manual for Courts-Martial, and each service has a regulation that gives particular details, processing guidance, and punishment limitations.[4]

Why This Unique Mechanism: The Theory of Nonjudicial Punishment

Less Formal than a Court, More Formal than a Woodshed: NJP Filling a Disciplinary Gap

Chapter 1 addressed the fundamental principles on which the unique military justice system is based. Several of these principles—efficiency, command control, discipline, and justice, exercised in a Constitutional manner, implemented by Congress in the UCMJ—converge when evaluating the unique mechanism of nonjudicial punishment. The need for NJP is as old as the military services. Commanders want to accomplish multiple goals: enforce discipline in a manner that is swift but fair; brings immediate consequences but is rooted in justice; and strengthens command authority while enhancing, not undermining, the rank and file's respect for the process and the commander. Most military discipline is relatively informal—the corrections, admonitions, and corrective training that are addressed in chapter 1.

Both extremes are highly unsatisfactory. On one hand is a system that is so informal that it has no structure or predictability and is open to abuse, in that commanders can conduct discipline off the books in a manner that is potentially capricious, abusive, and open to prejudice, favoritism, and exploitation. On the other hand is a system that carries all of the formalities and protections of court-martial, meaning it has the greatest potential to ensure justice (on the assumption that more due process and more procedural protections generally equate to a greater potential for reliable results and appropriate sanctions), but it is time consuming and can deter commanders from using it at all, when they need to be both fair and swift; courts-martial can take too much time for minor offenses or can risk inappropriately severe sanctions for conduct that does not warrant a full trial. NJP seeks to fill the gap between those two poles by creating a rule-based mechanism that enables commanders swiftly to discipline soldiers according to a set of rules that ensures a likelihood of reliable results; administers sanctions that are significant enough to arrest the attention of the misbehaving or underperforming soldier but does not crush the soldier, destroy her career, or carry such cumbersome procedural and review requirements that the commander is deterred by a leaden process from even pursuing it.

Minor Offenses

Article 15 applies to minor offenses. Congress did not further define the term, and the UCMJ does not elsewhere use the term in a manner that helps understand the phrase in Article 15.[5] The clear intent, drawn from the congressional hearings and staff reports that preceded the 1962 change to Article 15, was to provide a mechanism in which less serious offenses were adjudicated without the need for court-martial. The Manual for Courts-Martial (a document promulgated by the president that helps put flesh on the UCMJ, which is a federal statute) explains that it is ordinarily an offense for which the maximum punishment at court-martial would be no more than a year's confinement, but further provides that it depends on several factors, including the nature and circumstances of the offense and the duties, experience, and seniority of the soldier.[6] In practice, disputes are rare regarding what constitutes a minor offense, because the soldier receiving the NJP is not likely to insist that it is not minor when the alternative would be trying it at court-martial rather than at NJP, where the sanction and consequences are lower.

It does highlight, however, that any charge brought under Article 15 must be *an* offense—that is, Article 15 is only for violations of the Uniform Code of Military Justice. When a soldier receives the document notifying him that he is facing nonjudicial punishment, the violation is stated the same way that a charge is stated for violation of the UCMJ before a court-martial.

Commanders most commonly use NJP for military offenses such as being late for work (failure to repair to a place of duty), minor disrespect, short unauthorized absences, and minor derelictions such as sleeping on guard duty by a young soldier in a training environment. It is often used for minor drug offenses (use of drugs such as marijuana, frequently detected in urinalysis, or possession of small amounts of lesser drugs), but practices and customs vary among the services and are affected by other variables such as the location of the offense (for example, whether it occurred on a deployment) and the rank of the offender. NJP is also commonly used for drunk driving and relatively minor civilian offenses.

Correction and Deterrence

For most individuals in most circumstances, the intent of Article 15 is to correct a soldier—sting her with loss of pay, rank, or liberty, and then put her back to work. While Article 15 is literally (nonjudicial) punishment, it is by its nature—relatively summary, relatively swift, and without the power to discharge a soldier—a mechanism that vouches for the potential of its recipient to continue to perform military service. The purpose is to tailor a sanction to the offense and to the soldier's rank, maturity, and level of development.

While NJP generally is designed to correct and punish the soldier who receives the nonjudicial punishment, it also has the collateral impact of deterring those who might contemplate similar misconduct.[7] As discussed below, nonjudicial punishment hearings may be open to the public—which realistically means open to other members of the unit. Such openness serves two purposes. First, it serves the purpose of integrity, similar to the Sixth Amendment's requirement that criminal trials be open to the public: assuring the reliability of the process by exposing it to public scrutiny. The unit gets to see how the commander weighs evidence and makes quasi-judicial decisions. Second, it enables others to see what happens to those who violate the law, and, ideally, it discourages them from engaging in similar misconduct. This deterrent function is further effected by provisions in service regulations that permit commanders to publicize the results of NJP proceedings. This can be done publicly at unit formations and by posting the results of NJP. This should be accomplished in a manner that protects the privacy of the individual who received the NJP—for example, by masking the name of the person when posting the copy of the NJP proceeding and by not using the name when making the announcement to the unit, because it is the conduct not the transgressor that is important in deterring future violations. In practice, there is often minimal anonymity in such circumstances (intraunit communications are their own phenomenon), but the intent of this publicity is to let others know of the offense and to encourage them to calculate the sanction in determining whether they might be so inclined to similar misconduct. A confident and just commander seeks the opportunity to publicize the results of NJP to reinforce his practice or belief that he is accountable and fair, in the conviction that such transparency will gain the loyalty and respect of his subordinates, not merely their fear.

Commanders generally take seriously the corrective function of Article 15, but it is also not uncommon to administer nonjudicial punishment as a step toward "building paper" on a soldier, with the intent of administrative separation (see discussion later in this chapter) or court-martial. In that vein, senior leaders are attuned to such a practice and may evaluate a sudden spate of NJP skeptically—sometimes it reflects a "quitter" or a service member's incorrigibility, but sometimes it can reflect her leaders' determination to construct a case for her discharge. In addition, commanders who rely heavily on NJP might be leaders who run a particularly tight ship, or they may be leaders who are seen to be too quick to rely on formal disciplinary measures when less formal methods and more intensive leadership would be called for.

Speed and Efficiency

Efficiency is one of the key purposes that Congress had in mind when it debated creating this provision several times over the years. It is not speed at all costs, however. Commanders concurred that there was a need to address minor offenses in a way that was not too hard and not too soft. Although NJP dates in one form or another to the late 19th century, the current version only was put in place in 1962, when Congress amended the UCMJ to restructure this unique disciplinary mechanism with the intent of encouraging its use, especially as an alternative to courts-martial (see discussion in chapter 6). Commanders found that they were sending too many cases to courts-martial in general and to summary courts-martial in particular, and that summary courts-martial were relatively inefficient mechanisms—consumers of time and resources—to address offenses that commanders considered truly minor and for which speed was more important than the weight of the sanction. Leaders were willing to trade a lower level of potential punishment for speed—and gaining the consequently lesser due process for the soldier because the stakes of the proceeding were lower. Speed—ideally efficiency but not haste—is a key factor for most commanders when they make decisions about discipline, especially discipline that is designed more to correct misconduct than it is to bring someone to justice through the court-martial process. Most believe that the closer in time the adjudication and sanction are to the offense, the greater chance of success—both in grabbing the attention of the soldier and in deterring others who come to know of the conduct and the timely sanction. Under Article 15, there is no necessary delay other than the reasonable period that a soldier is given to consult counsel or review information the government gives him between notification and adjudication.

Inherent Authority

The mechanism of Article 15 is another illustration of the concept of a commander's inherent authority to discipline her troops. While this authority is never unlimited, the grant of such authority to a commander reflects the military's expectation that she have the tools available to accomplish her mission—and the essential tool is soldiers who respond to orders, a responsiveness that is rooted in discipline.

Individualized Treatment

As with all other dispositions decisions, the decision of whether to offer nonjudicial punishment and what punishment to adjudge must be made based on the individual offered the NJP and all of the circumstances of the offense. Commanders sometimes—and often in good faith—are inclined to follow punishment templates, but these are improper because they undermine the emphasis on individual justice and can carry implications of command influence by setting out particular offenses for command emphasis. For example, an air base commander who published guidelines for punishment of noncommissioned officers and commissioned officers facing NJP for drinking and driving was apparently motivated by a desire to put possible offenders on notice about the consequences of such potential misconduct—and thereby to deter it. From the standpoint of military justice, however, it deprived commanders of their authority to treat each case individually and, the Court of Appeals for the Armed Forces found, could imply an interest in severity of punishment for such offenses if they reached court-martial panels.[8]

Implementing Justice: The Practice of Nonjudicial Punishment

Levels of Nonjudicial Punishment

There are two types of nonjudicial punishment: formal and summary. Within formal NJP, there are two levels: company grade and field grade. The differences

There's More to Military Justice than Courts-Martial

among them relate mainly to the level of punishment available and the collateral consequences to those on whom NJP is imposed.

- *Summarized Article 15.* Under this mechanism, the details of which vary among the services and which is generally available only for junior enlisted soldiers, the maximum punishment is 14 days' extra duty and restriction (no correctional custody, no forfeitures of pay), and the soldier does not have the right to consult counsel or demand trial by court-martial. Summarized NJP was introduced in the 1980s in response to commanders' concerns that traditional NJP was becoming too cumbersome and that they needed a mechanism that provided a swift taste of discipline—hence the minimal due process and the relatively mild sanctions that are available.
- *Formal Article 15.* Most instances of NJP are formal, in that the soldier receives notice of the NJP, can consult counsel and demand trial by court-martial, and the available punishments depend on the soldier's and the imposing commander's rank. It is easiest to understand NJP by reference to levels of imposition authority: company grade and field grade.
  - NJP can first be imposed at the level of company or equivalent command. In the Army, a company is a unit of about 150 soldiers (the number can vary widely, depending on its mission), led by a captain or O-3. It is the lowest level of command, as platoon leaders (normally lieutenants in the Army, Air Force, and Marines, ensigns in the Navy) have leadership responsibilities and can give orders but generally do not formally have the authority and responsibility of command.
  - Field-grade officers are usually those in the rank of O-4 and above (major in all services but the Navy, in which they are lieutenant commanders). Because of their greater span of responsibility, they can impose greater punishment under Article 15. Most field-grade NJP is imposed by battalion commanders or equivalents, who usually hold the O-5 rank (lieutenant colonel in the Army and Air Force, commander in the Navy), and usually but not always are also summary court-martial convening authorities.
  - Commanding generals have wider authority under Article 15, but this mainly relates to their authority to impose NJP on officers. It is common but not required for commanding generals to withhold to themselves the authority to impose NJP on officers and on senior enlisted personnel, typically those of the top two or three enlisted ranks.[9]

Due Process

As discussed often in this text, the U.S. military justice system is committed to both discipline and justice. Therefore, nonjudicial punishment, though relatively summary and relatively efficient, must be justice based. It is especially true for this mechanism, because it is the ubiquitous justice mechanism in all of the services. If soldiers did not regard the system as fundamentally fair, it would corrode rather than reinforce justice. Over the years, the due process available at NJP has been refined, but these fundamentals remain:

- *Charges and evidence in advance.* A soldier is served with a copy of the NJP and given time to evaluate it and to make his decisions regarding whether to accept NJP, how to plead, and how to present his case. Presentation of charges normally consists of a commander or her designee, commonly the senior noncommissioned offers in the unit, presenting the soldier with a document that spells out the charge and also details his rights. The respondent should also receive the supporting paperwork, such as police report of investigation, sworn statements, or urinalysis test results so that his consultation with counsel, if he chooses to exercise that right, is meaningful.

- *Time to think.* The accused normally is given a few days in which to consult counsel and make her decisions regarding acceptance of NJP, her plea, and strategy. The amount of time varies according to service regulation, but is typically about 72 hours, a time period that has some flexibility in practice, depending on where the soldier is located and, when applicable, availability of defense counsel.
- *Availability of counsel.* A soldier facing NJP has the right to consult counsel except in rare circumstances. (As mentioned above, soldiers facing summarized proceedings do not have the right to consult counsel.) Soldiers have the right to consult independent military defense counsel provided free of charge by the military services (for details on independent military counsel, see chapter 7). The counsel are available to analyze the evidence and provide advice to the soldier. Ordinarily the defense counsel will review the evidence available to the soldier, advise him about the strength of the command's case, and talk him through all of his options—his procedural rights, including the right to demand trial by court-martial, and his plan for the NJP proceeding, should he decide to continue with the NJP process. The lawyer also will advise her client on how to present his case or make his best arguments for extenuation and mitigation, should the soldier plead guilty or be found guilty. The soldier does not have the right to the presence of counsel at the proceeding. He does have the rights to a spokesperson (discussed below). Occasionally, a military defense counsel will appear with a soldier at NJP. This is more common when officers face NJP, because the stakes for officers are higher (see discussion of collateral consequences below), but defense counsel generally are discouraged from representing soldiers in person at NJP because of the high volume of NJP, the extent to which it can take them from other duties, and the risk of unequal treatment by representing some soldiers but not others. A soldier may hire a civilian counsel to advise her, at no cost to the government, but the command need not delay the normal processing of NJP to accommodate a soldier's desire to consult civilian counsel or have a civilian appear as her spokesperson (discussed later in this chapter).
- *Right to object to NJP and demand court-martial.* Except in rare circumstances, a soldier need not accept NJP—he has an almost absolute right to reject NJP and to demand trial by court-martial. The only exception to this rule is for sailors embarked on or attached to a vessel; they have no such right to counsel, though the command may provide it anyway and often does. After a couple of well-publicized instances of abuse of this exception, the Navy has been especially vigilant to guard against its abuse. Of course, if a service member demands court-martial, the potential consequences are higher—greater punishment, federal conviction, and the possibility of a punitive discharge. The right to demand trial, however, is designed to protect the service member against unlawful command influence and to provide an option if, for whatever reason, the service member believes that the commander offering NJP would be prejudiced or unfair. The question of whether to accept NJP is a major reason that soldiers have the right to consult independent defense counsel before making the decision. While the consequences of court-martial obviously are greater, in some circumstances soldiers are willing to bear that risk because of their belief that they will not receive fair treatment at the NJP proceeding.

There's More to Military Justice than Courts-Martial

In practice, the vast majority of soldiers offered NJP decide to accept this mechanism, but a small percentage regularly reject it. When commanders are faced with a soldier who has turned down NJP, they ordinarily reanalyze the case in consultation with their prosecutor and sometimes after hearing an informal presentation from a defense counsel. Should a soldier turn down NJP, the command need not go forward with court-martial at all—the right to demand trial by court-martial does not guarantee that a court-martial will be held, it only guarantees that NJP will not be imposed. The command will choose from an array of options, including proceeding with court-martial for the charged offense, altering the offense charged, adding or deleting offenses, or conducting additional investigation. Sometimes commanders will pursue administrative sanctions, and sometimes commanders will conclude, after further analysis, that the soldier is not guilty of the offense or that trying the offense will unduly consume time and resources and will drop the charges altogether. It is possible that the command will reinvestigate the soldier's conduct and add charges before sending the case to court-martial. It should also be clear that the demand for court-martial does not bind the government only to offer her the lowest level of court-martial, summary court-martial, or to court-martial her only for the offenses that appeared on the NJP that she turned down. It is possible that the government will refer the case to a higher level of court-martial, but such a decision will draw significant scrutiny from defense counsel and military judges, because the government cannot—and cannot be seen to—punish an accused for his exercise of the right to turn down NJP and demand trial. In the absence of additional charges, it is most likely and generally most fair to first offer summary court-martial.

The decision on whether to accept NJP must be made before proceedings get underway. When the soldier returns to the commander after having deliberated on her choices—and had the opportunity to consult counsel, if it is not summarized NJP—she must make her election on whether to demand court-martial before the hearing begins. She may not begin the hearing—and certainly may not wait until a commander's decision on whether she has committed the offense or a decision on punishment—before making the decision. Conversely, once a decision is made to demand trial by court-martial, the command is under no obligation to permit the soldier to change that decision and revert to NJP; again, however, it is not uncommon in practice for a commander to permit a soldier to change his mind and return to NJP, especially if it seems the decision was hasty, emotional, or the result of poor advice from nonlawyer fellow soldiers. In permitting a soldier to make this decision, however, commanders must be careful to ensure that the soldier does not feel he is subject to command pressure to change his mind.

Burden of proof varies according to military service. Article 15 does not stipulate a burden of proof, so it can be set by the individual services. Traditionally, the Navy has set the standard at preponderance of the evidence, a standard used for many administrative proceedings and for some pretrial motions at courts-martial—commonly the burden of proof at administrative proceedings. The Army sets it at proof beyond a reasonable doubt, the highest burden of proof and that associated with criminal trials (because Article 15 does not stipulate a burden of proof and because NJP is not governed by the rules governing criminal trials, the burden of proof is up to individual services). The Navy's reasoning is that NJP's relative informality and relatively low level of sanction (as discussed above, it does not result in a criminal record, and its sanctions—loss of pay, status, and liberty—are internal to the military) do not warrant a higher burden of proof. The Army's reasoning is that the consequences of NJP to soldiers' careers can still be significant, and, more practically, every soldier has the right to turn down Article 15—at which point trial by court-martial is the next step and at which level proof beyond a reasonable doubt will be required; therefore, if that burden cannot be met at NJP, then a soldier will be more inclined to demand trial by court-martial at the outset, where the government would be unable to meet its burden.

The Military Rules of Evidence, which govern courts-martial, do not apply at NJP; the information presented only must be "relevant." Sometimes this complicates the analysis for an accused soldier and her counsel, because evidence that might be inadmissible at trial (e.g., some forms of hearsay) or difficult to obtain (testimony of reluctant, compromised, or difficult-to-locate witnesses) may be admissible at NJP because of its looser evidentiary strictures. Privileges still apply, which means that husband-wife, physician-patient, and clergy-penitent privileges, which apply to courts-martial, also apply at NJP.

The Hearing

The soldier has the right to attend his NJP hearing. He may waive this presence—a rarity—but otherwise must be permitted to attend. The soldier then has the right to speak at his own hearing.[10]

Acceptance of NJP does not mean acknowledgement of guilt. A soldier must make the threshold decision whether to go through the NJP process or whether to demand trial by court-martial. Choosing to go forward with NJP only means electing to continue with this adjudicative mechanism; it does not mean that she believes she is guilty or plans to plead guilty.

The soldier facing NJP has the right, except at summarized proceedings, to have a spokesperson present at the hearing. The spokesperson is not his advocate in the same sense that an attorney would be at trial, and certainly is not his counselor in the sense that only a defense lawyer can be; moreover, the soldier does not have the right to the presence of an attorney at NJP proceedings. The spokesperson's main role is to speak for the soldier before the command—she does not represent him, but she does assist in making his case. The commander imposing NJP need not permit the spokesperson to question witnesses, but this is a matter of discretion, and it is not uncommon to permit it. In practice, commanders try to accommodate the spokesperson in the interests of fairness and the appearance of fairness, but will constrict the role if the spokesperson turns the session into an unduly adversarial or protracted proceeding.

The accused may choose anyone as spokesperson, but no one may be obliged to serve in that role. The command should try to accommodate a soldier's choice of spokesperson, but it need not hold up the proceeding for the spokesperson and has no obligation to provide or pay for travel expenses. Although use of a spokesperson is not rare, it is not the norm in most of the thousands of instances of NJP administered in the services each year. Most soldiers find that presenting their cases directly is more effective, and the practice of directly and respectfully presenting their own cases—denying with firmness or taking responsibility while offering an explanation or extenuation—is more effective than using a spokesperson. Still, the soldier who is inarticulate, intimidated, or feels that he has little credibility with the command may choose to employ a spokesperson, and the command should accommodate him within the governing regulations.

A soldier must be advised of his Article 31 rights against self-incrimination when appearing at NJP. This is one of the settings for which the unique protections of Article 31—the provision that soldiers must be advised that they need not answer questions of superiors when the response might incriminate them (see chapter 4)—were designed. A soldier need not speak at NJP, nor must she present a case at all. In these regards, it is like a court-martial—the government solely bears the burden of proof.

In a typical proceeding, each military service has a script or NJP procedural guide that commanders generally follow to ensure that NJP proceedings run in an orderly manner, but its use is not required, and deviation from it does not necessarily invalidate or call into question the proceeding. It is only important that the hearing be conducted in a manner that establishes that the soldier was made aware of his rights and protections and that the proceedings were conducted fairly. The procedural matters include ensuring that the soldier does not demand trial by court-martial, re-advising her of her Article 31 right to silence, the right to present evidence, and the right to a spokesperson. Then the commander typically summarizes the evidence against the soldier, sometimes calling witnesses or referring the soldier to evidence—most often sworn statements and perhaps police or lab reports—that she has previously been provided. Then the soldier presents whatever evidence or witnesses she chooses and makes any statements she chooses. This can be accomplished alone, by the spokesperson, or in combination. An NJP proceeding is not bifurcated the way that a court-martial is neatly divided into a merits and sentencing phase, so evidence in extenuation and mitigation should be presented at the same time that the soldier contests the charge. A commander might close the proceedings to deliberate or proceed directly to findings and, if applicable, to punishment.

Often the commander has the senior noncommissioned officer present as an informal advisor, and often the members of the soldier's chain of command (his immediate supervisors) are present, but again neither is required. The common practice of requiring presence of the chain of command accomplishes multiple purposes: It emphasizes that the accused is still their soldier; reminds the soldier that the chain still is concerned about him (by choosing this mechanism, the command generally is vouching for the soldier's continued value to the military); and, to the extent that the soldier's conduct suggests poor leadership or accountability by his leaders, their presence can be uncomfortable or corrective in a way that the commander imposing NJP might find useful.

If the commander decides that the soldier did not commit the offense (the term *guilt* is not used at NJP, because it is not a court-martial, even though informally it is common to hear reference to having been found guilty at NJP), then she lines through the NJP form and the proceeding is over. If the commander imposes punishment, then she lines out any charges that she finds the soldier did not commit, annotates the form for punishment, and advises the soldier of his right to appeal (the commander's option includes finding that the soldier committed the offense—that is, imposing punishment under Article 15—and then imposing no punishment). The soldier then signs the document to acknowledge that he has received the punishment. He can make his decision regarding appeal at this point or after a couple of days' reflection.

Available Punishments

Generally, the sanctions available under NJP concern loss of military status and privileges—liberty, pay, and rank. The available punishments vary according to the type of NJP, the rank of the imposing commander, and the rank of the individual subject to NJP.

Admonition or Reprimand

These are censures that formally communicate to a soldier the command's and the military's displeasure with and disapproval of the misconduct. They carry no further sanction than the words themselves but are considered to be punishment. It is common for commanders to issue reprimands as part of punishment for officers, and sometimes for senior noncommissioned officers, but it is much less common for enlisted personnel. Reprimands can be oral or written or both. If a written reprimand is made part of the NJP punishment and the command decides to make the NJP part of the soldier's permanent record, the soldier has no opportunity to reply to the reprimand—unlike other reprimands, for which a soldier has a right to a written reply when the commander considers making it part of her permanent record. The difference is that a reprimand under NJP was preceded by due process—the opportunity to contest the government's case and to present a defense—while the administrative reprimand is the soldier's first notice of the government's intent to impose a sanction, and therefore a soldier must have a right to respond in writing before a decision is made whether to file it in her permanent file.

Deprivations of Liberty

There are several ways in which a soldier's liberty can be taken away or limited by NJP. This reflects the value that U.S. society places on liberty and the special place that liberty has in the life of military personnel, especially junior soldiers, who crave the freedom that their off-duty time promises. There are several ways in which liberty can be limited.

- *Restriction* is perhaps the most common sanction at NJP. The imposing commander sets the terms of the restriction—typically to specific limits on an installation. Ordinarily, soldiers placed on restriction continue to perform their routine military duties. The toughest restrictions are to place of duty, worship, mess hall, and perhaps gym. Less restrictive terms might include freedom to go anywhere on a military installation but no farther (commanders always retain authority to revoke pass privileges, which essentially restricts the soldier to the installation, but this authority may be exercised independent of NJP because, standing alone, it is an administrative and not a punitive measure). While restriction is a popular and effective sanction in a garrison or peacetime environment, it is not necessary or especially punitive in operational or deployed environments, where there often is little or no true liberty in the sense of freedom to go where one chooses. Restriction is characterized as a moral rather than a physical restraint, meaning that it is not enforced through confinement or constant monitoring of the restricted soldier, though he may be required to sign in from time to time or otherwise to comply with mechanisms designed to enforce accountability.
- *Arrest in quarters* is a rarely used sanction, available only for officers. It is similar to restriction in that it is a moral restraint, not usually enforced by the presence of military police or other enforcement. At its most severe, it literally restricts an officer to her military quarters—which could include a tent in an operational environment—severely limiting any nonduty activities.[11]
- At one time a popular mechanism, *correctional custody* is generally available only for junior enlisted personnel. It is not confinement in the same sense that soldiers are confined after courts-martial, a distinction reinforced by the requirement that soldiers serving correctional custody must be kept separate from those serving sentences to courts-martial. The emphasis of correctional custody is on the adjective—it is designed to correct, because all soldiers in corrective custody must return to duty (NJP cannot discharge a soldier). Many commanders find it effective to give a taste of jail to junior soldiers who show promise and only need to be jolted back to a path of effective service and compliance. The decline in the availability of military confinement facilities in recent years has contributed to this punishment becoming less widespread than it once was.

Extra Duty

Along with restriction, extra duty is the most widely used mechanism at NJP. Extra duty is the requirement that a soldier perform additional tasks to those he accomplishes during his ordinary duties. Typically this means a few hours' work at the end of the duty day, sometimes also on weekends, designed to fatigue the soldier and to prompt the reflection that, it is hoped, makes him aware of the consequences of his actions and deters him—as well as fellow soldiers who see him perform these duties—from further misconduct. Commanders must be careful not to assign hazardous duties, cruel and unusual punishments, or duties that would be demeaning to the rank of the person serving the punishment (this is especially pertinent with senior noncommissioned officers). This punishment may not be imposed on officers.

Loss of Pay

Loss of pay is another common sanction. It is also common for commanders to require the forfeiture of some pay but to suspend all or part of the forfeitures. This has two main purposes: It provides a powerful incentive for soldiers to conform their conduct and to regain the suspended forfeitures, and it acknowledges the potentially counterproductive impact of the forfeitures, especially for junior personnel with families and other financial obligations. Until the mid-1980s, a commander could detain a soldier's pay for a period of time, returning it to her at a later point. A consensus emerged that adjudging and suspending forfeitures might accomplish the intent of encouraging reform and improved behavior, whereas detention had no such motivational impact but still carried the potential costs of causing or aggravating a soldier's financial difficulties.

Reduction in Rank

Enlisted soldiers may lose rank at NJP, depending on the level of NJP and the rank of the soldier; officers may not be reduced in rank at NJP. The loss of rank is a powerful disincentive to misbehavior and a common sanction. Rank represents military achievement and authority, and soldiers are proud of their achievements and the status—as well as the pay and privileges—that accompany rank. Rank is hard to earn, and harder to re-earn after being busted. As with financial punishments, the imposing commander can impose the reduction and suspend it for a period of time, a common practice.

No Templates

Every commander imposing punishment under Article 15 is expected to make a judgment specific to that soldier and that offense. Commanders are forbidden from having guides, cheat sheets, or directives that they consult or follow in determining the punishment to adjudge. Senior commanders also may not publish such guides for junior commanders to employ.[12] This is a reinforcement of one of the core principles of military justice—individualized justice. Even though many offenses are similar and common (e.g., drunk driving, unauthorized absences), the system emphasizes that each soldier has a unique military record, unique background, burdens, and expectations, and the commander is obliged to make individual judgments.[13] Military courts, when deciding whether instances of NJP are admissible during the sentencing phases of courts-martial, have disallowed the admissibility of NJP that is found to have been imposed based on such templates. On the other hand, there is an expected level of predictability in commanders' approaches to the most common offenses—a predictability that should not translate as a guarantee or sure expectation for the soldier deciding whether to demand trial by court-martial, but a general pattern on which he and his counsel can rely in analyzing his prospects and likely outcomes and which service members see as reflective of a broad consistency and fairness on the part of their leaders.

Available Punishments for Enlisted Personnel at Company-Grade NJP

These are punishments that any commander down to the first level of command, most commonly a captain in the Army, Air Force, or Marines or a Navy lieutenant, may impose.

- *Deprivation of liberty.* Correctional custody for a maximum of seven days. This measure is not considered to be confinement, even though soldiers in correctional custody are held in confinement facilities or in separate spaces that they are not free to leave (sometimes in the same military confinement facilities as military prisoners who have been court-martialed but in different wings where they are not commingled and where their duties and supervision are different). Generally, only soldiers in the pay grade of E-3 or below may receive correctional custody, but that is a matter of service-specific regulation that can change.
- *Loss of pay.* Forfeiture of a maximum of seven days' pay.
- *Extra duty.* A soldier can be required to perform extra or "fatigue" duties for a maximum of 14 days. Typically these are maintenance duties or other arduous work (grass cutting, painting) that is performed after the duty day as a way of reinforcing the diminished prestige and loss of freedom that accompany such a minor violation.
- *Restriction.* For not more than 14 days.
- *Reduction in rank.* Reduction of a maximum of one pay grade, but only if promotion to that pay grade is within the authority of the commander who is imposing the NJP.
- *Admonition or reprimand.*

Available Punishments for Enlisted Personnel at Field-Grade NJP

These are punishments that may be imposed by any commander of the rank of major or, in the Navy, lieutenant commander, and above.

- *Deprivation of liberty.* Correctional custody for not more than 30 days for those eligible, generally pay grade E-3 or below. Restriction for a maximum of 60 days (but a maximum of 45 if combined with extra duty). It is up to the imposing commander whether to permit soldiers to fulfill their regular duties during the period of restriction.
- *Loss of pay.* Forfeiture of a maximum of one-half month's pay per month for two months.
- *Reduction in rank.* Generally one pay grade for E-5 or E-6 and below (the services vary), but service members in the grades E-4 and below can be reduced all the way to E-1.
- *Extra duty.* A soldier can be required to perform extra or "fatigue" duties for a maximum of 45 days. Typically these are maintenance duties or other arduous work (grass cutting, painting) that is performed after the duty day as a way of reinforcing the loss of prestige and freedom that accompanies such a minor violation.
- *Admonition or reprimand.*

Available Punishments for Officers at NJP that May Be Imposed by Any Superior Officer

- *Deprivation of liberty.* Officers may be restricted to specified limits for a maximum of 30 days. It is up to the imposing commander whether to permit them to fulfill their regular duties during the period of restriction.
- *Admonition or reprimand.*

Available Punishments for Officers at NJP that May Be Imposed by a General Officer or an Officer Exercising General Court-Martial Convening Authority

- *Deprivation of liberty.* Arrest in quarters for a maximum of 30 days. Officers may be restricted to specified limits for a maximum of 60 days. It is up to the imposing commander whether to permit them to fulfill their regular duties during the period of restriction.
- *Loss of pay.* Forfeiture of a maximum of one-half month's pay for two consecutive months.
- *Reduction in rank.* Officers may not be reduced in rank at NJP.

Combinations

Commanders often will combine several punishments at Article 15. Restriction and extra duty are popular punishments, especially for junior soldiers. While reduction in rank and forfeiture of pay also are common, commanders are especially careful about imposing such punishments, especially when soldiers have families, because they do not want to create additional problems—debt, for example, but also family stress and the problems that debt can cause military leaders—when addressing a different problem. It is common for commanders to suspend all or part of a forfeiture or reduction, meaning that it is not triggered unless a soldier commits an additional violation.

Suspending Punishment

Commanders may suspend almost all punishments under NJP, and frequently do so. The Manual for Courts-Martial encourages this practice:

> Commanders should consider suspending all or part of any punishment selected under Article 15, particularly in the case of first offenders or when significant extenuating or mitigating factors are present, . . . as an incentive to the offender and to give an opportunity to the commander to evaluate the offender during the period of suspension.[14]

This is another example of the tremendous discretion that commanders have in the military justice system, the amount of trust and authority placed in commanders, and the twin purposes of NJP: to punish and to provide a service member the opportunity to reform. Commanders may suspend all or part of a punishment for up to six months. It is common for commanders to impose two month's forfeitures but to suspend the second month's forfeitures or to suspend all or part of restriction or a reduction in rank. The condition on all suspensions, regardless of whether stated explicitly, is that the soldier not violate the UCMJ. A commander may place other conditions on suspensions, such as attending counseling or ceasing contact with a victim. Such conditions are intended to help the service member to overcome the factors that contributed to the offense and to provide incentives for reform and productive service. A commander may suspend the punishment at the time of imposing punishment under NJP (the most common practice), but may also choose to suspend the punishment any time up to four months after punishment is imposed—though only for portions of the punishment that remain unexecuted.

Vacating Suspended Punishments

If a commander believes that a soldier has violated the terms of the suspension—typically meaning she has again violated the UCMJ—then the commander has authority to vacate that suspension, meaning the rest of the original punishment will be imposed. Ordinarily, the commander must hold an additional hearing at which he determines whether the soldier violated the terms of the suspension; at a minimum, the soldier must be given the opportunity to present her case. Besides imposing the rest of the original punishment, the commander also may impose NJP—or court-martial, depending on the severity of the new offense—for the new offense.

Reducing Punishment

Just as the commander has authority to suspend punishments, he has the authority to reduce or eliminate punishments that have not been executed—to mitigate or remit them, in military language. This a less common practice, but commanders may choose to do so when a soldier shows extraordinary determination after imposition of NJP or has shown valor or otherwise distinguished herself. Commanders may also mitigate or remit unexecuted punishments if they determine that the punishment imposed was disproportionate for the offense or in light of the sanctions that other personnel involved in the offense may have received. There are various rules on how punishments may be reduced or converted to other punishments, but the availability of such postproceeding flexibility reflects the virtually unreviewable discretion of the commander on matters of discipline.

Appeals and Clemency after NJP

A commander's determination that a soldier committed an offense and his imposition of NJP does not necessarily end the matter. Again, the command's interest in discipline and efficiency is balanced against the system's need for due process sufficient to ensure that justice is fairly administered and that the result is one in which the system, society, the affected soldier, and those who know of her punishment, can have confidence. Accordingly, a soldier has a right to appeal Article 15, though on very narrow grounds, and the commander and his supervisor have plenary authority to exercise clemency—reduce the sanction—even if they believe the soldier committed the offense. Recall, as discussed earlier, they also had the authority to suspend the punishment at the time they imposed it.

Immediately after a commander imposes punishment under NJP, she returns the NJP form to the soldier, and explains that he has a right to appeal. The soldier may make his decision at that time, but he normally has five days in which to decide whether to appeal. The grounds for appeal are much narrower than they are at court-martial, where nearly any grounds are available, and where in fact they are broader than in most civilian courts (see chapter 6, discussing the fact that soldiers may appeal their courts-martial convictions on grounds of factual insufficiency as well as legal error). The only grounds for NJP appeals, however, are that the punishment is unjust or disproportionate to the offense. The soldier may not appeal on the grounds that he did not commit the offense—that is, that he is not guilty.

The soldier must submit her written appeal, explaining why the punishment is unjust or disproportionate, within five days of receiving punishment under Article 15. Although the soldier cannot directly contest the findings that she committed the offense, she can do so indirectly, by asserting that the punishment is unjust because, in effect, the original finding was erroneous. In practice, the most effective appeals are those that assert that the punishment is disproportionate either because of bias by the imposing commander or a marked and unexplainable disparity between the punishment the appealing soldier received and that received by confederates or similarly situated soldiers for the same or similar offenses.

The appeal goes to the commander who is immediately superior to the one who imposed punishment under Article 15. Before a commander acts on the appeal, he should receive a legal review from a judge advocate who acts as his legal advisor. The judge advocate may go beyond the material in the written appeal in analyzing the case and making her recommendation to the appellate authority. The commander who imposed NJP also may be asked to explain his reasoning. The superior authority may affirm the NJP or take any action she chooses regarding the findings or punishment, as long as she does not make them more severe. She may suspend, reduce, remit, or combine punishments in any of the manners that were available to the commander who imposed punishment under Article 15. The superior authority is not required to explain the reasons for any of her actions, including an action that leaves the NJP unchanged, but she must personally make the decision and personally sign the NJP record.

Even if the superior authority sets aside the NJP, he may authorize a new proceeding under Article 15. For example, he may choose to set aside the NJP on the grounds that the soldier did not receive a fair hearing or other concerns regarding fairness of the proceeding. He may then authorize a new proceeding under Article 15—but the sanction in any subsequent proceeding would be capped at the punishment actually imposed at the prior proceeding.

Starting the NJP appellate process does not mean that the soldier is absolved from serving the imposed punishment. As mentioned, most punishments take effect immediately, so the soldier should continue to serve her punishments while the appeal is pending. As an incentive for the command to act on appeals in a timely manner, however, if an appeal is not acted on within five days and if the soldier makes such a request, then she may be relieved of serving any part of the punishment involving deprivations of liberty or extra duty until the command acts on the appeal.

Final Observations

Not a Conviction

No matter how severe the sanction under NJP, it cannot follow a soldier out of the military. It is intended to be for internal military use only and is in no sense a federal conviction. A soldier need not disclose it when asked about his military record when seeking employment or security clearances. As discussed above, this is often the factor that tips a soldier toward accepting adjudication under Article 15, rather than taking the risk of contesting the Article 15—and ending up with a federal conviction.

Not "Guilty"

Because NJP is not a court-martial and the decision to impose punishment is not a conviction, soldiers should not be referred to as having been found guilty at NJP. Strictly, this is inaccurate, though not uncommon in informal speech.

Collateral Consequences

While the record of NJP does not travel outside the military, the impact within the military can be considerable. When a commander determines that a soldier has violated the UCMJ and decides to impose punishment under NJP, she must then make a decision where to file the record of the proceeding. The services vary in their regulations governing this, but the essential decision is whether to make it part of the permanent record (Official Military Personnel File) or to file it locally, meaning that it is expunged from the soldier's file when he leaves an organization or within a certain maximum period of time, typically two years. In recent years, the services have modified the rules on filing determinations so that most first-time instances of NJP for junior enlisted personnel must be filed locally. This is designed to enforce the original theory of nonjudicial punishment—that it is an internal military disciplinary measure intended to both punish and reform; if a filing decision carried a permanent stigma, then the opportunity to reform could become only theoretical. In practice, it is not unusual for enlisted personnel to achieve senior rank despite an instance or two of NJP. It is much less likely for officers, a concern reflected throughout the history of NJP, and a recurring theme in analyses of NJP since the Powell Report. A commander's decision to file an instance of NJP in an officer's permanent record makes it highly unlikely that the officer will advance in rank and be able to make the military a career. In light of this widely shared perception, the focus of many officers' cases at their NJP hearings is an effort to avoid placing the NJP in their permanent files.

Popularity, Enduring Mechanism

The great majority of soldiers who receive nonjudicial punishment continue to serve honorably and do not face administrative separation or further direct consequences to their misconduct. The great number of instances of nonjudicial punishment in all services reflects commanders' general satisfaction with this measure—they vote with their operating practices and signify their general contentment with the balance that NJP provides between command authority, efficiency, correction, and justice.

Corrective Training, Admonition

It is important to remember that the U.S. military invests a considerable amount of money into each recruit who joins the all-volunteer force. The goal of the military is to provide a leadership structure in which each volunteer has the opportunity to succeed. In recognition of the fact that soldiers come from all educational and social backgrounds, the system is geared to train and mold them and to provide as many corrective opportunities as possible so that the investment in them pays off in the form of a productive member of the military. Employment of the formalities of military justice is considered a last resort. Consequently, the spectrum of military discipline consists of many nonpunitive steps and lightly punitive measures short of separation, before the system gets to the point of sending someone home or prosecuting her. This emphasis on leadership and correction recurs in regulations, leadership training, and even in the Manual for Courts-Martial. In the section on nonjudicial punishment, the Manual provides that, "Generally, discipline can be maintained through effective leadership, including, when necessary, administrative corrective measures."[15] It counsels that NJP is appropriate for minor offenses only "when administrative corrective measures are inadequate due to the nature of the minor offense or the record of the servicemember." Corrective training, admonition, and other nonpunitive (or prepunitive) measures are limited only by the creativity of a leader, regulations that require the corrective training be linked to the infraction, and the ordinary limits on abusive leadership, hazardous conditions, and resources.

| Counseling | Admonition | Reprimand | Administrative Separation | Nonjudicial Punishment | Court-Martial |

Company Grade / Field Grade — *Summary / Special / General*

Source: Illustration by Jude Morris.

Administrative Separations

Thousands of soldiers are discharged by the military each year, many with discharges for conduct ranging from incompetence to a pattern of minor misconduct, inability to adapt (trainee discharges), personality disorder, or homosexuality. All service members facing involuntary separation receive some level of due process that is tied to their length of service or to the type of discharge that the military seeks to impose for their conduct or condition. By far, more individuals leave the military through this process than through courts-martial.

Administrative separations are designed to release from the military those whose conduct or characteristics make them unfit for further service. In some instances, this is because of conduct, character, or performance shortcomings, but it can also be for status such as single parenthood or mental health difficulties.

Common grounds for administrative discharge include patterns of minor misconduct and displaying characteristics that are incompatible with military service but that do not constitute criminal conduct or do not warrant the time and resources required to move a case through the military justice system.

In all proceedings in which someone's livelihood is in jeopardy, some level of due process is required, because the respondent is said to have a property stake in the job and perhaps in avoiding or moderating the stigma that might attach to the fact of being involuntary separated from the military or the characterization of service that attaches to that separation. The extent of the due process generally depends on either or both of two factors: the length of time the person has served in the military and the type of discharge that the military seeks to impose.

Due Process—"Job Right" or "Stigma"

In most circumstances, if the military seeks to discharge a soldier with less than six years' service and does not seek to invoke an other than honorable discharge, the soldier only has the right to notification that the military seeks his discharge and the right to reply in writing, after consultation with counsel, petitioning either for retention or for a more favorable discharge. The available "good" discharges are an honorable discharge, which is issued to all soldiers who complete their terms of service, and a "general discharge under honorable conditions," still considered a "good" discharge in that the bearer is entitled to all significant veterans' benefits, even though the general discharge hints that the service was not optimal in all respects. An "other than honorable discharge," called an undesirable discharge in prior generations, deprives the member of most veterans' benefits[16] and is considered—and intended—to carry a stigma into the civilian world. This makes the characterization of discharge a significant matter for contention between advocates at separation hearings.

If the military seeks an other than honorable discharge, regardless of the respondent's length of service, or seeks to discharge a soldier with more than six years' service, regardless of the type of discharge sought, then that soldier is entitled to have her case heard by a board of three service members, typically two officers and a senior enlisted soldier, but these rules generally are set by the service secretaries and can vary. The soldier also has the right to be represented by military defense counsel at the hearing. The respondent has certain due process rights before the hearing commences, including the right to review all of the evidence the government intends to produce, notice of witnesses the government intends to call, and reasonable (though relatively short) time to prepare. He also has a right to request that witnesses be produced on his behalf, though the government need not produce out-of-town witnesses, and these are matters of discretion for the board president; telephonic or video teleconference testimony is permitted, unlike in courts-martial and most criminal trials. The procedures in this area are intended to strike a balance between the military's right to discharge soldiers it believes are not ready or fit to serve and a soldier's right to reasonably and effectively defend herself. It is a balance between the government's right to an efficient process that is truth-seeking but without the Constitutional rigor of a court-martial and the relative stigma attaching to the grounds for discharge and the nature of the discharge.

A soldier facing administrative separation may waive his right to a hearing before an administrative board or may waive the right to respond in writing. If he does so, however, he bears the risk of having the worst discharge available (of which he has received written notice) approved. In addition, most service members facing adverse administrative separation boards may waive the board hearing in exchange for a more favorable characterization of service—like courts-martial plea bargains, it is in the discretion of the separation authority (the administrative equivalent of the convening authority) to decide whether to accept such an offer, and, as with plea bargains, it is a balance of factors that determine whether it is wise and efficient.

Common Bases for Administrative Separation

Misconduct

The most common grounds asserted for administrative separations are misconduct and poor performance. Misconduct can be addressed under the UCMJ, and most administrative rules counsel against using the administrative process to avoid the UCMJ (see the discussion spurred by Air Force General Harmon and others in the late 1950s and early 1960s in chapter 7), but commanders frequently consider other factors in choosing to pursue the administrative route for discharge. These factors include the difficulty of proving a case beyond a reasonable doubt, evidentiary issues such as unlawful or questionable searches or interrogation practices that nonetheless yield reliable evidence, or the fact that the respondent may have committed many minor acts of misconduct but no one act that is significant enough to warrant the investment of resources that a court-martial requires, nor to warrant the stigma of a criminal conviction that would follow a soldier to civilian life. The discharges available under this provision are honorable and general and, if the respondent appears before a board, other than honorable. Another circumstance in which a service member can be discharged for misconduct is for a civilian conviction. Often this is essentially a housekeeping matter, because a service member convicted by a civilian court for a significant offense is simply unavailable for military duty. Those convicted of significant civilian offenses but perhaps on probation may also face separation under such provisions.

Unsatisfactory Performance

Discharges for poor performance are designed to separate individuals who are not guilty of criminal misconduct and may have no character shortcomings at all—but simply cannot perform their military duties adequately. A subset of this discharge are trainee discharges, available for those with very short periods of service (typically six months, though most of these rules are service-specific and not statutory), for which a soldier has nearly no rights to respond (the discharge is "uncharacterized" and therefore virtually stigma free, and the soldier has no credible claim of a property right in her military status so early in her enlistment). Most discharges for poor performance, however, concern those who cannot perform to standard. The focus of a separation board or a leader faced with a recommendation for discharge under these grounds is whether the individual has been given adequate opportunity to perform and whether there is something in his current job or unit that might suggest a deviation from prior good performance. Because this discharge is not based on character problems or misconduct, the only available discharges are honorable or under honorable conditions. Therefore, only those with at least six years of service are entitled to contest them before a board.

Rehabilitation

Most regulations that govern administrative discharges, especially the portions regarding poor performance and misconduct, create a preference if not a requirement for attempts at rehabilitation. Poor performers ordinarily should be counseled in writing and, when possible, given the opportunity to perform in another unit. Those who commit minor misconduct should receive rehabilitative transfers when that is workable. The rehabilitation requirements can be waived and are not required in cases of major misconduct (some offenses are serious enough that offering rehabilitation undermines the seriousness of the offense itself), and there are other factors, including operational requirements that leaders may cite to justify waiving the rehabilitation requirement. Still, the regulatory preference for rehabilitation reinforces the military culture of "footlocker counseling" and the military's institutional confidence in its ability to turn most poor performers and most immature individuals who commit minor misconduct into reliable warriors. Moreover, leaders are mindful of the public investment in the training and development of each service member and do not casually separate them. Administrative separation hearings typically bore in closely on the chain of command, both officer and enlisted, and try to gauge whether the soldier received a fair chance to perform or whether she may have latent talent and character that did not have a fair opportunity to bloom.

Discharge in Lieu of Court-Martial

A soldier who is facing court-martial charges may request to be administratively discharged instead of facing court-martial. There are several advantages to the accused soldier: He need not plead guilty to the offense, he avoids a federal conviction, he does not receive a sentence of confinement (or financial penalty), and he does not receive a punitive discharge. He also does not face the public embarrassment or humiliation of a trial, if that is a concern. He does, however, have to admit his guilt—albeit in his application for discharge rather than in open court, and not under oath—and he does leave the service. In addition, he faces the possibility, and in most circumstances the likelihood, of an other than dishonorable discharge, considered a "bad" discharge, which likely deprives him of most benefits associated with honorable military service.

The benefits to the government are largely those of efficiency and, to a lesser degree, of deterrence. In a circumstance in which the government is not confident that certain evidence might be admissible at trial or has concerns about a victim's credibility, availability, or durability, it may entertain a request for discharge in lieu of court-martial, even when it believes the offense warrants trial and conviction. There are a range of cost-benefit factors that could also affect the government's judgment, essentially balancing the resource consumption of a contested criminal trial against the likelihood of a conviction and appropriate sentence. Attitudes toward willingness to entertain such discharges vary among and within the services and according to the relative strength of the many variables suggested above. Defense counsel have to evaluate the case in determining whether to recommend that a client seek such a discharge as opposed to contesting the case, and the government needs to analyze the extent to which such a discharge meets its broad interest in good order and discipline as well as its specific interest in the case. Sometimes defense counsel will float a request for discharge under this chapter to see whether the government accepts or begins to frame the terms of possible pretrial negotiations; in addition, sometimes a defense counsel will use the submission and denial of a request for discharge to communicate to the client the seriousness of the government's commitment to the case and perhaps to encourage a realistic appraisal of the case. Too many separations under this provision can lead to charges or perceptions that a command is too tentative about bringing tough cases to trial, whereas an inflexible unwillingness to entertain such requests can mean that the command does not sufficiently discriminate in the allocation of prosecutorial energy and resources, making it difficult in some circumstances to give appropriate attention to the most important cases. Concerns and impact on victims are also a factor that commanders must consider in evaluating whether and when to employ this option—while recognizing it is only available when sought by an accused.

There are several other provisions for discharge, but they do not generally involve misconduct and consequently are not relevant to the use of administrative measures as an alternative to court-martial. These include pregnancy, by which a soldier may seek discharge because an anticipated inability to serve while a mother (often but not always as a single mother), alcohol or drug rehabilitation failure (often tied to misconduct, but a recognition that, at some level and in some instances, it is more related to a disease or disorder—and therefore a force management decision—than it is to criminality), and homosexuality. Although homosexual conduct remains a violation of the UCMJ, the basis for discharging homosexuals has narrowed in recent years, and the basis is what the military considers to be its incompatibility with the close-quarters, high-solidarity environment of military units rather than the morality or criminality of homosexual conduct itself. Because of the unique sensitivity to this issue, investigations must be managed at a relatively high level.

Discharge as a Last Resort

Over generations of time, the military has shifted from a philosophy of weeding out those not fit for military service to committing itself to investing in the physical and character development of the volunteers who present themselves for service. This does not mean accepting all who volunteer; nor does it mean indulging all behavior (or there would be no need for discipline, a justice system, and this book). Leaders have tended to emphasize that leadership is more than creating an environment in which those who stumble are discharged and emphasizing that good leaders can take fallible, flawed, and limited volunteers and turn them—not all of them in all circumstances but most of them in most circumstances—into productive and honorable members of the military. General John A. Wickham, Jr., served as chief of staff of the Army from 1983 to 1987 and issued a memo in which he urged leaders to conduct "footlocker counseling" of soldiers, meaning that leaders would do all they could to invest their energy and talents into the development of a soldier, so that when a soldier failed, it was not due to a lack of leadership or attention, but a matter of lack of ability or physical or moral fitness. "Because we have gotten away from the 'zero-defects' mentality to a point where leaders are now willing to let mistakes be made without crucifying people soldiers can grow," he wrote.[17] "I want to get rid of the 'zero-defects' Army, to develop a leadership that truly does mentor."

Notes

1. Manual for Courts-Martial, Part V, paragraph 1c.

2. As becomes clear later in this chapter, one instance or repeated instances of NJP can contribute to forming grounds for administrative separation and a less favorable characterization of discharge. The record of NJP, however, is internal to the military and not discoverable or releasable to civilian employers, criminal data bases, credit agencies, or other entities that could affect a former service member's reputation, prospects, or prosperity.

3. For example, in fiscal year 2006, the Army tried about 1,600 courts-martial and adjudicated about 42,000 incidents of nonjudicial punishment, a ratio of about 26 instances of nonjudicial punishment for every court-martial. Source: Office of the Clerk of Court, Army Court of Criminal Appeals (reports on file with author).

4. Article 15, UCMJ, permits "such additional regulations as may be prescribed by the Secretary concerned . . . with respect to the kind and amount of punishment authorized," who may impose NJP, and the level of court-martial to which case may be referred upon demand of the soldier who turns down NJP.

5. R.C.M. 907(b)(2)(D)(iv) requires offset against courts-martial punishment in the event that the accused previously had been punished for the offense under Article 15, but only if it is a minor offense.

6. The concept is defined and discussed in greater detail in Part V, paragraph 1e of the Manual for Courts-Martial.

7. Manual for Courts-Martial, Part V, paragraph 1c.

8. See *United States v. Martinez*, 42 M.J. 327, 331-34 (C.A.A.F. 1995).

9. The power to withhold punishment authority has two primary purposes: consistency and protection against unlawful command influence.

10. In the rare instance that NJP is based on the record of a court of inquiry or other investigative body, the soldier need not be given the opportunity to personally appear at an NJP proceeding. The theory behind this is that the soldier already had the chance to contest the government evidence and present his case at the prior proceeding. In these circumstances, the soldier still has the due process right to be informed that the command contemplates NJP; he still has the right to submit written materials on his behalf in defense, extenuation, or mitigation; and he has the right to demand trial by court-martial. NJP based on courts of inquiry and such bodies is rare.

11. Lieutenant William Calley, convicted in 1971 of murder for his role in the 1969 killings in My Lai, Vietnam, famously served several years of house arrest after his conviction (though he ultimately spent a short time in prison), but that was part of post–court-martial clemency, unrelated to NJP, though the terms of the confinement are similar.

12. Manual for Courts-Martial, Part V, paragraph 1d(2), provides that "No superior may . . . issue regulations, orders, or 'guides' which suggest to subordinate authorities that certain categories of minor offenses be disposed of by nonjudicial punishment . . . or that predetermined kinds or amounts of punishments be imposed for certain classifications of offenses."

13. Manual for Courts-Martial, Part V, paragraph 1d(1), tells commanders to "consider the nature of the offense, the record of the servicemember, the needs for good order and

discipline, and the effect of nonjudicial punishment on the servicemember and the servicemember's record."

14. Manual for Courts-Martial, Part V, paragraph 1d(3).

15. Manual for Courts-Martial, Part V, paragraph 1d(1).

16. The details regarding veterans' benefits are arcane, and they vary depending on numerous factors, including whether a soldier has prior "good" discharges.

17. General John A. Wickham, Jr., On Leadership and the Profession of Arms, Memorable Words of the Thirtieth Chief of Staff of the United States Army. http://www.army.mil/family/2008/pdf/onLeadership.pdf (accessed October 22, 2009).

CHAPTER 9

Back to the Future: Military Commissions to Try War Criminals

The central purpose of the military justice system is to enforce good order and discipline among soldiers. It is not its only purpose, however. It also provides a vehicle for bringing to justice those who violate the law of war, whether they are lawful or unlawful combatants. Throughout U.S. history, military commissions have been the judicial forum most commonly employed to accomplish this. This mechanism, which lay dormant for almost 60 years after extensive use during World War II, was brought back to life by President George W. Bush in the wake of the September 11, 2001, terrorist attacks on the United States, sparking considerable debate and protracted litigation. Military commissions have deep roots in U.S. history and were used during several wars before the Supreme Court validated their use in 1942—after which Congress included commissions in the Uniform Code of Military Justice (UCMJ) in 1950, virtually unchanged from the military commission provision in the Articles of War.

The law of war refers to the body of law that has developed with the intention of regulating the initiation and practices of modern warfare. Because there are relatively few formally declared wars, the law of war is now more commonly referred to as the *law of armed conflict*. A significant amount of the law of war can be found in the 19th- and 20-century treaties Hague and Geneva Conventions, but it also includes historical practices, and is considered to be a dynamic body of law affected by practices that evolve into customs, as well as the writings of leading publicists. The law of armed conflict seeks to stop wars before they start and moderate their conduct by minimizing harm to civilians and infrastructure, and minimizing suffering by civilians and combatants. It is founded in several assumptions about the proper conduct of war, and among them is the preference that combatants be clearly distinguished from unlawful combatants—not only to improve the chances of a "fair fight," but to enhance accountability for conduct and to reduce the chances of involving and harming civilians in the conflicts.

What Is a Commission?

A commission is a judicial body, a panel of officers that has the power to adjudicate the guilt or innocence of someone charged with a war crime. Unlike a court-martial, for which there is a fixed definition and set of rules (see chapters 2 and 3 for a discussion of the types of courts-martial and their corresponding rules and procedures), there is no singular concept of a military commission—and their configuration and rules have varied significantly in each conflict in which they have been employed. Despite these differences, the concepts underpinning commissions have remained constant. Some commissions have attracted more attention at the time they were employed than other times (the commissions conducted during the Mexican War and World War II were not nearly as controversial as those surrounding the Civil War), as the nature of the war, the status of the individual tried, the offenses charged, and the political environment all contributed to the extent to which they enjoyed public acceptance. The popular press sometimes refers to commissions as *military tribunals,* an inexact synonym because it can describe a wide range of proceedings; *military commissions* is the most accurate historical term for U.S. war crimes trials conducted by the military, and commissions are the long-used statutory term, both in the Articles of War and their successor, the UCMJ. Tribunals are best understood as proceedings that find facts but do not adjudicate guilt; for example, courts of inquiry, which find facts that might later be introduced in disciplinary proceedings, and Article 5 tribunals, which are sometimes convened under Article 5 of the Geneva Convention to determine whether detainees are lawful combatants under the law of war, are variants of tribunals. Commissions may be convened by any senior commander, and most commissions in U.S. history have been convened by theater-level commanders. A small number of, and some of the more well-known commissions, have been convened by presidents, to include the Nazi saboteurs ordered to trial by President Franklin Roosevelt and the post–September 11 military commissions initially ordered by President George W. Bush.

War Crimes

In the post-9/11 debates over military commissions, the discussion often centered on whether commissions were justified by an expressed need; that is, whether a commission was necessary because the ordinary federal courts (often referred to as Article III courts, because they are grounded in the judicial authority in Article III of the Constitution) or courts-martial (Article I courts) would be unable to handle them for reasons of evidence or national security. Often those were the key factors in explaining or justifying commissions, but that has not historically been the case and is not necessary from a legal standpoint. In other words, commissions are not courts of last resort reserved for war crimes that cannot be tried in conventional courts. They are courts that historically have been employed to try violations of the law of war and would be a legally available mechanism even if the conventional courts were able to accommodate the trials. Further debate, of course, concerns whether that choice would be wise or just, given the availability of conventional courts, but that is different from the assertion that such a finding would be a prerequisite for convening a commission. Therefore, it is a recognized ground to use commissions simply because the offender is suspected of violating the law of war.

National Security

National security is both a theoretical basis and, increasingly, a practical reason for military commissions. The theory concerns the offenses themselves, violations of the law of war, and it recognizes that a nation—a sovereign—has the right to prosecute violations of the law of war. Practically, national security is a key factor, because sometimes the way that evidence has been gathered precludes its use in a conventional court. This is especially true when evidence is gathered initially and primarily for intelligence purposes but later also becomes valuable for use in a judicial proceeding. In such circumstances, the conventional courts might not be a workable forum for presenting such evidence because of the requirements that the defense have the opportunity to evaluate the evidence and to test it in open court or because prosecutors are unable to establish its authenticity with sufficient rigor or are unable or unwilling publicly to disclose where it obtained the evidence or by whom.

For example, a conversation captured by a wiretap might be very valuable and trustworthy evidence—the words of those involved in a crime—but the government would maintain that the fact of the wiretap and the way the government obtained the information (technology, listening posts, and the like) should not be shared publicly, because it would compromise further such efforts, weakening the U.S. government in the process of bringing someone to justice. This same principle would be involved in deciding how to present in court evidence that was gathered by a covert operative, whether by a member of the U.S. government or someone working for the United States. Similar factors would be involved if evidence were gathered primarily by or in coordination with foreign governments, whether by their militaries or intelligence agencies—disclosure of which could harm those governments domestically, politically, and internationally. Obviously, such evidence can be extremely valuable, but just as obviously, knowledge of information such as an informant's identity makes it unlikely for that person to be useful in the future, requiring a balancing of national security and the interests in a fair result that are grounded in the defense's ability to test evidence by reviewing it in advance and through cross-examination. National security concerns are central to the process by which the nation holds a potential war criminal accountable for his actions and the ways in which it protects the assets and operations of military and intelligence agencies. Commissions provide evidentiary mechanisms, discussed in more detail below, that are fundamental to a criminal trial, but they also involve the judge and others in crafting a process that accommodates national security, the interests of the defense, and society and an accused's interest in a reliable result. This is a foundational concern, and one of the more controversial areas involving military commissions.

Necessity and Military Operations

The job of service members is to fight and win our nation's wars and to keep the peace during periods of tranquility. When fighting wars, it is generally not their job to act as police or criminal investigators.[1] At the same time, information and evidence that they might seize in undertaking their operational tasks could end up being made available for use in a criminal trial. Unlike conventional law enforcement, however, the soldiers who seize evidence or information generally do not have the time or ability—and, most believe, are under no U.S. legal requirement—to collect evidence in the same way and according to the same standards and restrictions as those applicable in U.S. domestic courts. Therefore, commissions can serve the purpose of providing a forum in which evidence can be introduced into a criminal proceeding that might not be admissible in ordinary courts but would still be reliable. For example, soldiers conduct battlefield interrogations without reading rights to those whom they are questioning, generally not providing the option to decline interrogation or to consult a lawyer. They do this for two reasons: (1) Their main purpose usually is to find information that can assist in military operations, helping to refine tactics and plans and keep people safe ("where are the weapons?" "who is your boss?" "what is the escape route?") rather than to obtain information for a criminal proceeding; and (2) the Constitutional privilege against self-incrimination generally does not extend to noncitizens overseas, and the Fourth Amendment requirement for reasonable searches and seizures (including a preference for search warrants and arrest warrants) does not ordinarily apply outside the United States and on a battlefield.

Regardless of these factors, evidence that is presented at a criminal trial must be reliable—a jury must be able to trust it, so they must be told the circumstances by which the evidence was gathered, providing them a basis for making a judgment about how much weight to give to it, if any. While some of the evidence concerns words out of people's mouths—hearsay—it also involves records and items seized in military operations. Such evidence normally would have to be supported by a strict chain of custody that would enable prosecutors to establish that it was collected appropriately and safeguarded in a manner that avoided contamination or loss of control that could call into question its trustworthiness. Often it is not practically possible to comply with such requirements when evidence is seized from a battlefield and then passed through multiple channels and handlers without the time and ability to carefully execute receipts and the kind of tracking, verification, and authentication documents that accompany the products of most law enforcement operations. Besides the fact that most military members are not trained in the details of evidence collection, many military leaders would consider it operationally perilous for soldiers, operating in a volatile and lethal environment, to be distracted by concerns about matters of evidentiary integrity.[2] Prosecutors, on the other hand, must be willing to bear such a risk—that a jury might find it untrustworthy—in making a case before a military commission that such evidence is reliable anyway, seeking to introduce other information that might be considered sufficiently corroborative to make the evidence worthy of consideration.

Personal Security

It is axiomatic that bringing unlawful combatants to justice should not require those who participate in the process to risk their safety or security. Because military commissions provide the opportunity to adapt rules and procedures in light of security concerns, military commissions can ensure that witnesses, jurors, victims, and others critical to a system of justice do not bear additional risks because of their participation. For example, panel members (jurors) need not be publicly identified, and witnesses can testify under pseudonyms and remotely.[3] In fact, the civilian justice system has adapted in some circumstances—such as the trials of organized crime kingpins, gang leaders, and other sophisticated criminals—but commissions, by their nature and history, are attuned to such measures and may implement them with lesser scrutiny or risk of appellate reversal than civilian courts.

Reliability and Due Process

The rules and procedures used by military commissions have changed each time they have been employed, generally because the accepted procedures in domestic courts have changed—broadly, in the direction of greater openness, greater due process, and more protections for the accused. While efficiency remains a key attraction of commissions, it cannot be a shortcut for expediency if it means to maintain its credibility as an evidence-based vehicle for justice; the ultimate test of a criminal judicial system is reliability of the result, and most procedures are geared to ensuring that the verdict is one in which participants and society can have confidence. There was, for years, a consensus, though not universal view, that the Fourth, Fifth, and Sixth Amendments to the Constitution did not apply to unlawful combatants and to evidence gathering in a war zone, though many of the protections underlying those amendments were incorporated into commissions procedures, often with adjustments—in the belief that such procedures still contributed to reliable results. For example, the Fifth Amendment provides that an individual may not be compelled to give testimony against herself. Over time, U.S. courts have expanded that to include a prohibition against custodial questioning unless an individual is provided the right to consult an attorney. In the most recent military commissions, the prohibition against questioning did not apply before trial, but the centuries-old privilege against self-incrimination at trial was incorporated because of the belief that it is a fundamental protection and that the alternative—compulsory testimony of the person on trial—put him to the dilemma of testifying truthfully and incriminating himself or lying, neither of which harmonizes an interest in justice and truth-seeking.[4]

Commissions through U.S. History

Early American History

George Washington convened a proceeding to determine whether Major Andre, the British spy, was guilty of espionage, and many historians refer to it as a military commission. The tribunal was a board of officers convened to make a recommendation to Washington on whether Andre was a spy. Scholars and historians, therefore, dispute whether it should be classified as a military commission because it did not have direct authority to adjudicate guilt and had no ability to assess punishment. The inability to establish guilt is, to some degree, consistent with courts-martial and commissions, because the convening authority (the person who ordered the commission into existence) has the power to reject the findings of a court and to alter the sentence, in both instances only in favor of the accused. Regardless, the Andre tribunal was a mechanism, convened by a commander in the field, to find evidence in a particular case about an enemy soldier suspected of violating the laws of war; therefore, but for its lack of adjudicative authority, it was similar to a commission if it was not actually one. (It should be noted that courts-martial have been used from time to time to try soldiers from other nations, and, in recent years, some critics and human rights advocates have urged trying suspected war criminals by courts-martial.) In one of the more controversial exercises of commissions, General Andrew Jackson—in his capacity as a field commander, not president (which he became in 1825)—convened military commissions during the War of 1812 and during the First Seminole War. In the latter conflict, he approved the recommendation of a military commission in 1818 to execute two British adventurers from the Bahamas who were found to have been instigators among the Seminoles.[5]

Mexican War

The little-remembered Mexican War represented a major expansion of the military commission to operation outside U.S. territory, the first precursor of later commissions convened overseas. U.S. forces commanded by General Winfield Scott occupied Mexico in 1847 and immediately had two major law and order concerns: (1) prosecuting Mexicans who were suspected of guerrilla warfare or encouraging desertion of American soldiers and (2) keeping law and order in the country, ideally by applying Mexican law. The use of commissions to prosecute law of war violations was consistent with the fundamental purpose of military commissions—the prosecution of those who would undermine U.S. military effort, increase risk to civilians, and increase bloodshed and acrimony by violating the law of war.

General Scott emphasized to his troops that they had to respect the rights of the Mexicans whom they conquered, insisting on compliance with the rule of law by his soldiers as well as by the Mexicans. His General Order Number 20 establishing military commissions is as interesting for the way in which it makes the case for the need for commissions as it is for the particulars that relate to that war. Scott's order, of which there are several versions, because it was republished with clarifications in different locations during 1847, starts with the recognition that the commissions are meant to fill a gap in the law—that there were "many grave offenses not provided for in an Act of Congress."

Scott's Councils of War tried Mexican citizens accused of violations of the law of war. In addition, he convened courts that enforced martial law, though his preference was to stand up or revitalize indigenous Mexican courts on the theory that such courts were best equipped to handle violations of domestic law. In addition, using indigenous courts would reduce the sense of an imperialist occupation. Scott was careful to limit the scope of commissions, so that they did not cover every conceivable offense but only those offenses that were not "clearly cognizable by court martial." The order also stipulated that commission sentences could not be more severe than those that an accused person might have received in U.S. courts.

Winfield Scott's Use of Military Commissions in the Mexican War

Military commissions lurched back into public consciousness after President Bush resurrected the long-dormant judicial mechanism after the attacks of September 11, 2001. While the president patterned his order closely after Franklin D. Roosevelt's order in the *Quirin* case, General Winfield Scott's order of 1847 establishing military commissions during the Mexican War is noteworthy and forward looking in at least two respects: (1) It acknowledges that Congress has not adequately—or at least not specifically—provided for prosecution of law of war violations that occur in locations outside the United States (this was the first major campaign outside U.S. soil), an acknowledgement that arose repeatedly through history and after September 11, 2001, when a gap relating to bringing "non-state actors" to justice was a major concern; and (2) it specifically delineates the crimes over which commissions would have jurisdiction, limiting them to those that could not be tried by courts-martial and to punishments available in U.S. civilian courts. Scott, whose reputation for broad-mindedness and foresight (while associated with the Trail of Tears, he also was a loyal Unionist despite his Virginia heritage) exceeds, among most historians, his "Fuss and Feathers" reputation for vanity, provides a peek into the future with his wartime order: The Order appears with its original spellings and syntax.

General Orders, Headquarters of the Army,

National Palace of Mexico, (No. 287.) September 17, 1847.

The General-in-Chief republishes, with important additions, the General Orders, No. 20, of February 19, 1847 (declaring Martial Law), to govern all who may be concerned.

1. It is still to be apprehended that many grave offences, not provided for in the Act of Congress "establishing rules and articles for the government of the armies of the United States," approved April 10, 1806, may again be committed—by, or upon, individuals of those armies, in Mexico, pending the existing war between the two Republics. Allusion is here made to offences, any one of which, if committed within the United States or their organized Territories, would, of course, be tried and severely punished by the ordinary or civil courts of the land, [sic]
2. Assassination, murder, poisoning, rape, or the attempt to commit either; malicious stabbing or maiming; malicious assault and battery, robbery, theft; the wanton desecration of churches, cemeteries or other religious edifices and fixtures; the interruption of religious ceremonies, and the destruction, except by order of a superior officer, of public or private property; are such offences.
3. The good of the service, the honor of the United States and the interests of humanity, imperiously demand that every crime, enumerated above, should be severely punished.
4. But the written code, as above, commonly called the rules and articles of war, does not provide for the punishment of any one of those crimes, even when committed by individuals of the army upon the persons or property of other individuals of the same, except in the very restricted case in the 9th of those articles; nor for like outrages, committed by the same class of individuals, upon the persons or property of a hostile country, except very partially, in the 51st, 52d, and 55th articles; and the same code is absolutely silent as to all injuries which may be inflicted upon individuals of the army, or their property, against the laws of war, by individuals of a hostile country.
5. It is evident that the 99th article, independent of any reference to the restriction in the 87th, is wholly nugatory in reaching any one of those high crimes.
6. For all the offences, therefore, enumerated in the second paragraph above, which may be committed abroad—in, by, or upon the army, a supplemental code is absolutely needed.
7. That unwritten code is Martial Law, as an addition to the written military code, prescribed by Congress in the rules and articles of war, and which unwritten code, all armies, in hostile countries, are forced to adopt—not only for their own safety, but for the protection of the unoffending inhabitants and their property, about the theatres of military operations, against injuries, on the part of the army, contrary to the laws of war.
8. From the same supreme necessity, martial law is hereby declared as a supplemental code in, and about, all cities, towns, camps, posts, hospitals, and other places which may be occupied by any part of the forces of the United States, in Mexico, and in, and about, all columns, escorts, convoys, guards, and detachments, of the said forces, while engaged in prosecuting the existing war in, and against the said republic, and while remaining within the same.
9. Accordingly, every crime, enumerated in paragraph No. 2, above, whether committed—(1) By any inhabitant of Mexico, sojourner or traveler therein, upon the person or property of any individual of the United States forces, retainer or follower of the same; (2) By any individual of the said forces, retainer or follower of the same, upon the person or property of any inhabitant of Mexico, sojourner or traveler therein; or (3) By any individual of the said forces, retainer or follower of the same, upon the person or property of any other individual

of the said forces, retainer or follower of the same—shall be duly tried and punished under the said supplemental code.

10. For this purpose it is ordered, that all offenders, in the matters aforesaid, shall be promptly seized, confined, and reported for trial, before military commissions, to be duly appointed as follows:

11. Every military commission, under this order, will be appointed, governed, and limited, as nearly as practicable, as prescribed by the 65th, 66th, 67th, and 97th, of the said rules and articles of war, and the proceedings of such commissions will be duly recorded, in writing, reviewed, revised, disapproved or approved, and the sentences executed—all, as near as may be, as in the cases of the proceedings and sentences of courts martial, provided, that no military commission shall try any case clearly cognizable by any court martial, and provided, also, that no sentence of a military commission shall be put in execution against any individual belonging to this army, which may not be, according to the nature and degree of the offence, as established by evidence, in conformity with known punishments, in like cases, in some one of the States of the United States of America.

12. The sale, waste or loss of ammunition, horses, arms, clothing or accoutrements, by soldiers, is punishable under the 37th and 38th articles of war. Any Mexican or resident or traveler, in Mexico, who shall purchase of any American soldier, either horse, horse equipments, arms, ammunition, accoutrements or clothing, shall be tried and severely punished, by a military commission, as above.

13. The administration of justice, both in civil and criminal matters, through the ordinary courts of the country, shall nowhere and in no degree, be interrupted by any officer or soldier of the American forces, except, 1. In cases to which an officer, soldier, agent, servant, or follower of the American army may be a party; and 2. In political cases—that is, prosecutions against other individuals on the allegations that they have given friendly information, aid or assistance to the American forces.

14. For the ease and safety of both parties, in all cities and towns occupied by the American army, a Mexican police shall be established and duly harmonized with the military police of the said forces.

15. This splendid capital—its churches and religious worship; its convents and monasteries; its inhabitants and property are, moreover, placed under the special safeguard of the faith and honor of the American army.

16. In consideration of the foregoing protection, a contribution of $150,000 is imposed on this capital, to be paid in four weekly installments of thirty-seven thousand five hundred dollars ($37,500) each, beginning on Monday next, the 20th instant, and terminating on Monday, the 11th of October.

17. The Ayuntamiento, or corporate authority of the city, is specially charged with the collection and payment of the several installments.

18. Of the whole contributions to be paid over to this army, twenty thousand dollars shall be appropriated to the purchase of extra comforts for the wounded and sick in hospital; ninety thousand dollars ($90,000) to the purchase of blankets and shoes for gratuitous distribution among the rank and file of the army, and forty thousand dollars ($40,000) reserved for other necessary military purposes.

19. This order will be read at the head of every company of the United States' forces, serving in Mexico, and translated into Spanish for the information of Mexicans.

By command of Major-General Scott. H. L.
SCOTT, A. A.–
General.

The offenses that he chose to highlight in his general order provide a window into his greatest concerns as commander of an army in a foreign land: "Any Mexican or resident or traveler, in Mexico, who shall purchase of any American soldier, either horse, horse equipments, arms, ammunition, accoutrements or clothing shall be tried and severely punished, by a military commission." This was well before the sophisticated logistics train that came to characterize the U.S. Army, but Scott's message also carries a hint of what would later be characterized as unlawful command influence or convening authority inflexibility in the reference to "severely punish[ing]" violators.

All in all, Scott continued to build and reinforce his reputation for enlightened leadership by grounding commissions in mid-century's advanced sense of the rule of law, while also admonishing his troops to protect "[t]his splendid capital . . . its inhabitants and property," placing them "under the special safeguard of the faith and honor of the American army."

Copperheads, Milligan, and Civilian Courts: Commissions during the Civil War

Winfield Scott concluded his extraordinary and extraordinarily long military career in the Civil War, which provided the next occasion for employing military commissions, obviously in the unique circumstance of a country being at war with itself. More than 2,000 commissions were convened during the Civil War, providing the opportunity to refine the concept still further.

Two of the most famous cases involved rebellious northerners who were sympathetic with the Confederacy but who did not take up arms against the government of the United States. Both cases reached the Supreme Court, and both reflected a level of deference that courts continue to provide to military leaders in time of war—but they also showed the limits of any national authority's law enforcement powers, especially when involving the writ of habeas corpus. In the same controversial order in which he claimed to suspend the writ of habeas corpus ("claimed" because the Constitution entrusts that responsibility to the Congress, and it has remained an unresolved matter of controversy since), President Lincoln provided for trial by military commissions. The March 1863 document, issued at what turns out to have been about the halfway point in the bloody war, did not provide implementing detail, because the custom remained that commissions were convened by battlefield commanders. Lincoln did, however, briefly explain why commissions were an appropriate measure at that time, writing in the first paragraph of the order: "That during the existing insurrection, and as a necessary means for suppressing the same, all rebels and insurgents, their aiders and abettors, within the United States, and all persons discouraging volunteer enlistments resisting militia drafts, or guilty of any disloyal practice, affording aid and comfort to rebels, against the authority of the United States, shall be subject to martial law, and liable to trial and punishment by courts martial or military commission." It was not long before zealous commanders convened such commissions, the legality of which was called into question.

In *United States v. Vallandingham*,⁶ the Supreme Court held in 1864 that military commissions could not be reviewed by the ordinary appellate courts of the United States, which indirectly upheld the conviction of Clement Vallandingham, the "Supreme Grand Commander of the Sons of Liberty," by a military commission convened by General Ambrose Burnside. His fellow traveler, however, Lamdin Milligan, escaped the consequences of his military commissions conviction on grounds having nothing to do with his guilt but on the basis that military commissions could not be employed against U.S. citizens for domestic offenses (not law of war violations) when the ordinary courts were open and operating—as they were at that time in Indiana. Milligan was tried for violations of the law of war, inciting insurrection and disloyalty, but the Court did not reach the merits of the case—whether Milligan actually committed the offenses—because it concluded, in a decision not published until 1866, after the war was over, that military commissions were an inappropriate mechanism to try U.S. citizens, even during wartime, when the courts were available.⁷

Before that decision was issued, Abraham Lincoln was assassinated in April 1865, and President Andrew Johnson was persuaded to try eight of the conspirators, who included Mary Surratt and Samuel Mudd, the physician who set John Wilkes Booth's broken leg, by military commission for violations of the law of war. Many have criticized the commission for having had loose procedures, arguing that the prosecution exploited the fact that a commission was not bound by conventional rules for criminal courts and therefore could manipulate a military jury and public sympathy in a trial that occurred only weeks after the assassination. The criticisms also illustrate that military commissions generally follow the legal tenor of the times, and, at that time, accused persons did not enjoy nearly the rights and procedural protections or oversight by layers of appellate courts that they did a century later. Among other factors, several accused did not have counsel when the trial convened, none had their charges in advance, and the government did not provide them the opportunity to review the evidence against them in advance—a far cry from the broad discovery procedures that have become such an integral part of the criminal trial process in contemporary America. Portions of the trial were closed, based on the claim by General Joseph Holt, the judge advocate general, who also served as legal advisor to the commission, that witnesses might be intimidated if they had to testify publicly. The dual role of serving as prosecutor and legal advisor persisted in various incarnations in the military justice system through the mid-20th century.

Critics also argued that a military commission, even if it had defensible procedures, was an inappropriate forum under these circumstances, because civilian courts were open and operating, and, therefore, there was no real military necessity that required using this unusual forum for eight civilians. There was no federal crime of assassination at that time (the federal criminal code was thin until well into the 20th century), and opponents argued that a straightforward charge of murder would have been more appropriate. They also have argued that the government conjured new crimes in relying on the laws of war as the source of the crimes. All of the defendants were charged with conspiracy as well as offenses such as providing horses, advice, or shelter to John Wilkes Booth, but the grand conspiracy charge enabled the government to place before the commission large amounts of evidence regarding the Southern war effort, often spiced with evidence about atrocities. All recognized that none of the eight knew about or participated in the atrocities, but it was considered to be relevant evidence because of the sweep of the conspiracy and the broadly shared objective of bringing down the government. A century and a half later, several al Qaeda members or supporters implicated in terrorism related to the September 11, 2001, attacks and related events also were charged with a grand conspiracy, again based on the settled legal principle that conspirators need not know all of the details of their co-conspirators' acts as long as they can be shown to have shared the same criminal intent.[8]

The government relied on the theory that assassination of a head of state by such means constituted a violation of the law of war. Attorney General James Speed also issued an opinion in 1865 justifying the commission on the ground that, unlike Vallandingham and Milligan, whose activities were open and public, the covert nature of the Lincoln assassination conspiracy made it appropriate for adjudication as a war crime by commission. After about six weeks of testimony by more than 350 witnesses and presentations by eight different counsel of varying levels of competence, all eight of the conspirators were convicted, four of them receiving death sentences, three receiving life in prison, and one receiving a six-year sentence for aiding and abetting Booth's escape. The voting process itself was controversial, because General Holt unilaterally decided just before the court closed that a simple majority could adjudge a life sentence and that a two-thirds vote would permit a death sentence. The end of the trial brought the speed that has been associated with commissions throughout history. The commission of nine general officers issued its verdict on June 30, 1865, and there was no appellate process of any kind available. President Johnson approved the sentence on July 5, and the four who received death sentences, including Mary Surratt, were hung at Fort McNair, in Washington, DC, on July 7, 1865.[9]

The Supreme Court never reviewed the case of the Lincoln conspirators, but it was, by a unique procedural oddity, reviewed indirectly by the federal courts from the late 1990s until 2002. Mudd's kin long had contended that his involvement was either innocent or misunderstood. His great-grandson brought an action to correct his military record and to invalidate the military commission—on the *Milligan*-related grounds that the commission had no jurisdiction over a Maryland citizen when the courts were available to try him (President Andrew Johnson ultimately pardoned Mudd in 1869 because of his work, while imprisoned in the Dry Tortugas, caring for many individuals, both prisoners and guards, during a yellow fever outbreak). While the Army Board for Correction of Military Records, had found that Mudd was entitled to relief because the Lincoln commission did not have jurisdiction over someone in Mudd's status (civilian when the ordinary courts were open and operating), the lower federal courts found that the military commission was an appropriate exercise of jurisdiction, because he had been charged with a violation of the law of war, even though the courts were open at the time. Ultimately, the Washington, DC, Circuit Court of Appeals ruled in 2002 that Mudd (through his ancestors) could not use a military board designed to correct military records as an avenue for relief, because he had never been a member of the military.[10] Still, no citizen has been tried by military commission since the Civil War for offenses committed on U.S. soil.

World War I

The United States did not employ military commissions during World War I, a decision influenced by the legal analysis of the attorney general, who conservatively interpreted the Constitutional and statutory authority governing military commissions.

A Russian national, Pable Waberski, was arrested in 1918 coming into the United States from Mexico, suspected of crossing the border to commit sabotage on behalf of the Germans. He was charged with spying. Thomas Watt Gregory, President Woodrow Wilson's attorney general for the entire course of the war, did not dispute whether commissions could be employed by the United States, but believed—in a precursor to issues that arose anew in the Bush military commissions almost 90 years later—that a commission would not have jurisdiction over such an offense because it did not occur in hostile territory or in an area under U.S. military control. In his 1918 formal opinion, Watt also relied on the fact that the ordinary courts of the United States were operating in that area and could have been used to try Waberski.[11]

Watt's analysis did not question the availability of the mechanism of military commissions, as he referred approvingly to their prior use, especially during the Mexican War and the Civil War, but he also believed that jurisdiction did not extend to trying Waberski for spying under these circumstances. He cited the Hague Convention of 1917 as partial support for his conclusion, writing that "Congress can not constitutionally confer jurisdiction upon a military court to try and sentence any man not a member of the military forces and not subject to the jurisdiction of such court under the laws of war or martial law." Watt believed that spying was only an offense when it occurred behind enemy lines (see chapter 4 for a discussion of spying and the lurking requirement, which happened to figure significantly in Watt's opinion), and, because Waberski was not spying under these circumstances, Watt concluded that Congress did not intend it to be triable by military commission. He also concluded that the language in the Articles of War that said spying could occur behind enemy lines "or elsewhere" was legally invalid. He believed that Waberski could be tried by the United States, but for some other offense and by civilian courts. He wrote: "If [Waberski] could constitutionally be tried by court-martial, then it would logically follow that Congress could provide for the trial by military courts of any person, citizen or alien, accused of espionage or any other type of war crime, no matter where committed and no matter where such person be found and apprehended." Consequently, the Wilson administration adhered to the view that commissions were unavailable in circumstances like Waberski's and did not employ them during that conflict.

The law has changed in three significant respects since World War I, any of which might have altered the attorney general's opinion. First, later versions of the Articles of War (and then the UCMJ) authorize military commissions for violations of the law of war or statute. This means that, even if a future attorney general were to conclude that an offense was not a violation of a law of war but was a violation of a Congressional statute, then it could be tried by military commission (this is the case with the Military Commissions Act of 2006, discussed later in this chapter).[12] Second, Congress has continued to include the "or elsewhere" language in its codification of the offense of spying. Finally, Congress has expressly provided that the UCMJ has worldwide jurisdiction, an assertion that was not explicit early in the 20th century, when a large standing army with routine worldwide deployments was not yet the norm.

Submarines and Saboteurs: The Source of Modern Authority for Military Commissions

In late spring 1942, when the United States had been at war barely six months, the Nazis sent two sets of saboteurs to land on U.S. soil. Their purpose was to infiltrate the United States and cause destruction, one group landing on Long Island and the other at Ponte Vedra, Florida. Though dressed in uniforms in the hopes of gaining treatment as prisoners of war if caught, they buried the uniforms shortly after landing. All eight were born in Germany, but two were U.S. citizens. They were tried by a swiftly convened military commission of seven general officers ordered into existence by President Franklin D. Roosevelt. The commission convened in a conference room at the Department of Justice in Washington, DC, and was closed to the public. The accused were represented by a distinguished advocate, Kenneth C. Royall, who won a reputation for thoroughness and probity, petitioning the president directly and asking that the cases be tried in civilian court on the grounds that the president did not have authority to convene military commissions in such circumstances. The president refused, and Royall took his plea to the federal courts, ultimately to the Supreme Court. The eight saboteurs were apprehended on June 13 and June 17, and the military commission convened on July 2, the same day it was ordered by President Roosevelt. The case was argued before the Supreme Court on July 29 and 30, a decision issued the next day—extraordinary speed by any measure—and six of the eight were executed on August 8 (President Roosevelt commuted two of the sentences to life in prison).

The Court issued a more complete ruling on October 29, 1942.[13] The case has been much criticized, but it was a unanimous decision by the FDR Supreme Court, the central holding of which remained unchallenged in fall 2001, when the Bush administration began to consider whether to convene commissions: "Lawful combatants are subject to capture and detention as prisoners of war by opposing military forces. Unlawful combatants are likewise subject to capture and detention, but in addition they are subject to trial and punishment by military tribunals for acts which render their belligerency unlawful." The *Quirin* saboteurs were considered unlawful combatants because they were guilty of espionage; of course, their intentional disregard for the law of war, which included discarding their uniforms so that they could avoid identification as combatants, deprived them of the protections of "privileged combatants" who could lawfully attack an enemy in compliance with the laws of war. This was a central consideration in the 2001 decision of the Bush administration to convene military commissions for 9/11-related conspirators and other combatants captured in or near the theater of war in Afghanistan.

Quirin also stood for the principle that such unlawful combatants could be tried by military commission even though the civilian courts were open and operating—a different conclusion than the one drawn by Attorney General Watt during the Wilson administration, who interpreted the Civil War–era *Milligan* decision to compel use of civilian courts for such individuals, though Watt himself might have seen a distinction between Waberski, caught trying to gain entry into the United States, and the Nazis, who were apprehended on U.S. soil. The unanimous *Quirin* court distinguished Milligan on the grounds that he had never been a part of conventional military, but it did not further elaborate on where the line could be drawn, content to make clear that Quirin and his co-conspirators clearly qualified as unlawful enemy combatants.

Quirin was far from the only exercise of military commissions during World War II, which saw hundreds of commissions convened in both the European and Pacific theaters. The trial of General Tomoyuki Yamashita, one of the most senior leaders of Japan's Imperial Army, was especially noteworthy both because of his position and the legal principles on which it was based. Yamashita was tried after the war mainly for war crimes committed by those under his vast command. This raised two important issues: (1) whether commissions could be convened *after* a conflict and (2) the extent to which a commander can be held to account for the offenses of those under his command. The Supreme Court found that the end of hostilities did not terminate the jurisdiction of military commissions, because they are grounded more in the nature of the offense—law of war violations by enemy combatants—than they are in the fact that a conflict might be ongoing.[14] The Court also held, in a decision with landmark significance beyond the issue of military commissions, that "command responsibility" was a valid legal concept by which a military leader could be held criminally liable, even when she might not know the particular acts of specific subordinates. The Supreme Court's review did not touch on the facts of the case itself—it deferred to the commission that heard the evidence—but it affirmed that commissions were an appropriate mechanism and rejected the argument that the Geneva Conventions required that Yamashita be tried by court-martial. The Court interpreted the Geneva provision that requires prisoners to be tried by courts-martial to mean that courts-martial were required for offenses committed *while* a prisoner, not necessarily for those who had been taken prisoner. Justice Frank Murphy wrote a lengthy and passionate dissent, arguing that the Yamashita commission was so procedurally weak as to constitute a violation of the Fifth Amendment's due process clause—which, he argued, encompassed universal concerns that should not be interpreted as inapplicable to a noncitizen.[15] Murphy, a Roosevelt appointee, had served as governor general of the Philippines before World War II and had dissented in the *Korematsu* decision that upheld the internal relocation of Japanese Americans earlier in the war. In his *Yamashita* dissent, Murphy wrote that the rights secured by the Fifth Amendment "belong to every person in the world, victor or vanquished, whatever may be his race, color, or beliefs. They rise above any status of belligerency or outlawry. They survive any popular passion or frenzy of the moment."[16] He argued that Yamashita could not be found to have violated the law of war by attributing the acts of subordinates to him, and that the ordinary courts were appropriate to the extent that any criminal case against Yamashita could have been fashioned. He continued: "No military necessity or other emergency demanded the suspension of the safeguards of due process. Yet petitioner was rushed to trial under an improper charge, given insufficient time to prepare an adequate defense, deprived of the benefits of some of the most elementary rules of evidence, and summarily sentenced to be hanged. In all this needless and unseemly haste, there was no serious attempt to charge or to prove that he committed a recognized violation of the laws of war. He was not charged with personally participating in the acts of atrocity, or with ordering or condoning their commission."[17] Justice Wiley Blount Rutledge also dissented, but the Court clearly approved the trial and the underlying concept; the dissenters' views resurfaced about 55 years later.

Nuremberg and International Tribunals

The Nuremberg Trials were not military commissions. The post–World War II trials at Nuremberg, Germany, were created for the specific purpose of trying senior Nazi leaders for atrocities committed during World War II. Nuremberg was actually two sets of trials—the International Military Tribunal at which 21 senior Nazis were tried, and the Nuremberg Military Trials, that tried another group of senior leaders, including a set of trials for medical personnel and a set of trials for judges. Although the trials merit the considerable debate they have generated since their conclusion in 1949, they were not military commissions in the same sense of those convened by the United States under its own authority and are therefore beyond the scope of this book. Critics and observers of the post-2001 military commissions process frequently cited a desire to reach a "Nuremberg Standard," though the procedures at Nuremberg featured far fewer protections for the defendants than those of later commissions, including the most recent ones. International tribunals have been convened in recent years in the former Yugoslavia (starting in 1993 and projected to expire in 2010), Rwanda, Sierra Leone, and Cambodia. These proceedings have a common feature absent from the U.S. commissions in that they follow extraordinary rebellion and oppression or are convened in failed or successor states in whose judicial processes citizens and the world community would have little grounds to have confidence. In contrast, the U.S. military commissions received considerable criticism, but not often on the core issue of the nation's ability to exercise a rudiment of sovereignty in convening courts for attacks on itself and its citizens.

Lockerbie Renews Discussion of Military Commissions

In December 1988, terrorists blew up a Pan Am flight as it passed over Lockerbie, Scotland, en route from Frankfurt, Germany, to New York. It quickly became clear that the bombing was the act of terrorists, who may have had the indulgence or tacit support of sovereign governments but were not soldiers or in any credible sense lawful or privileged combatants. Those on board the flight were innocent civilians, and 189 of the 259 on board were Americans. The Reagan administration, only weeks from leaving office, was concerned that bringing the terrorists to justice would be a protracted, if not futile, process. It also was concerned that bringing them to justice in a conventional criminal trial would fail to highlight the essential nature of the bombing—that it was an act of war, not simply a crime. Administration officials, under the leadership of Acting Attorney General William Barr, resurrected the concept of military commissions and studied whether they might be an appropriate mechanism, in that they would reinforce the message that the attacks were more in the nature of an act of war—by unlawful combatants—than a crime, and would move faster than traditional criminal processes. Ultimately, the decision was made not to pursue military commissions, but the practical and philosophical discussions that Lockerbie generated quickly came to the fore about a dozen years later.

To those in the George W. Bush administration in 2001, the frustrations of Lockerbie also highlighted the need for and value of other than conventional judicial processes for dealing with terrorist attacks that could be considered acts of war. Ultimately, two Libyan men were arrested for the attacks in 1991 and were brought to trial in a Dutch courtroom applying Scottish law in a trial that concluded early in 2001. One individual was convicted and given a life sentence (requiring him to serve a minimum 27 years),[18] and the other was acquitted. Many U.S. officials and victim family members considered this to be unsatisfactory for several reasons. It took more than a dozen years to get to trial, providing attenuated justice to the many kin of the victims.[19] The trial occurred in the Netherlands, a nation unconnected to the offense (and as a result of years of negotiation), and the law applied in the trial was from a nation in whose skies the bombing occurred and which lost 11 innocent civilians on the ground, but which was not the target of the attack—it was clearly meant to murder as many Americans as possible.

September 11: The Resuscitation of Military Commissions

Shortly after the September 11 attacks, members of the Bush administration began studying military commissions as part of a comprehensive review of executive

Back to the Future

authority and the range of judicial options available in responding to the attacks. Within two months, the president made a decision to authorize military commissions, and, on November 13, 2001, he signed a military order in which he made military commissions available for the trial of noncitizen unlawful combatants involved in the attacks and anyone who was a member of the al Qaeda terrorist organization or harbored al Qaeda terrorists. The president's order was styled a military order,[20] after President Roosevelt's Military Order of 1942 that authorized the *Quirin* commissions, and was intended to emphasize that it came from the president as commander-in-chief, not merely as head of the executive branch.

In March 2002, Secretary of Defense Donald Rumsfeld published an order that provided rules and procedures for the commissions. Key features included:

- Right to military defense counsel upon being charged with an offense.
- Right to civilian counsel of choice, as long as the counsel was a member of any state bar in the United States; the accused could retain his civilian counsel even if he hired a civilian, the same right as an accused at court-martial.
- Privilege against self-incrimination at trial. This right was not extended to detainees before trial, a major departure not only from military practice but from U.S. Constitutional law as it has evolved in recent generations. Since the *Miranda* ruling of 1964, no one who is in custody may be questioned by law enforcement unless read her rights, which include the right to have counsel present during questioning. There were several reasons for not extending this protection to detainees, chief among them that it could inhibit intelligence gathering and that, in many circumstances, especially overseas, it was unworkable.[21] Because most questioning of those detained on suspicion of terrorism was designed, at least initially, to obtain intelligence information, incorporating *Miranda* advice—the right to choose not to talk and the right to engage an attorney—would make that problematic. Most commissions advocates believed that Constitutional law made clear that the Fifth Amendment did not apply to noncitizens overseas in any event, but this ended up a contentious matter even through the Supreme Court's decision in *Boumediene v. Bush*[22] in 2008. Although there was no pretrial privilege against self-incrimination, there was a consensus that it should apply at trial, because it is a fundamental attribute of Western truth-seeking criminal processes. In addition, the rules forbade a commission to draw a negative inference from a decision not to testify, an inference that some European countries and others do permit.
- Right to a copy of all charges and supporting documents, translated to the accused's native language. This is considered a fundamental of a fair trial; if an accused does not know what he is to defend against in advance of trial, he cannot prepare for trial in any meaningful way.
- Two-thirds vote to convict, the same as in military practice. The two-thirds vote was required in noncapital cases, with two-thirds concurrence also needed on a sentence, but three-fourths were needed to approve a sentence of 10 years to life. While the two-thirds vote seems to offer less protection for an accused than the unanimity typical in civilian jurisdictions, the first vote is binding, unlike in civilian jurisdictions that will revote until unanimity. This is the same as courts-martial.
- Unanimous vote was required for imposition of the death penalty, a provision not in effect at the time of *Quirin* but reflecting developments in the law of capital punishment

in the time since that decision. In fact, three unanimous votes were required for the death penalty, because the rules also incorporated the even more recent (post–*Gregg v. Georgia*)[23] requirement for pleading aggravating factors. In any capital case, then, unanimity was required on a finding of guilt, on a finding of an aggravating factor, and then on a sentence of death.
- Open trials. Trials would be presumptively open to the press and public, and the government would have to make a showing to the satisfaction of the presiding official (equivalent of judge) for any part of the proceeding to be closed.

The Supreme Court Intervenes

Most drafters of the 2001 military commissions rules assumed that the federal courts would not intervene and that charged individuals would not have had access to them until after trial—basing their assumption in large part on the fact that the *Quirin* defendants received appellate review directly from—but only from—the United States Supreme Court and only after their verdicts. There was no intermediate court, and there was no opportunity for an accused individual to collaterally attack the process through the writ of habeas corpus or other extraordinary petition to the federal courts before a trial was held. Soon, however, the Bush administration faced several suits in various forums that contested the entire process, from the president's authority to order commissions in the way he did and the type he did to the ways in which the published procedures differed from traditional civilian courts. In 2006, the Supreme Court validated the mechanism of military commission, but, in *Hamdan v. Rumsfeld*,[24] ruled that President Bush had acted contrary to the UCMJ and the Geneva Conventions in ordering military commissions in his November 2001 military order. The majority opinion, written by Justice John Paul Stevens, found that commissions had to be authorized by statute or be conducted in accordance with the laws of war, as implemented by the Geneva Conventions or the UCMJ. The president had cited Article 36 of the UCMJ in his original order, finding that the rules and procedures of the UCMJ and federal courts were impracticable for commissions.[25] The five-member majority found that certain deviations from such rules and procedures, including the fact that, under some circumstances, evidence could be submitted that the defense counsel and accused could not see, invalidated the process. Justice Thomas wrote a vigorous dissent, which he delivered from the bench, the first time he had delivered an oral opinion in more than six years. He emphasized that the congressional action was not required, because Congress had authorized military commissions in the UCMJ itself and had signified additional deference to presidential authority in its post-9/11 enactments, including the Authorization for Use of Military Force.[26] Justice Alito, writing separately in dissent, argued that the Constitutional authority for commissions preceded *Quirin*, which he considered to be appropriate precedent for the commissions at issue. He also argued that the commissions were "regularly constituted courts" and that any procedural disputes could be resolved through the appellate process set up in the rules that the secretary of defense had set for these commissions.

Congress Acts

After the *Hamdan* ruling, Congress acted with uncommon speed. It held hearings in summer 2006 and then passed the Military Commissions Act of 2006 (MCA), which President Bush signed into law in October that year. The MCA was patterned after the UCMJ and was aimed at providing the explicit congressional authorization for commissions that the *Hamdan* majority had considered necessary (Justice Breyer, in a separate concurrence to the *Hamdan* majority, had written that the Court was likely to approve a commissions scheme if Congress explicitly authorized it). The MCA authorized the secretary of defense to promulgate procedural rules, which he did in publishing the Rules for Military Commissions, which appeared in the Manual for Military Commissions, itself patterned closely after the Manual for Courts-Martial. These rules included the protections mentioned above from the secretary of defense's rules published in March 2002. Rather than the several-page document that highlighted those essential protections, which was the format of the 2002 rules, the Manual for Military Commissions (MMC) followed the framework of the long-tested Manual for Courts-Martial, deviating where the drafters believed it necessary to accommodate the security and operational concerns of military commissions designed for the current war. Among the major changes from or additions to the 2002 rules:

- *Institutionalizing a military judge.* The earlier rules relied on the *Quirin*-era military justice construct by which a "law member" sat with the commission panel but did not have conclusive authority to issue rulings that were binding at trial. The MMC adopted the post-1968 model of an independent military judge who issued binding rulings.
- *Clarifying and expanding discovery.* The MMC provided for government production of documents and other items that the government planned to introduce and was "material to the preparation of the defense" or would be exculpatory or tend to reduce the sentence. The discovery standards for commissions were nearly as broad as courts-martial and arguably broader than in federal criminal courts.
- *Codified national security privilege.* Congress imposed a slightly altered version of the Classified Information Procedures Act (CIPA) and Military Rule of Evidence 505, which tracks CIPA closely. Military Commission Rule of Evidence 505 differed from those rules in that it reduced a judge's discretion in handling classified information and permits a prosecutor to insist on a closed session if lesser remedies such as admitting unclassified summaries of evidence were unworkable.
- *Introduced a more robust appellate process.* One of the persistent criticisms of the original commissions rules was that they did not provide for appellate review beyond the in-house process created by the rules. The MCA set up a procedure that was similar to courts-martial appeals and guaranteed access to conventional federal courts. Every commission conviction automatically would be appealed to the Court of Military Commissions Review (CMCR), which was patterned after the Courts of Criminal Appeals of the individual services (see chapter 6), though the CMCR, unlike the service appellate courts, would have at least one civilian member. After review by the CMCR, cases could then be appealed through the U.S. District Court for the District of Columbia, a traditional federal court, and then through the Washington, DC, Circuit Court of Appeals and then by petition to the U.S. Supreme Court.

Trials Begin

In 2007, there was a single trial, the negotiated guilty plea of Australian David Hicks, an early Taliban sympathizer who was captured in Afghanistan while fighting with al Qaeda forces; the agreement permitted him to return to Australia to serve most of his sentence. In 2008, the first contested cases were tried, the much publicized trial of Salim Hamdan, which received considerable attention because of Hamdan's prior path to the Supreme Court and because it was the first contested proceeding. A panel convicted him of material support to terrorism for being a long-time member of al Qaeda and for providing security to Osama bin Laden, but acquitted him of conspiring with other al Qaeda members to conduct terrorist activity. He received a sentence of five and a half years' confinement. The military judge who presided over the trial applied a version of "time served" for five years of the sentence, based on the theory that Hamdan should have received credit for time spent in Guantanamo Bay pending charges. While the government failed in its effort to contest this theory at trial, applying the theory would have meant that Hamdan only had to serve six additional months in confinement beyond his conviction in July 2008. Prosecutors appealed the ruling, arguing that a "time served" concept was inapplicable to military commissions, because the detainees were already lawfully held under the law of war, meaning that he was not really held pending charges in the same way that accused persons typically are held pending criminal trial or courts-martial. Because the U.S.'s authority to hold Hamdan was independent of the commissions process and because the conditions of detention were the same for those facing commissions trials as for the hundreds held without anticipation or likelihood of trials, the government believed that the ordinary set-off or credit for pretrial confinement should not apply. Consistent with this argument, the government intentionally would not use the word *confinement* in the pretrial context, preferring the term *detained,* as it sounded in the law of war and international conventions. Without conceding the point, and prepared to litigate it in future cases, the U.S. government returned Hamdan to his home country of Yemen in late 2008; the legal issue never was definitively resolved in his case.

In November 2008, Ali Hamza Ahmed Suleiman, known as al-Bahlul, was convicted of conspiracy, terrorism, and material support for terrorism for serving as a chief propagandist for al Qaeda, and a panel sentenced him to life in prison. While al-Bahlul, also a Yemeni, insisted he was "boycotting" his trial, he appeared for all sessions, speaking occasionally, but neither he nor his military defense counsel questioned any witnesses or presented independent evidence. During the sentencing phase of the trial, al-Bahlul spoke at length about his commitment to al Qaeda and his hatred of the United States.

Major Issues Litigated

- *Jurisdiction over the person—unlawful combatancy.* A threshold consideration for military commissions is the status of those whom they try—that is, whether a military court, as opposed to a civilian court in the United States or the location of capture or offense, is the more appropriate forum. Unlawful combatants, sometimes characterized as "unprivileged combatants" because they do not enjoy the combatant privilege that protects them from criminal responsibility for killing opposing soldiers in combat, generally are subject to war crimes trials such as military commissions, because they are being charged with violations of the laws of war. As Chief Justice Stone wrote in *Quirin* in 1942, "the law of war draws a distinction between the armed forces and the peaceful populations of belligerent nations and also between those who are lawful and unlawful combatants. Lawful combatants are subject to capture and detention as prisoners of war by opposing military forces. Unlawful combatants are likewise subject to capture and detention, but in addition they are subject to trial and punishment by military tribunals for acts which render their belligerency unlawful."[27] With those definitions in mind, Stone explained why the Nazi saboteurs in that case were properly classified as unlawful combatants. "The spy who secretly and without uniform passes the military lines of a belligerent in time of war, seeking to gather military information and communicate it to the enemy, or an enemy combatant who without uniform comes secretly through the lines for the purpose of waging war by destruction of life or property, are familiar examples of belligerents who are generally deemed not to be entitled to the status of prisoners of war, but to be offenders against the law of war subject to trial and punishment by military tribunals."[28] The prosecution's threshold task in a military commissions case is to establish that the person being tried is lawfully before the court because she was not a lawful combatant, meaning that she was not a member of an armed force as generally understood—featuring a chain of command, distinctive insignia, carrying arms openly, and conforming to the laws of war.[29] Once that was established, then the government would prove that her acts violated the law of war. In Hamdan, the defense argued that he was not an unlawful combatant just because he was apprehended with surface to air missiles in his vehicle. The trial judge ultimately ruled that such conduct was sufficient proof that Hamdan had "engaged in hostilities" under the Military Commissions Act and that he was not a privileged combatant because of his loyalty to al Qaeda, a terrorist organization.

The post-9/11 military commissions also faced what many considered to be a more difficult judgment on jurisdiction regarding Afghan citizens or members of the Taliban. While the government was able to show in several cases that the conduct of charged individuals violated the law of war or the Military Commissions Act—for example, by maiming or attempting to kill U.S. military personnel, storing weapons, or emplacing mines—prosecutors never brought a case in which a member of the Taliban asserted that he was essentially a member of the nation's military and therefore a lawful combatant.

- *Taking statements and collecting evidence—the Fourth and Fifth Amendments.* One of the key attractions of military commissions is their flexibility regarding the rules of evidence, built in part on the assumption that Constitutional considerations regarding the gathering and production of evidence do not apply. The government generally argues that the Fourth Amendment—normally requiring a warrant based on probability for obtaining evidence, except in exigent circumstances—is inapplicable as a matter of law and functionality. As a matter of law, the government argues, the Constitution does not apply overseas and especially does not apply overseas to the collection of evidence against individuals who are not U.S. citizens and are engaged in unlawful combatancy. As a practical matter, the government argues, much of the evidence against unlawful combatants is collected in combat zones by soldiers who are not trained in the niceties of law enforcement and whose primary mission—winning a war and staying alive while doing so—could be jeopardized if the conventions of civilian law enforcement were applied to them. Defense counsel argue that the Fourth Amendment should apply any time that U.S. officials, whether soldiers or otherwise, are involved in evidence collection, wherever in the world and whatever the circumstances. They argue that the Constitution has been found to apply outside the United States in some circumstances and that, even if there were concerns about extending the protection to noncitizens, the strictures of the Fourth Amendment help buttress the evidentiary integrity of the court in which the evidence is offered and therefore the entire process. Judges generally have ruled that the Fourth Amendment does not apply to commissions.

The Fifth Amendment protects against compulsory self-incrimination, and the Supreme Court has interpreted that protection, in *Miranda v. Arizona*,[30] to extend to any custodial questioning by law enforcement officials, entitling suspects not only to refuse to talk but to the assistance of a lawyer should they request it. The government argues, as with the Fourth Amendment, that the Constitution does not apply at commissions and to evidence adduced overseas, but also argues that it is particularly impractical and inappropriate to impose those restrictions under circumstances in which the primary purpose of questioning often is for intelligence purposes—or a mix of intelligence and law enforcement purposes that the government should not have to defend or sort for litigation. The commission rules apply the protection against self-incrimination only in the courtroom and permit unlimited questioning of suspected war criminals without a rights advisement The government requestioned several of the more significant detainees years after their questioning in Central Intelligence Agency (CIA) custody, under a plan that emphasized to the detainees that they did not have to talk, that they were not in custody of the CIA, and that interrogators were not concerned with and had not relied on their prior statements; even this advice, designed to ensure voluntary statements, intentionally did not include advice regarding the right to counsel.

- *Authenticity of evidence.* It is a fundamental requirement that the government be able to show that evidence that it offers in court is what its proponent purports it to be—in other words, it must be authenticated through the rules of evidence that have evolved over time. As discussed above, much evidence involving violations of the law of war is collected under battlefield conditions or by clandestine means, sometimes in coordination with foreign governments. Battlefield evidence simply cannot meet the chain of custody standards of conventionally gathered evidence, because service members often gather it under the stressful, dangerous, volatile, and austere environment of combat by individuals ordinarily without training or experience in the conventions of law enforcement.
- *Hearsay.* This concept also relates to authenticity but extends beyond physical evidence to statements and records—and any information that constitutes an out-of-court statement that is offered by either party in court "for the truth of the matter asserted." Hearsay, then, can be a statement by someone not in court if it is offered as truth and can also

be other than oral statements offered as truth—commonly bank and medical records, lab reports, or other government documents. It is the use of statements by people not present in court that is most controversial in military commissions, and it provides a vehicle for using detainees' statements against each other. The relaxed hearsay rule means that a proponent of hearsay—and both the prosecution and defense can and have used the rule—may argue for its admissibility if it can establish sufficient reliability and trustworthiness (commissions rules also require 30 days' notice to the opponent), a standard used in European courts and most international criminal tribunals. This area received much of the attention of critics, including the American Bar Association and other interest groups, which denounced commissions based on the view that too much hearsay could be admitted before a commission and that the advantage of the more liberal rule would flow toward the government in an unbalanced manner.

- *National security information.* In some circumstances, the government could establish that chain of custody but would prefer not to do so—because the evidence was obtained through intelligence means—signal intelligence, informants, other sophisticated surveillance—that the government would prefer not to disclose, because it would expose to others the way that the United States obtained the information or risk relationships with people or governments who may have cooperated. Military Commissions Rule 505 is similar to equivalent rules in courts-martial and federal courts (the Classified Information Procedures Act) in that it provides the government the opportunity to make individual presentations to the military judge and seek authority to introduce evidentiary substitutes (e.g., a summary of an intercept or permission to obscure the actual location of an arrest or a seizure of information). Uniquely, RMC 505 also provided the option of closing the courtroom—an opportunity the government was determined not to employ and had not done so through 2009.

One of the consistent themes of President Barack Obama's 2008 presidential campaign was his pledge to close the Guantanamo Bay detention facility. Shortly after taking office, he announced plans to close the facility within a year and convened several study groups to examine not only the detention facility itself but whether military commissions or some other method was best suited for bringing to justice that number of accused terrorists. He directed the secretary of defense to order prosecutors to cease charging and trying commissions cases while the entire process was reviewed. In May 2009, the president announced that he was prepared to go forward with an altered commissions process, but the review process went slower than expected. After pledging to discontinue the "failed" military commissions, the Obama administration supported the Military Commissions Act of 2009, which they believed moderated some of the evidentiary rules of the prior commissions to their satisfaction, and the President signed the act on October 27, 2009, making some changes to the admissibility of coerced evidence, procedures for handling classified evidence, and rules governing the admissibility of hearsay. Still to be determined at that time were the precise wording of changes to rules and procedures, and which cases if any would be tried by future military commissions or federal court, how to decide whether a case would be tried by commission or elsewhere, and where commissions trials would be held if commissions were to continue.

Notes

1. All services have law enforcement personnel, and their missions can include investigation of war crimes and battlefield misconduct, but they are not normally attached to front-line units; consequently, their investigations and evidence gathering tend to be after-the-fact and not contemporaneous with the events they are charged to investigate.

2. Some elite military organizations, such as special operations forces, will incorporate evidence gathering and preservation as part of raids and other well-planned and often rehearsed encounters. This is in contrast to conventional forces fighting in less controlled and manageable environments, which will not normally have law enforcement or law enforcement-like capabilities.

3. Witnesses may not testify from outside the courtroom in U.S. criminal courts without the consent of both parties.

4. For an excellent overview of military commissions, as well as broad treatment of President Bush's November 2001 military order, see Jennifer Elsea, CRS Report for Congress, *Terrorism and the Law of War: Trying Terrorists as War Criminals before Military Commissions* (Congressional Research Service, 2001).

5. *American Military History*, vol. I, Center for Military History, at 160–62. Timothy Johnson, *Winfield Scott: The Quest for Military Glory* (University Press of Kansas, 1998).

6. 68 U.S. 243 (1863)

7. *Ex parte Milligan*, 71 U.S. 2 (1866).

8. Among other distinctions, of course, none of the 9/11-related conspirators was a U.S. citizen.

9. A well-researched popular treatment of the Lincoln commissions appears in Michael W. Kauffman, *American Brutus, John Wilkes Booth and the Lincoln Conspirators* (2004), at 342–74.

10. In this regard, the court of appeals did not have to address the underlying issue of the whether the commission was properly constituted—consistent with courts' general desire to rule on the narrowest grounds possible. *Mudd v. White*, D.C. Circuit Court of Appeals (No. 01–5103) (November 8, 2002).

11. By most accounts, Waberski (whose first name was also reported as Pablo) was an alias for Lothar Witzke, an officer in the Germany navy who posed as Waberski, ostensibly a Russian national. Waberski/Witzke ultimately was convicted by court-martial. Wilson commuted his death sentence to life in prison in 1920, and President Coolidge pardoned him in 1923 after he helped rescue fellow inmates in a prison fire. He was deported and sent back to Germany, which decorated him.

12. The Constitution gives Congress the authority to "define and punish Piracies and Felonies committed on the high Seas, and Offenses against the Law of Nations." United States Constitution, Article I, Section 8.

13. 317 U.S. 1 (1942) (per curiam).

14. In re Yamashita, 327 U.S. 1 (1946).

15. He quoted the language of the amendment itself, which provides that it applies to "any person." *Yamashita* at 26 (Murphy, J., dissenting).

16. Id. at 26.

17. Id. at 27–28.

18. The Scottish released him in August 2009. It was a decision hailed in Libya and harshly criticized elsewhere, including in the U.S.

19. Obviously, if the accused were innocent, then waiting more than a decade for trial also would be intolerable and unjust.

20. Rather than as an executive order, the normal vehicle for promulgating most presidential exercises of authority.

21. It was considered unworkable at least in the sense that authorities overseas could not guarantee the availability, much less the quality, of counsel located overseas. Those on the other side argue that this is less persuasive in the era of instant communications.

22. 553 U.S.; 128 S.Ct. 2229 (2008).

23. 428 U.S. 153 (1976), the Supreme Court decision that set conditions for resuming capital punishment in the states, it having effectively declared capital sentence schemes constitutionally deficient in the 1972 decision, *Furman v. Georgia,* 408 U.S. 238 (1972).

24. 548 U.S. 556 (2006).

25. Article 36 provides, in part: "Pretrial, trial, and post-trial procedures, including modes of proof, for cases arising under this chapter triable in courts-martial, military commissions and other military tribunals . . . may be prescribed by the President [and] . . . shall, so far as he considers practicable, apply the principles of law and the rules of evidence generally recognized in the trial of criminal cases in the United States district courts, but which may not be contrary to or inconsistent with this chapter."

26. The Joint Congressional Resolution of September 14, 2001, which gave extraordinary if not precisely defined authority to the president to respond to the attacks of September 11, 2001. *Authorization for use of Military Force against Terrorists,* Pub. L. 107–40, 115 Stat. 224. Among other language, it authorized the president to use all "necessary and appropriate force" against those whom he determined "planned, authorized, committed or aided" the September 11 attacks, or who harbored them.

27. *In re Quirin* at 30–31 (citations omitted).

28. Id. at 31.

29. These four criteria generally define a lawful combatant, who would then be eligible for the treatment of a prisoner of war, even when not a member of a conventional military organization in a nation-state: "(a) That of being commanded by a person responsible for his subordinates; (b) That of having a fixed distinctive sign recognizable at a distance; (c) That of carrying arms openly; (d) That of conducting their operations in accordance with the laws and customs of war." Geneva Convention relative to the Treatment of Prisoners of War, Article 4 (1949).

30. 384 U.S. 436 (1964).

Glossary

Terms

Accused
: The service member accused of an offense, either before courts-martial or nonjudicial punishment. The individual is still referred to as the accused during the sentencing phase of trial.

Administrative separation or administrative discharge
: Representing a wide range of regulatory bases for discharging soldiers, these are not courts-martial and not federal convictions (see chapter 8).

Article 15
: Article of the Uniform Code of Military Justice that provides for nonjudicial punishment.

Article 31
: Article of the Uniform Code of Military Justice that provides protection against self-incrimination and requires warnings before official questioning.

Article 32
: Article of the Uniform Code of Military Justice that requires independent pretrial investigation and hearing conducted by a military officer before a charge is referred to a general court-martial.

Bad-conduct discharge
: Less severe of the two punitive discharges available to enlisted members at general courts-martial and the only discharge available at special courts-martial.

Benchbook
: Official publication used by military trial judges of all services, contains elements of offenses, draft instructions, and other guidance for judges.

Glossary

Charge	A statement of a violation of the Uniform Code of Military Justice (UCMJ). A service member facing court-martial or punishment under Article 15 must have a charge sworn against him that cites a specific provision of the UCMJ (see specification below).
Convening authority	Commander who has legal authority to convene courts-martial at a certain level, depending on the officer's rank and level of command.
Court-martial	A military criminal trial.
Dishonorable discharge	The more severe of the two punitive discharges that can be adjudged against enlisted personnel, but never against commissioned officers and only at general courts-martial.
Dismissal	The only punitive discharge that can be adjudged against a commissioned officer and only by a general court-martial.
Flyer	Document given to a court-martial panel after the court is assembled; contains the charges and specifications and no other information.
General articles	Articles 133, conduct unbecoming an officer, and 134, service discrediting conduct or conduct prejudicial to good order and discipline (see chapter 5).
General court-martial	Highest level of military court-martial, the equivalent of felony-level court.
JAGMAN	Judge Advocate General's Manual, the Navy's all-purpose procedural guide to a wide range of investigations and procedures; JAGMAN also is a Navy colloquialism for an investigation.
Law member	Judge advocate who sat with and advised court-martial panels until replaced by military judges in 1968.
Manual for Courts-Martial	Sometimes referred to as "the Manual," it is the compendium of Rules for Courts-Martial and Military Rules of Evidence, along with several appendices, that provide ready references to the full text of the United States Constitution and Uniform Code of Military Justice, and analyses of the Rules for Courts-Martial and Rules of Evidence.

Glossary

Mast or Captain's Mast	Navy term for nonjudicial punishment.
Military judge	Military trial judge, introduced in 1968 (previously the "law member").
Other than honorable discharge	The military's most unfavorable administrative discharge, it cannot be adjudged by a court-martial and cannot be adjudged against a service member unless the service member seeks it (sometimes as an alternative for court-martial) or is offered the opportunity to appear before a board of officers (not a court-martial panel).
Panel	Military equivalent of jury.
Panel member	Individual who sits on a court-martial panel.
Panel president	Senior member of the court-martial panel.
Preferral	The first stage in the formal process of bringing court-martial charges against a service member under the Uniform Code of Military Justice.
Punitive discharge	One of the three discharges that only can be adjudged by a court-martial. For enlisted members, the bad-conduct or dishonorable discharge and, for officers, the dismissal.
Referral	The decision by a convening authority to send a case to trial by court-martial.
Special court-martial	The military's "misdemeanor court," generally having a maximum punishment of one year's confinement, forfeiture of two-thirds pay per month, and a bad-conduct discharge.
Specification	Statement on a charge sheet that provides a specific, concise factual allegation for a charge. There must be at least one specification for every charge. Whereas charges are numbered by Roman numerals, specifications are enumerated by Arabic numerals. A "form spec" is the suggested but not required draft wording for a violation of the Uniform Code of Military Justice that appears in the Manual for Courts-Martial immediately following the manual's description of the offense.
Summary court-martial	The lowest level of court-martial, consisting of a single officer who adjudicates guilt and punishment.
Undesirable discharge	Predecessor to the other than honorable discharge.

Uniform Code of Military Justice	Statute passed by Congress in 1950 that provides a single criminal code for all members of the military; has been amended several times since then.

Acronyms or Colloquialisms

AWOL	Absence without leave (see Article 36, UCMJ).
BCD	Bad-conduct discharge.
BCD Special	Term long used to distinguish a court-martial empowered to adjudge a bad-conduct discharge (BCD) from "straight specials," that did not have that authority. This term has become archaic since the maximum punishment for all courts-martial was increased to include authority to adjudge a BCD.
CA	Convening authority. Commonly abbreviated by the level of court—for example, GCMCA for general court-martial convening authority, sometimes abbreviated (especially in the Navy) as OEGCMCA, for officer exercising general court-martial convening authority.
CAAF	Court of Appeals for the Armed Forces, the all-civilian, senior civilian court in the military services.
Chapter 10	Army shorthand for discharge in lieu of court-martial. All services have equivalents for it. Chapter 10, Army Regulation 635–200.
CMA (sometimes COMA)	Predecessor name for Court of Appeals for the Armed Forces, 1951–1994.
DC	Defense counsel.
DD	Dishonorable discharge.
Kick	A punitive discharge.
NJP	Nonjudicial punishment (see chapter 9).
OTH	Other than honorable discharge.
PTR	Post-trial review. Predecessor to the staff judge advocate review (SJAR), it was a detailed and extensive recounting of a court-martial that had to be prepared before a convening authority could take final action on a case; modified in scope in 1984.

Glossary

SJA	Staff judge advocate. The senior legal advisor in a military organization that has an officer who has authority to convene a general court-martial. Military officer and lawyer who advises convening authorities on whether a case should be referred to trial.
SJAR	Staff Judge Advocate Review. Document required by Rule for Courts-Martial 1106 that summarizes the result of court-martial and contains recommendations for convening authority action regarding findings and sentence.
TC	Trial counsel; formal term for military prosecutors.
TDS	Trial Defense Service, the name for the organizations of military defense counsel who defend service members at courts-martial and other adverse proceedings.
UCMJ	Uniform Code of Military Justice.

Bibliography

Bishop, Joseph W. *Justice under Fire: A Study of Military Law*. New York: Charterhouse Publishers, 1974.
Borch, Frederic L. III. *Judge Advocates in Vietnam: Army Lawyers in Southeast Asia, 1959–1975*. Honolulu, HI: University Press of the Pacific, 2004.
Davidson, Michael J. *A Guide to Military Criminal Law*. Annapolis, MD: U.S. Naval Institute Press 1999.
DiMona, Joseph. *Great Court-Martial Cases*. New York: Grosset & Dunlap, 1972.
Elsea, Jennifer. *CRS Report for Congress, Terrorism and the Law of War: Trying Terrorists as War Criminals before Military Commissions*. Washington, DC: Congressional Research Service, 2001.
Fidell, Eugene R. *Military Justice: Cases and Materials*. Newark, NJ: LexisNexis/Matthew Bender, 2007.
Fidell, Eugene R., and Dwight H. Sullivan. *Evolving Military Justice*. Annapolis, MD: U.S. Naval Institute Press, 2002.
Fisher, Louis. *Nazi Saboteurs on Trial. A Military Tribunal and American Law*. Lawrence: University Press of Kansas, 2003.
Generous, William T., Jr. *Swords and Scales*. Washington, NY: Kennikat Press, 1973.
Gilligan, Francis A., and Fredric I. Lederer. *Court-Martial Procedure* (3d ed.). Newark, NJ: Lexis Law Publishing, 2007.
Hillman, Elizabeth Lutes. *Defending America: Military Culture and the Cold War Court-Martial*. Princeton, NJ: Princeton University Press, 2005.
Huie, William Bradford. *The Execution of Eddie Slovik*. 1954. Reprint, Yardley, PA: Westholme Publishing, 2004.
Index and Legislative History: Uniform Code of Military Justice. 1950.
Lindley, John M. *A Soldier Is Also a Citizen: The Controversy over Military Justice in the U.S. Army, 1917–1920*. Durham, NC: Duke University Press, 1974.
Lowry, Thomas. *Don't Shoot That Boy! Abraham Lincoln and Military Justice*. Cambridge, MA: Da Capo Press, 1999.
Lurie, Jonathan. *Arming Military Justice: The Origins of the United States Court of Appeals, 1775–1950*. Princeton, NJ: Princeton University Press, 1992.
Lurie, Jonathan. *Pursuing Military Justice: The History of the United States Court of Appeals for the Armed Forces, 1951–1980*. Princeton, NJ: Princeton University Press, 1998.
Manual for Courts-Martial, United States. Washington, DC: Government Printing Office, 2008.

Morgan, Edmund M. "The Background of the Uniform Code of Military Justice." *Vanderbilt Law Review* 6 (1953).

Pasley, Robert, and Felix E. Larkin. "The Navy Court-Martial: Proposals for Its Reform." *Cornell Law Quarterly* 33 (1947).

Report of Committee on a Uniform Code of Military Justice to the Secretary of Defense 1949. http://www.loc.gov/rr/frd/Military_Law/pdf/morgan.pdf (accessed October 22, 2009).

Richards, Peter. *Extraordinary Justice: Military Tribunals in Historical and International Context*. New York: New York University Press, 2007.

Saltzburg, Stephen A., Lee D. Schinasi, and David A. Schlueter. *Military Rules of Evidence Manual* (6th ed.). Newark, NJ: LexisNexis/Matthew Bender, 2006.

Schlueter, David A. *Military Criminal Justice: Practice and Procedure*. Newark, NJ: Lexis Law Publishing, 1999.

Staff, The Judge Advocate General's School, U.S. Army. *The Advocacy Trainer*. 1997. Reprint, Charlottesville, VA: The Judge Advocate General's School, 2008.

Weiner, Frederick B. "American Military Law in the Light of the First Mutiny Act's Tricentennial." *Military Law Review* 126 (1989).

Weiner, Frederick B. "Courts-Martial and the Bill of Rights: The Original Practice." *Harvard Law Review* 72 (1958–59).

West, Luther C. *They Call It Justice: Command Influence and the Court-Martial System*. New York: Viking, 1977.

Westmoreland, William C., and George S. Prugh. "Judges in Command: The Judicialized Uniform Code of Military Justice in Combat." *Harvard Journal of Law and Public Policy* 3 (1980).

Winthrop, William. *Military Law and Precedents*. 2nd ed. Washington, DC: Government Printing Office, 1920.

Index

Adams, John, 17, 72
Administrative separations: due process provided, 167–68; grounds for, 168–69; in general, 134–35, 167–72
Ansell, Samuel, 21–23, 25, 29, 32, 128
Ansell-Chamberlain Bill, 30
Appeals: by government (interlocutory) 93–94, 138; in general, 27, 30, 114–20, 126
Articles for the Government of the Navy, 17, 122
Articles of War: in general, 10, 14–15, 17, 18–21, 30, 127, 175, 187; 1806 Code, 15; 1786 amendments to, 14; 1775 version, 14
Article 31, UCMJ, 9, 47, 48, 50–51, 126, 132, 133, 143, 157. *See also* self-incrimination
Article 32 investigation, 9, 29, 54–57, 61, 126, 132–33

Boards of Review, 31, 115, 136
British, influence on military justice system, 2, 14, 16–17, 18, 20, 23

Capital offenses: in general, 25, 72–74, 105–6, 124; unanimous vote required, 32
Charges: disposition of, 52–53; processing and recommendations, 53–55, 58. *See also* preferral; referral
Code of Conduct (non-punitive), 73
Commander's authority: disposition of charges, 52, 57–62; individualized disposition, 6, 7, 52–3, 152; in general, 4, 26, 52–54, 57, 130, 145; inherent authority, 5, 9–10, 53, 152; lowest level of disposition, 6–7, 30, 52, 59; post-trial authority, 113–15
Congress: authority to define crimes, 63; authorization of military justice system, 16, 17; oversight of military justice system, 19, 25
Conspiracy, 74
Constitution, applicability of: 2, 9–10, 16, 34; applicability of Fifth Amendment, 35; applicability of Sixth Amendment, 41
Contemptuous words, using (Art. 88), 66–67
Convening authority: in general, 41, 56; post-trial and clemency responsibilities, 13–15, pretrial agreements, 61
Corrections: in general, 17–18, 119–20; United States Disciplinary Barracks (Fort Leavenworth), 18, 119
Corrective training, 166
Court of Appeal for the Armed Forces, 55, 117, 129, 138, 152
Court of Military Appeals, 117, 127–29, 132, 138
Courts-martial. *See* general courts-martial; pleas; pretrial agreements; punishments;

special courts-martial; summary courts-martial
Crowder, Enoch, 18–23, 25–30

Death penalty. *See* capital offenses
Defense counsel: competence and independence, 22, 27; for nonjudicial punishment, 154; in general, 31–32, 51, 92–93, 126–27, 135 142–44
Dereliction of duty (Art. 92), 69–70
Desertion (Art. 85), 32
Deterrence, 1, 100, 101, 123–24, 150, 170
Discharges: bad-conduct, 105; dismissal, 105; dishonorable, 105; in general, 171–72; in lieu of court-martial, 170–71; punitive, 104–5
Dismissal. *See* discharges
Disobedience of lawful general order (Art. 92), 69
Disobedience of lawful order (Art. 90, 91), 67–68
Disrespect, superior commissioned officer (Art. 90), 70
Double jeopardy, 40
Dynes v. Hoover, 16

Elston Act, 125–27
Espionage (Art. 106a), 72

Fraudulent enlistment or separation (Art. 83), 65

General courts-martial, 16, 41, 45–46
Geneva Conventions, 174–75, 188, 192, 292, 295, 323
Good order and discipline, 1, 3, 4, 7, 16, 23, 52, 58, 72–73, 74

Hague Convention, 71
Hickey, Thomas, 14, 15
Houston riots, 23–25

Insubordination (Art. 91), 70–71
International Criminal Court, 8
Investigations: in general, 47–48, 54, 126; preliminary, pretrial, 26, 31, 126, 132

Judge advocates, 12, 57–58
Judicial deference, 8–9

Jurisdiction: over the person, 34–36, 134; over the offense, 36, 40; reservists, 36
Jury. *See* panel members
Justice: in general, 1, 5, 12; perception of, 4–5, 7, 16

Law of war (or law of armed conflict), 76, 79, 80, 174, 175–76, 179, 184–89, 194–96

Malingering, (Art. 115), 75–76
Manual for Courts-Martial, in general, 11, 139, 193
Military commissions: evidentiary issues and procedures, 190–92; Hamdan, Salim, 192, 194; history of, 179–90; in general, 174–97; Military Commissions Act of 2006, 193; Military Commissions Act of 2009, 197; military necessity, 177–78; national security concerns addressed, 176–77; *Quirin, Ex parte*, 180, 187–89; reliability and due process, 178–79
Military Extra-Territorial Jurisdiction Act, 35
Military judge: in general, 1, 30, 39, 135; trial by judge alone, 31
Military Justice Act of 1983, 137–38
Military Justice Act of 1968, 115, 122, 129, 135–36, 139–40
Military Justice Act of 1920, 25, 30
Military justice system: early history of, 1–2, 114–15; future of, 143–44; reliability of, 7; servicemembers' faith in, 5, 7
Military law, sources of, 10–12
Military offenses, in general, 64–65
Military Rules of Evidence: in general, 90–92, 137–38; inspections, 90–91; national security-related, 92; polygraph results, bar against, 91–92, 117
Mitchell, Billy, 76–79
Misbehavior before the enemy (Art. 99), 73–74
Misconduct as prisoner (Art. 105), 74–75
Morgan, Edmund M., 127–29
Mutiny and sedition (Art. 94), 72–73

Index

Nonjudicial punishment: burden of proof, 155–56; categories, 152–53; defense counsel, eligibility for, 154; due process provided, 153–58, 162–65; individual treatment, 160–61; in general, 30, 31, 131–32, 134, 148–66; in 1920 Military Justice Act, 31; minor offenses, 150; punishments, 158–63; purpose of, 150–52; right to demand court-martial, 154

O'Callahan v. Parker, 37–38, 39, 40, 140

Panel members: enlisted members, 127; in general, 18, 30, 60–61, 114, 136, 145, 178
Plea bargaining. *See* pretrial agreements
Pleas, 107
Post-trial procedures: clemency, 113–14; in general, 15, 23, 28–29, 30, 112–15, 132, 138; post-trial review, 138; record of trial, 112–13; reforms, 132; revising trial results, 22–23
Powell Report, 129–32, 133
Preferral of charges, 31, 51–52; specification, 51–52
Presidential authority to determine punishments, 32
Pretrial agreements: in general, 60–62, 108–12; *Care* inquiry, 108–11
Pretrial advice, 29, 58–59
Pretrial confinement, 48–49
Pretrial punishment, 49–50
Principal, charging as (Art. 77), 63–64
Punishments, courts-martial: fine, 103; forfeiture, 102–03; hard labor without confinement, 103; in general, 101–7; reprimand, 102. *See also* capital offenses; discharges

Quirin, Ex parte. See military commissions

Referral of charges, 30, 58–60, 128
Regimental courts (or garrison courts), 19
Reid v. Covert, 34–36, 134

Releasing prisoner without authority (Art. 96), 76–77
Relford v. Commandant, 38, 140
Ruckman, John Wilson, 24

Scott, Winfield, 3, 179–83
Self-incrimination, privilege against, 50–51. *See* Article 31
Sentencing: effective dates, 107, extenuation and mitigation, 98–99; factors, 100–101; in general: 28, 95–101, 107, 112–13, 130. *See also* capital offenses; discharges
Sentencing guidelines, absence of, 6, 95, 97, 101
Separate society, military as, 2–3, 9, 66
Service connection, 37–40, 140
Slovik, Eddie, 123–25
Special courts-martial, 20, 29, 31, 40, 41, 44, 131, 136
Specification. *See* preferral
Spencer, Philip, 16
Spying (Art. 106), 15, 71
Staff Judge Advocate, 27–28, 59, 61, 114
Status of Forces Agreements, 8, 35, 40, 48
Stimson, Henry L., 18
Stimson Report, 37–38, 59
Subordinate compelling surrender (Art. 100), 74
Summary courts-martial, 2, 16, 19, 41–44, 126, 127

Uniform Code of Military Justice (UCMJ): in general, 2, 3, 6, 10–11, 122; worldwide applicability, 7, 8, 139–40, 145. *See also* jurisdiction
United States v. Care, 108. *See also* pretrial agreements
United States v. Solorio, 37–39
United States v. Vallandingham, 184
Unlawful command influence, 4, 26, 28, 58, 125, 126, 131, 135, 141–42; "10 Commandments of," 142

Washington, George, 14, 15, 179

About the Author

LAWRENCE J. MORRIS served as an Army judge advocate from 1982 until his retirement as a colonel in 2009. His duties included multiple tours as a prosecutor and defense counsel and supervisor of trial advocates. He also served as professor and chair, Criminal Law Department, The Army Judge Advocate General's School; staff judge advocate, 10th Mountain Division; chief of criminal law, U.S. Army; staff judge advocate (general counsel), United States Military Academy; chief public defender, U.S. Army; founding executive director, Law & Order Task Force, Baghdad, Iraq; and chief prosecutor, Office of Military Commissions. He deployed to Bosnia-Herzegovina with the 10th Mountain Division, where he served as the chief counsel for Multi-National Division (North), and later deployed to Iraq. Colonel (Ret.) Morris has published numerous articles about military justice and has taught criminal law, constitutional law, and criminal procedure at the Columbus School of Law, Catholic University of America, and the George Mason University School of Law. He has lectured widely on military justice, trial advocacy, military commissions, national security, and leadership. Colonel Morris has undergraduate and law degrees from Marquette University; an LLM from the Judge Advocate General's School, and an M.S. in national security strategy from the National Defense University, where he was a distinguished graduate.

CPSIA information can be obtained at www.ICGtesting.com
Printed in the USA
BVOW06*0031140916

461675BV00021B/167/P